THE ELEMENTS OF
NEW TESTAMENT GREEK

THE ELEMENTS OF
NEW TESTAMENT GREEK

A METHOD OF STUDYING THE GREEK
NEW TESTAMENT WITH EXERCISES

By

REV. H. P. V. NUNN, M.A.

ST JOHN'S COLLEGE, CAMBRIDGE, SOMETIME
LECTURER AT ST AIDAN'S COLLEGE, BIRKENHEAD

WIPF & STOCK · Eugene, Oregon

Wipf and Stock Publishers
199 W 8th Ave, Suite 3
Eugene, OR 97401

The Elements of New Testament Greek
A Method of Studying the Greek New Testament with Exercises
By Nunn, H. P. V.
ISBN 13: 978-1-62564-877-8
Publication date 4/22/2014
Previously published by Cambridge University Press, 1962

PREFACE

THIS book is intended principally for those who wish to take up the study of Greek after they have left school with a view to reading the Greek Testament. Generally speaking, it is concerned only with such words and forms as are found in New Testament Greek. The words used in the exercises are those which occur frequently in the Gospels and the Acts of the Apostles: they are collected in vocabularies at the end of the book, and it is believed that, if these vocabularies are carefully committed to memory, the student will find himself supplied with such words as are necessary to enable him to read these portions of the New Testament with ease and rapidity.

The author attaches great importance to the accurate knowledge of the meanings of the most common words as an aid to the thorough and rapid acquirement of a language. Fortunately the words used in the Gospels and in the Acts are comparatively few, and this fact together with the simplicity of their style makes these books in many respects very suitable first reading books even for those who do not intend to limit their study of the Greek language to the New Testament.

The most common irregular verbs are gradually introduced into the exercises and are also collected in a table at the end of the book. The sentences in the later exercises are taken almost verbatim from the Greek Testament. The verbs in μι are not introduced until the end of the book and the author therefore recommends that the Greek Testament itself should not be studied until these verbs have been mastered and all the Greek into English exercises in the book have been written out. Those who wish to become proficient in the subject should also write out all the English into Greek exercises.

In no study is the saying of Bacon that writing maketh an exact man so thoroughly exemplified as in the study of languages.

The order in which the forms and constructions treated in the exercises are placed, with the exception of the verbs in $\mu\iota$, is determined by the principle that those are treated first which occur most frequently.

Syntax is only treated so far as to enable examples to be given of the use of the Subjunctive and Infinitive moods and of the Participle. The author ventures to refer those who desire further information on this subject to his *Short Syntax of New Testament Greek* published by the Cambridge University Press, to which reference is occasionally made in footnotes in this book.

The Introduction to that book on the subject of English Grammar is reprinted here immediately after the table of contents, and the author would urge that it should be studied at the beginning by those to whom its contents are partially unfamiliar.

It is hoped that a student who has been carefully through this book will be able to read the easier portions of the New Testament with the aid of a dictionary. As however the subject-matter of the New Testament is already so familiar to most people in an English translation, such a power does not really imply much knowledge of Greek. Those who wish to gain an intelligent knowledge of the language should study some easy Greek author whose meaning is not already familiar to them. Such may be found in any of the many elementary editions of Xenophon or Lucian which are published[1], or even in Plato's Apology of Socrates studied with or without the help of a translation. The latter book is so interesting and important in its contents and so perfect and yet so simple in its style that it should be studied in the original language by all those who have the opportunity. Translations of Lucian and of Plato's Apology are published in a convenient form by the Oxford University Press.

If these books are thought to be too difficult the writings of the Apostolic Fathers, especially the Epistle of St Clement and the Shepherd of Hermas, may be recommended. These latter books are however not published in a form adapted for beginners, and the author has therefore attempted to meet this need by publishing selections from them and from other Christian authors of the first two centuries with notes at the end of the "Syntax" referred to above.

In conclusion he wishes to record his obligation to Messrs Bradley and Horswell for their "New Testament Word Lists," which were of great service in preparing the exercises in this book, and to his father for the care with which he looked over the proofs. The text of the Greek New Testament recommended is that published by the Bible Society.

H. P. V. NUNN.

November 6, 1913.

---

[1] See the "Elementary Classics" series published by Macmillan.

PREFACE TO THE EIGHTH EDITION

SOME additional matter has been added in an appendix to this edition to which reference is made at the appropriate places in the text. Other small changes and corrections have been made. The author wishes to acknowledge the help received from the late Mr H. Scott, from the Rev. Erle Homer Merriman, from Mr Lawson, from Dr Howard and from the Rev. J. Wenham which enabled him to make these changes and corrections.

H. P. V. NUNN.

17 DAVENPORT PARK ROAD,
    STOCKPORT,
        CHESHIRE.

CONTENTS

LESSON		PAGE
	Tense-Characteristics	xi
	English Grammar	xiii
I	The Alphabet	1
II	Breathings, accents, iota subscript	5
III	The Present Indicative Active	7
IV	The Present Indicative of contracted verbs in εω	9
V	Nouns of the Second Declension ending in ος	10
VI	The Genitive and Dative cases, the Definite Article	13
VII	Neuter Nouns of the Second Declension	14
VIII	Feminine Nouns of the First Declension	16
IX	Masculine Nouns of the First Declension, etc.	17
X	Adjectives of the Second Declension, Present Tense of "To be"	19
XI	The Imperfect Indicative Active, Accentuation of verbs	21
XII	Imperfect of the verb "To be," Demonstrative Pronouns, αὐτός	25
XIII	The Present and Imperfect Indicative Passive	27
XIV	Deponent Verbs, the Present Imperative, the Relative Pronoun	31
XV	The Present Infinitive, Personal and Possessive Pronouns	35
XVI	The Future Indicative Active and Middle, the Middle Voice	40
XVII	Two stems of verbs, the Reflexive Pronoun, questions	43
XVIII	The First Aorist Active	47
XIX	The Second Aorist Active, Object clauses after verbs of saying or thinking	51
XX	The Future and Aorist Active of liquid verbs, Temporal clauses	55

CONTENTS

LESSON		PAGE
XXI	The Third Declension	58
XXII	Nouns with stems ending in a vowel, Neuter Nouns of the Third Declension	62
XXIII	Adjectives of the Third Declension, Irregular Adjectives	65
XXIV	The First and Second Aorist Passive, the Future Passive	68
XXV	Participles	72
XXVI	The Genitive Absolute, Interrogative and Indefinite Pronouns, certain Prepositions	77
XXVII	The First and Second Aorist Middle, the comparison of Adjectives, Adverbs	82
XXVIII	Contracted Verbs ending in αω and οω	87
XXIX	The Perfect and Pluperfect Tenses	91
XXX	The Subjunctive Mood	95
XXXI	Subjunctive of Contracted Verbs and of εἰμί, further uses of the Subjunctive	99
XXXII	Further uses of the Infinitive	102
XXXIII	The Verbs in μι: δίδωμι	106
XXXIV	τίθημι	110
XXXV	ἵστημι	112
XXXVI	Other Verbs in μι	116
XXXVII	The Optative Mood, Periphrastic Tenses	119
XXXVIII	Prepositions	121
XXXIX	Conditional Sentences	133
	Reading Exercises	136
	Accentuation	140
	The Regular Verb	144
	Table of Principal Parts of Verbs	151
	VOCABULARIES	156
	ENGLISH-GREEK VOCABULARY	176
	APPENDIX	184
	ENGLISH INDEX	189
	GREEK INDEX	191

CHARACTERISTIC LETTERS OF THE TENSES IN THE REGULAR VERB AND SOME REMARKS ON ITS FORMS

The matter on this page is inserted here for convenience of reference, but should not be used until the tenses of the regular verb are being learned

FUTURE ACTIVE. Characteristic letter σ inserted before the endings of the Present Active. No Subjunctive.

FUTURE MIDDLE. Characteristic letter σ inserted before the endings of the Present Passive. No Subjunctive.

FUTURE PASSIVE. Characteristic letters $\theta\eta\sigma$ inserted before the endings of the Present Passive. No Subjunctive.

1ST AORIST ACTIVE. Characteristic letters generally σa.
    Subjunctive formed by putting σ before the endings of the Present Subjunctive Active.

1ST AORIST MIDDLE. Characteristic letters generally σa.
    Subjunctive formed by putting σ before the endings of the Present Subjunctive Passive.

1ST AORIST PASSIVE. Characteristic letters $\theta\eta$ $\theta\epsilon$.
    Subjunctive formed by putting θ before the endings of the Present Subjunctive ACTIVE.

2ND AORIST ACTIVE. Endings in the Indicative mood same as endings of the Imperfect Active, in other moods same as those of the Present Active, but added to the VERBAL STEM and not to the Present stem. (Note differences in accent in Inf. and Part.)

2ND AORIST MIDDLE. Endings in the Indicative mood same as those of the Imperfect Passsive, in other moods same as those of the Present Passive, but added to the VERBAL STEM and not to the Present stem.

2ND AORIST PASSIVE. Characteristic letters η or ϵ.
    Subjunctive formed by adding endings of Present Subjunctive ACTIVE to the VERBAL STEM and not to the Present stem.

TENSE-CHARACTERISTICS

1st PERFECT AND PLUPERFECT ACTIVE. Characteristic letter κ.
> Reduplication in all moods. Subjunctive and Optative formed by putting κ before endings of Present Subjunctive and Optative Active.

PERFECT AND PLUPERFECT PASSIVE. Reduplication in all moods. Subjunctive and Optative formed by using the corresponding mood of εἶναι with the Perfect Passive Participle.

Past tenses have the augment in the INDICATIVE mood only.

The Perfect is not a past tense in Greek. If it has an augment it is because the first letters of the form are of such a nature that they cannot be reduplicated.

ENGLISH GRAMMAR

1. PARTS OF SPEECH

By **parts of speech** we mean the various classes under which all words used in speaking and writing may be arranged.

The names of the parts of speech are as follows:

Noun. Pronoun. Adjective.

Verb. Adverb.

Preposition. Conjunction. Interjection.

The Article, definite and indefinite, is also sometimes classed as a separate part of speech.

A NOUN is the name of anything. (Latin *nomen*, name.)

    Examples: John, boy, sweetness.

A PRONOUN is a word used instead of a noun. (Latin *pro*, for: *nomen*, name.)

    Examples: I, you, they, who, that.

AN ADJECTIVE is a word joined to a noun to limit its application. (Latin *adjectum*, a thing thrown to.)

    Examples: Good, many.

A VERB is a word by means of which we can make a statement, ask a question, or give a command about some person or thing. (Latin *verbum*, a word, so called as being the principal word in the sentence.)

    Examples: I run, we see.

AN ADVERB is a word joined to a verb, adjective or other adverb to qualify its meaning.

    Examples: Slowly, very, there.

A PREPOSITION is a word joined with, and generally placed before a noun or its equivalent[1], so that the preposition together with the noun forms a phrase equivalent to an adverb or adjective. (Latin *praepositum*, placed before.)

    Examples: At, with, by.

A CONJUNCTION is a word that joins together sentences, clauses or words. (Latin *conjungo*, I join.)

    Examples: And, but, for.

---

[1] See page xxvii.

AN INTERJECTION is a word thrown into a sentence to express a feeling of the mind. (Latin *interjicio*, I throw in.)
Examples: Hallo, ha.

The DEFINITE ARTICLE *The* and the INDEFINITE ARTICLE *A* are always joined with nouns like adjectives.

2. PARSING

As this book is intended for older students it has not been thought necessary to adopt the method of deriving the reason for the names of the different parts of speech from examples.

This is excellently done in a little book called *How to tell the Parts of Speech*, by the Rev. E. A. Abbott, published by Seeley, which the student who is altogether unacquainted with this subject is advised to get.

A few rules and examples are however given which may be of assistance in determining the parts of speech.

The first principle to be remembered is that no word should ever be parsed without careful reference to the function which it performs in the sentence where it occurs.

In English many words having exactly the same form must be regarded as entirely different parts of speech, according to the place which they occupy in the sentence, and must be translated by wholly different words in Latin and Greek, according as their meaning varies.

For example the word *that* may be (1) A demonstrative Pronoun. (2) A demonstrative Adjective. (3) A relative Pronoun. (4) A Conjunction[1].

(1) That is the man. (2) Give me that book. (3) This is the book that I want. (4) He said that this was the book. (4) He came that he might find the book.

Again, the word *considering* may be (1) A verbal noun. (2) A participle.

(1) Considering is slow work. (2) He went away considering the matter.

Many words may be nouns or verbs, according to the place which they occupy in the sentence.

---

[1] Consider the meaning of the word *that* in the following sentence, *He said that that that that man said was false.*

Some such words are: Bite, fly, rose, scale and sign.

Other words may be adjectives or nouns, such as: Base, last, stout, spring, kind.

Other words may be adjectives or verbs, such as: Lean, clean, blunt, idle, free.

Remembering then always to consider the word in connection with its sentence, the student should ask himself the following questions before parsing a word. They will help him to find out what part of speech it is.

(1) Is it the name of anything?
   Then it is a **noun**.

(2) Can a noun which is mentioned or thought of before be substituted for the word without altering the meaning of the sentence?
   Then it is a **pronoun**.

(3) Does it answer any of the questions: *What kind? How many? How much? Which? Whose? In what order?* with regard to some noun?
   Then it is an **adjective**.

(4) Does it make a statement, ask a question, or give a command?
   Then it is a **verb**.

(5) Does it answer the questions *How? When? Where?*
   Then it is an **adverb**.

Note. The words *How? When?* and *Where?* are themselves adverbs.

(6) Does it stand before a noun or its equivalent making with it a phrase which is equivalent to an adverb or adjective?
   Then it is a **preposition**.

(Another test of a preposition is that it is a word which is not a verb but which can stand before *him* and *them*, but not before *he* or *they*.)

(7) Does it join sentences, clauses or words?
   Then it is a **conjunction**.

The words in the following sentence are parsed as an example.
The man went quickly down the street and did not turn to his right hand or to his left.

THE	Limits the application of the word *man*. Tells us which man it was, i.e. some man already known.	Therefore it is that kind of adjective to which the name Definite Article is given.
MAN	Is the name of something.	Therefore it is a noun.
WENT	Makes a statement about the man.	Therefore it is a verb.
QUICKLY	Qualifies the verb *went*, tells us how he went.	Therefore it is an adverb.
DOWN	Stands before the noun *street*, making with it a phrase equivalent to an adverb because it qualifies the verb *went*, telling us where he went.	Therefore it is a preposition.
THE	See above.	
STREET	Is the name of something.	Therefore it is a noun.
AND	Joins together two clauses.	Therefore it is a conjunction.
DID TURN	Makes a statement about the man.	Therefore it is a verb.
NOT	Qualifies the verb *did turn* because it tells us how he did turn, i.e. not at all.	Therefore it is an adverb.
TO	See *down* above.	
HIS	The noun *man's* can be substituted for this.	Therefore it is a pronoun.
	But it also qualifies the noun *hand*, telling whose hand it is.	Therefore it is an adjective as well. Such words are called Pronominal adjectives.
RIGHT	Qualifies the noun *hand*, telling us which hand it is.	Therefore it is an adjective.
HAND	Is the name of something.	Therefore it is a noun.
OR	Joins together the two clauses *did not turn to his right hand* and (*did not turn*) *to his left*.	Therefore it is a conjunction.
TO	See above.	
HIS	See above.	
LEFT	See above.	

8. NOUNS

There are **four** kinds of nouns:

(1) **Proper Nouns.** A Proper noun is the name appropriated to any particular person, place or thing (Latin *proprius*, belonging to a person).

Examples: John, Mary, London, England.

(2) **Common Nouns.** A Common noun is the name which all things of the same kind have in common (Latin *communis*, belonging to all).

Examples: Boy, girl, town, country.

(3) **Collective Nouns.** A Collective noun is the name of a number of persons or things forming one body.

Examples: Committee, jury, army.

(4) **Abstract Nouns.** An Abstract noun is the name of some quality, state, or action considered apart from the person or thing in which it is embodied (Latin *abstractus*, withdrawn).

Examples: Goodness, whiteness, purity, servitude, running, walking.

Number, Gender, Case

Number. Nouns are inflected or changed in form to show whether they are singular or plural in number.

A noun in the **Singular number** is the name of a single person or thing, unless it is a Collective noun (see above).

A noun in the **Plural number** is the name of more than one person or thing.

Examples:	Singular	Plural
	Horse	horses
	Man	men
	Ox	oxen.

Gender. In English all names of men or male animals are in the Masculine gender, all names of women or female animals are in the Feminine gender, all names of things without life are in the Neuter gender. Nouns used to denote persons of either sex such as *parent, sovereign*, are said to be of Common gender.

In Latin and Greek, although all names of men and male animals are Masculine, and all names of women or female animals are Feminine, names of things without life may be Masculine or Feminine in gender as well as Neuter. The gender of a noun is generally determined by the ending of the Nominative Singular.

Case. Nearly all traces of case-endings have disappeared from English nouns. The only surviving ending is that of the Possessive or Genitive case which is formed by adding *'s* to the end of a noun in the singular and *s'* to the end of the noun in the Plural.

Example	Nominative	Possessive Singular	Possessive Plural
	horse	horse's	horses'

4. ADJECTIVES

In English, adjectives are never inflected, but have the same ending whether they qualify singular or plural, masculine or feminine nouns.

In Latin and Greek they are inflected to show gender, number, and case.

5. VERBS

Verbs are of two kinds—Transitive and Intransitive.

(*a*) **Transitive Verbs.** Transitive verbs are so called because they denote an action which necessarily affects or passes over to some person or thing other than the subject of the verb (Latin *transire*, to pass over).

Examples: I *throw*, I *take*. These statements are not complete; we ask immediately, What do you *throw* or *take?* The name of the person or thing affected by the action of the verb must be supplied in order to make a complete sentence—*I throw a ball, I take an apple*. The name of the person or thing which is affected by the action of the verb is called the **direct object**.

A transitive verb is one which must have a direct object expressed in order to make a complete sentence.

Intransitive Verbs. Intransitive verbs are so called because they denote an action which does not affect or pass over to any person or thing besides the subject of the verb.

Examples: I *stand*, The sun *shines*. These sentences are complete statements in themselves.

(*b*) **Active Voice.** A verb is said to be in the Active voice when its subject is spoken of as acting or doing something (Latin *ago*, I act).

Passive Voice. A verb is said to be in the Passive voice when its subject is spoken of as suffering or being acted upon (Latin *patior*, I suffer).

Examples: Active, I love, I was hearing.
Passive, I am loved, I was being heard.

N.B. Only Transitive verbs can have a Passive voice.

There are certain verbs such as *I fall, I slip*, etc. which do not speak of the subject as acting; these are however regarded as Active verbs because they are Intransitive.

(c) **Deponent Verbs.** In Latin and Greek there are many verbs which are called Deponent verbs. These are verbs which have the form of Passive verbs, but which are Active in meaning.

They are called *Deponent* because they have *laid aside* (Latin *depono*) a passive sense and assumed an active.

Examples: *patior*, I suffer. ἀποκρίνομαι, I answer.

(d) **The English Passive voice** of any verb is formed by using the proper tenses of the verb *to be* with the PASSIVE PARTICIPLE (which usually ends in *ed*) of the verb of which we desire to form the Passive voice.

Present simple Active	I love.
Present simple Passive	I am loved.
Past simple Active	I loved.
Past simple Passive	I was loved.
Future simple Active	I shall love.
Future simple Passive	I shall be loved.

This formation must be carefully distinguished from the use of the same Auxiliary verb *to be* with the ACTIVE PARTICIPLE which forms the Continuous Active tenses of the verb.

Present continuous Active	I am loving.
Past continuous Active	I was loving.
Future continuous Active	I shall be loving.

The student should be able to tell readily what voice, tense, and person any English verb is in; unless he can do this he cannot possibly translate from another language with accuracy.

It is good practice to go through the tenses of an English verb, first in the Active, and then in the Passive.

(e) **Auxiliary Verbs.** Auxiliary verbs are verbs which are used as aids (Latin *auxilia*) to enable other verbs to form moods and tenses, which cannot be expressed within the compass of one word.

Examples: I SHALL go. I WOULD HAVE gone. I SHALL HAVE BEEN sent.

In English the use of these verbs is very common, no tense in the Active Voice except the Past can be formed without them, and they are used in every tense of the Passive voice.

In Latin and Greek they are rarely used. The only verb used in these languages as an auxiliary verb is the verb *to be*.

Impersonal Verbs. Impersonal verbs are verbs which are not used in the first and second persons, but only in the third.

Examples: It rains, it snows.

The Copulative Verb, Verbs of Incomplete Predication.

The verb *to be* has two meanings:

(1) It is used in the sense of *to exist* as in the sentence *God is*.

(2) It is used to join together two nouns or noun equivalents which denote the same person or thing when the person or thing denoted by the one is said to be identical with the person or thing denoted by the other.

Examples: William was Duke of Normandy. I am the governor. This is he.

As the nouns or noun equivalents joined together by the verb *to be* denote the same person or thing, they must always be in the same case. It is grammatically incorrect to say *I am him, It is me*, because *him* and *me* are in the Accusative case, and *I* and *it* are in the Nominative case.

It is necessary to observe this rule very carefully in Latin and Greek where the Nominative and Accusative cases generally have different forms.

This rule is sometimes stated as follows:

"The verb 'to be' takes the same case after it as before it."

The verb *to be* may also join together a noun or a noun equivalent and an adjective, making a sentence which asserts that the quality denoted by the adjective is an attribute of the person or thing denoted by the noun or noun equivalent. This adjective always agrees with the noun in number, gender and case, in such languages as Latin and Greek.

Examples: The king is proud. He is good. To err is human.

From its power of joining nouns to other nouns or adjectives the verb *to be* is called the **Copulative Verb.** (Latin *copulo*, I link.)

It is also called a verb of **Incomplete Predication** because it does not make sense when it stands by itself (except when used in the sense of *to exist*), but requires to be followed by a noun or an adjective which is called the **Complement,** because it fills up the sense (Latin *compleo, I fill up*).

There are other verbs of Incomplete Predication besides the verb *to be*, some Intransitive and some Transitive.

Such verbs are: Intransitive—become, seem, appear, etc.
Transitive—make, declare, choose, think, consider, etc.

When a verb of Incomplete Predication is Intransitive, or Transitive and in the Passive voice, the Complement refers to the same person or thing as the subject of the sentence, and must therefore be in the Nominative case.

Examples: Peter became an Apostle.
This place seems healthy.
He is called our king.

But when a verb of Incomplete Predication is Transitive and in the Active voice, the Complement refers to the same person or thing as the object of the sentence, and is therefore in the Accusative case.

Examples: They made him captain.
We choose you king.
You consider me happy.

This principle is obviously of great importance in Greek and Latin.

(*f*) Person and Number.

The **First Person** of the verb is used when the speaker is speaking of himself.

The **Second Person** is used when the speaker is speaking to another person or thing.

The **Third Person** is used when the speaker is speaking of another person or thing.

Examples: 1st person, I love. 2nd person, You love. 3rd person, He loves.

The use of the **Singular Number** denotes that only one person or thing is being spoken about.

The use of the **Plural Number** denotes that more than one person or thing is being spoken about.

Rule. **The verb agrees with its subject in Number and Person.**

Note. The Plural of the second person *You* is almost always used in modern English instead of the second person Singular, even where only one person is being spoken to.

But in Latin and Greek the Singular is always used when one person is being spoken to.

(*g*) **Tense.** Tenses are forms which verbs assume to show at what time the action of the verb is represented as taking place.

The times when the action may take place are (i) Past, (ii) Present, (iii) Future.

The tenses in English have further subdivisions to show whether the action is represented as being (1) continuous or in progress, (2) indefinite or simple, (3) perfect or completed.

Below is a table of the Tenses of an English verb in the Indicative Mood with the corresponding tenses of a Greek and Latin verb, given, where possible, with the names by which the tenses are generally called in Latin and Greek Grammars.

It will be seen that there are more tense-forms in English than in Latin and Greek.

The Latin and Greek Present stands both for the English Present Continuous and Present Simple, and the Latin and Greek Future for the English Future Continuous and Future Simple.

The Latin Perfect has two meanings, one of which corresponds to the English Past Simple, and the other to the English Present Perfect or Perfect, as it is generally called.

TIME

STATE	Past	Present	Future
Continuous	I was loving I used to love Amabam (Imperfect) ἐφίλουν	I am loving Amo φιλῶ	I shall be loving Amabo φιλήσω
Simple	I loved Amavi (Perfect) ἐφίλησα (Aorist)	I love Amo φιλῶ	I shall love Amabo φιλήσω
Perfect	I had loved Amaveram (Pluperfect) ἐπεφιλήκειν	I have loved Amavi (Perfect) πεφίληκα	I shall have loved Amavero πεφιλήσομαι
Perfect Continuous	I had been loving None	I have been loving None	I shall have been loving None

(*h*) **Moods.** Moods are forms which verbs assume to show the way in which the action denoted by the verb is to be regarded, i.e. if it is a statement or fact, a command, a wish, or a thought.

The **Indicative Mood** generally makes a statement, or asks a question.

Examples: He goes. We shall run. Were you listening?

The **Imperative Mood** gives a command.

Examples: Go. Come. Make haste.

The **Subjunctive Mood** expresses a thought or wish rather than an actual fact.

The uses of the Subjunctive Mood are so various, and its use in English is so different from its use in Latin and Greek, that it is impossible to bring it under any more exact definition.

The student is warned against connecting any particular English meaning with the Latin and Greek Subjunctive, or with the Greek Optative such as *that I might love, I should, or would, love.*

Practice, and the observance of seemingly arbitrary rules, will alone enable him to use these moods correctly.

The use of tenses formed with *may, might, should, would,* etc. in English is a most unreliable guide to the use of the Subjunctive and Optative in Latin and Greek.

(*i*) **Participles.** Participles are verbal adjectives resembling verbs in that they can have subjects and objects, tenses and voices, and resembling adjectives in that they can qualify nouns.

There are two Participles in English—the Active Participle ending in *ing*, and the Passive Participle ending generally in *ed* or *d*.

Examples: *Loving, Loved.*

There is also a Past Active Participle formed with the auxiliary *having* and the Passive Participle.

Example: *Having loved.*

The Past Passive Participle is formed with the auxiliary verbs *having been* and the Passive Participle.

Example: *Having been loved.*

The Present Participle Passive is *being loved.*

There is no Past Participle Active in Latin except in the case of Deponent verbs, nor is there any Present Participle Passive. Both however are found in Greek.

As the verbal noun or Gerund in English ends in *ing* as well as the Active Participle care must be taken to distinguish them.

If the word is a Participle, it can always be replaced by such a clause beginning with a Conjunction or a Relative.

When it is a verb-noun it cannot be replaced by a clause.

Examples: (1) Skating is a fine exercise.

Here *skating* is a verb-noun and the subject of the sentence.

(2) I like to see the boys skating.

Here *skating* can be replaced by the clause *when they are skating,* and is therefore a Participle.

(3) There is a dancing bear.

Here *dancing* can be replaced by the Relative clause *that is dancing.* Therefore it is a Participle.

Participles are also used with auxiliary verbs to form certain tenses of the verb as shown above.

(j) **Verbal Nouns, Infinitive, Gerund.** The so-called Infinitive Mood *to go, to see, to hear* is really a verbal noun.

The other verbal noun in English is called the Gerund, and ends in *ing—going, seeing, hearing.*

Verbal nouns resemble verbs in that they can have a subject and an object, tenses and voices: they resemble a noun in that they themselves can be the subject or object of another verb.

Examples of the use of the Infinitive.

(1) As Subject—*To err is human.* Here *to err* is the subject of the sentence.

As is explained more fully in section 12, sentences in which the Infinitive stands as a Subject are more usually expressed in the following form with an anticipatory *it* standing as the grammatical subject before the verb:

It is human to err.

It is a pleasure to see you.

It is advisable to make haste.

The object of an Infinitive standing as the subject of a sentence may be expressed as in the following example: *To forgive such crimes is difficult,* or *It is difficult to forgive such crimes.*

Here *such crimes* is the object of *to forgive.*

The only way in which the subject of an Infinitive standing as the subject of a sentence can be expressed in English is by inserting *for* in front of it and making it depend on the predicate of the principal clause: *It is difficult* **for a king** *to forgive such crimes.*

(2) As Object—*They wish to live.* Here *to live* is the object of *they wish.*

I wish him to live. Here *him* is the subject of *to live* and the clause *him to live* is the object of *I wish.*

I wish him to see you. Here *him* is the subject, and *you* the object of *to see* and the clause *him to see you* is the object of *I wish.*

The use of the Gerund is seen in the following examples:

As Subject—Playing the violin is a delightful occupation.

As Object—He loves playing the violin.

(3) The Infinitive is also used after certain nouns and adjectives in an explanatory or epexegetic sense.

Examples: I have not the heart to do it.
We are not worthy to gather up the crumbs under His table.
It is time to depart.
He was not able to answer a word.

The Infinitive and the Gerund must be always treated as verbal nouns, and then their use, in the various constructions in which they occur, will explain itself.

Notes on the form of the English Infinitive. The English Infinitive is nearly always found with the preposition *to* in front of it.

This preposition is no part of the Infinitive, but is a relic of the Dative case of the verbal noun in Old English. The force of the preposition has become so weakened that its presence in the sentence is generally quite neglected, and another preposition may even be put in front of it, as for example— *What went ye out for to see?*

This Dative case of the verbal noun originally expressed purpose, and this use still survives in such sentences as *I came to see you, He went to hear the band.*

The preposition *to* may be omitted after certain verbs such as *may, can, shall, bid, let, make*, etc.

Examples: *I can do this, Let him go, Make him stay.*

Contrast with these the following examples, *I am able to do this, Allow him to go, Force him to stay.*

6. SENTENCES

A sentence is a group of words expressing a statement, a command, or a question. (Abbott.)

Every sentence must consist of at least two parts:

(1) **The Subject**—the name of that which is spoken about[1].

---

[1] The definition of the Subject of a sentence given above is not satisfactory. In the sentence *Caesar conquered the Gauls*, the Gauls are spoken about quite as much as Caesar.

It is however the definition generally given.

Dr Abbott suggests the following definition: "The Subject of a verb in a stating sentence is the word, or collection of words answering the question asked by putting *Who* or *What* before the verb."

(2) **The Predicate**—the word, or group of words which expresses the assertion that is made, the command that is given, or the question that is asked about the subject.

N.B. The Predicate is not necessarily identical with the verb, it includes the extensions of the verb and the objects, if any, as well as the verb.

If the verb in the Predicate is Transitive it must have an Object. **The object of a verb is the name of that towards which the action of the verb is directed.**

In considering a sentence, first pick out the verb.

The best way to find the Subject is to ask the question *who?* or *what?* before the verb.

The best way to find the Object is to ask the question *whom?* or *what?* after the verb.

Example : Caesar conquered the Gauls.

Who conquered? answer *Caesar*. Therefore *Caesar* is the Subject.

Caesar conquered whom? answer *the Gauls*. Therefore *the Gauls* is the Object.

Either the Subject or the Predicate can be omitted when it can easily be supplied from the context. It is therefore possible for a sentence to consist of only one word.

Examples : Go.   Come.   (Subject omitted.)
Who did this? I.   (Predicate omitted.)

The omission of the Subject often occurs in Latin and Greek because the forms of the verbs in these languages leave no doubt as to the number and person of the subject. It only occurs in English in the Imperative mood. When any part of the sentence is omitted it is sometimes said to be *understood*.

Every sentence must fall into one of five forms:

(1) **Subject and Intransitive Verb.**

Example : SUBJECT   PREDICATE
           The sun   *shines.*

(2) **Subject, Transitive Verb, Object.**

Example : SUBJECT   PREDICATE
                   Verb   Object
           Caesar *conquered*   *the Gauls.*

(3) Subject, Transitive Verb, two Objects.

Example:

SUBJECT	PREDICATE		
	Verb	Indirect Object	Direct Object
Socrates	*taught*	*Plato*	*philosophy.*

(4) Subject, Copulative Verb or Intransitive Verb of Incomplete Predication, Predicate Noun or Adjective.

Example:

SUBJECT	PREDICATE	
	Verb	Predicate Noun
William	*was*	*a king.*
	Verb	Predicate Adjective
He	*is*	*happy.*
Alexander	*was called*	*great.*

(5) Subject, Transitive Verb of Incomplete Predication, Object, Predicate Noun or Adjective.

Example:

SUBJECT	PREDICATE		
	Verb	Object	Predicate Noun
Tyranny	*makes*	*men*	*slaves.*
	Verb	Object	Predicate Adjective
They	*call*	*him*	*happy.*

Note. As was mentioned above the Predicate of a sentence is not necessarily identical with the verb. It includes the verb and the object or complement with all the words which qualify them.

Any part of a sentence may be amplified or extended by the addition of qualifying words. The learner must get into the habit of picking out the Verb and Subject first, and then finding out to which of the above forms the sentence, which he is going to translate, belongs.

Take for example the following sentence:

CAESAR, the great Roman general, completely CONQUERED the Gauls, the inhabitants of modern France, at the siege of Alesia.

This is a sentence of form 2 with amplifications.

A noun or pronoun may be amplified or extended in meaning by an adjective or an adjective equivalent.

A verb, an adjective, or an adverb may be amplified or extended in meaning by an adverb or an adverb equivalent.

7. EQUIVALENTS

The Noun, the Adjective, and the Adverb may be replaced by other parts of speech which can do the same work in the sentence.

A word doing the work of a different part of speech, or a group of words doing the work of a single part of speech, is called an **equivalent**.

A group of words forming an equivalent, and not having a subject or predicate of its own, is called a **phrase**.

In the above example the words *the great Roman general*, *inhabitants of modern France* and *at the siege of Alesia* are all Phrases.

A group of words forming an equivalent and having a subject and predicate of its own is called a **subordinate clause**.

Example: Caesar, *who was a great Roman general*, completely conquered the Gauls, *who inhabited modern France*, *when he took Alesia*. Here all the groups of words in italics are Subordinate Clauses.

NOUN EQUIVALENTS. A noun equivalent may be

(1) A **pronoun**. *You* are happy. *I* am miserable.

(2) A **verb-noun**, an Infinitive or Gerund. I like *to run*. *Sleeping* is pleasant.

(3) An **adjective**.
Both *wise* and *foolish* know this.

(4) A **clause**, generally called a noun or substantival clause.
That you have wronged me doth appear in this.
I see *that you know him*.
I declare *him to be a thief*.

ADJECTIVE EQUIVALENTS. An adjective equivalent may be

(1) A **verbal adjective** or participle, or a participial phrase.
A *loving* mother. A *loved* spot. We saw a man *carrying wood*.

(2) A **noun** in apposition.
Queen Victoria. Edward *the peacemaker*

(3) A **noun** preceded by a preposition, or in the possessive case.
The Houses *of Parliament*.
Maids' Causeway.
The King *of Britain*. (Compare His Britannic Majesty.)
Dogs *for hunting*.

(4) An Adjectival **Clause**.
> The horse *which I saw* is there.   At evening *when the sun did set.*

ADVERB EQUIVALENTS.   An adverb equivalent may be

(1) **A noun** preceded by a preposition.
> He lives *in the woods.*
> He walked *for six hours.*

(2) **A noun** sometimes qualified by an adjective, but without a preposition.
> He died *last night.*
> They went *home.*
> We hope to live *many years.*

(3) An Adverbial **clause**.
> I will see you *when you come.*
> I have come *in order to see him.*
> I will see you *if you come.*

(4) A participle or a participial phrase.
> We stood *amazed.*
> *Hearing this* I went home.
> *The sun having set* we went to rest.

(5) An Infinitive.
> We came *to see the spectacle.*
> He is too foolish *to be trusted.*

8. SENTENCES SIMPLE AND COMPLEX

A simple sentence is a sentence which contains a single subject and a single predicate.

A complex sentence is a sentence which contains a principal clause and one or more subordinate clauses depending on it, or on one another, as noun, adjective or adverb equivalents.

It will be found convenient to keep the name **sentence** for complete statements occurring between two full stops.

Groups of words forming part of a compound or complex sentence, and having a subject and predicate of their own, should be called **clauses.**

Groups of words forming an equivalent to some part of speech, and not having a subject and predicate of their own, should be called **phrases**.

Two or more clauses which are not dependent on one another, but which make equally important and independent statements, are said to be combined by coordination, and to form a **compound sentence**. Such clauses are generally joined together by the coordinating conjunctions *and, but, or, for,* etc.

Example: You do this, and I do that.

Example of a Complex Sentence.

When the captain drew near to the coast, he sent some of his men to land in order that he might get help, if the other ships, which had not yet arrived, should need it.

(1) Main Clause: *he sent some of his men to land.*

Subject: He.   Predicate: Sent some of his men to land.

(2) *when the captain drew near to the coast*
is an Adverbial Clause qualifying *sent.*
It tells us when he sent the men.

(3) *in order that he might get help*
is an Adverbial Clause qualifying *sent.*
It tells us why he sent the men.

(4) *if the other ships should need it*
is an Adverbial Clause qualifying *get help.*
It tells us under what conditions he would need the help.

(5) *which had not yet arrived*
is an Adjectival Clause qualifying *ships.*
It tells us more about the ships.

9. SUBSTANTIVAL OR NOUN CLAUSES

A **Substantival or Noun Clause** is a clause which stands in the relationship of a noun to the principal clause or to some other clause in a complex sentence.

(1) **As Subject.** *That he is coming* is certain.

(2) **As Object.** He said *that he was king.* (Statement.)

He commanded *that bread should be set before them.* (Command.)

He besought him *that he might be with him.* (Petition.)

Do you know *who he is?*
He asked *how it happened.* } (Questions.)
Tell me *where he lives.*

You see *how unjust he is.* (Exclamation.)

(3) As **Complement, or Predicative Noun.**
My hope is *that you may succeed.*

(4) In **Apposition** to another noun.
I had no idea *that you would oppose me.*

When a Noun Clause which is the object of a verb states a fact, it is generally called a **Dependent Statement.**

When a Noun Clause gives the words of a command or petition, it is generally called a **Dependent Command or Petition.**

When a Noun Clause begins with an interrogative or exclamatory word such as *who, what, where, whether, if, how,* it is generally called a **Dependent Question or Exclamation.**

All the Noun Clauses given above with the exception of the Dependent Questions and Exclamations are introduced by the conjunction *that* and contain a finite verb.

In certain cases however an infinitive or a gerund may be used in Noun Clauses instead of a clause introduced by *that* and containing a finite verb. This is natural because the infinitive and gerund are verbal nouns.

The infinitive is used frequently in Noun Clauses in Greek and Latin, it is therefore important to see how far the same construction prevails in English.

It is used in English as follows:

(1) As Subject. *To err* is human.
It is a pleasure *to see you.* (See section 12.)

(2) As Object. I declare him *to be guilty.*
We believe him *to be innocent.* } (Statements.)
He commanded them *to go away.* (Command.)

(3) As Complement or Predicative Noun.
My hope is *to succeed.*

The use of the infinitive in a dependent statement is only found after a few verbs in English, such as *I declare, I assert, I proclaim,*

I believe, etc. A clause introduced by *that* is by far the most common way of expressing a dependent statement in English, and can be used after any verb.

The infinitive is frequently used in dependent commands or petitions in English, and indeed is the most usual way of expressing them.

There are certain verbs such as *I wish, I hope, I am able, I can*, etc. which always take an Infinitive as their object.

These are sometimes called **Modal Verbs** because they are considered to add to the verb new ways of expressing its meaning.

Examples: I wish *to see the king.*
          We hope *to live many years.*
          They can *do nothing without you.* (See 5*j*.)

The use of the Gerund is seen in such sentences as:

Subject: *Healing the sick* is a noble work.
Object: I deny *using the expression.*

10. ADJECTIVAL CLAUSES

Adjectival clauses are introduced by the relative pronouns *Who, Which, That*, and their equivalents *when, where, such as*, etc. and qualify some noun in another clause just like an adjective.

        This is the man *who sent me.*
        This is the man *whom I saw.*
        We will do this in the evening *when we meet.*
        This is the place *where I was born.*
        I can sell you a house *such as you require.*

The word to which the relative pronoun refers, and which the clause which it introduces qualifies, is called the **antecedent**.

In the first two sentences the word *the man* is the antecedent, in the others *evening, place*, and *house*.

A Participle qualifying the Antecedent may take the place of an Adjectival Clause.

We may write:

        I saw a man clinging to a mast, or
        I saw a man who was clinging to a mast.

11. ADVERBIAL CLAUSES

Adverbial Clauses are clauses which stand in the relationship of an adverb to the verb in another clause.

Example: I will do this *on condition that you do that*.

Here the clause *on condition that you do that* qualifies the verb *I will do* just like an adverb.

The sentence might have been written: I will do this *conditionally*.

Example: I will do this *when to-morrow comes*.

Here *when to-morrow comes* is an adverbial clause qualifying *I will do*. The sentence might have been written: I will do this *to-morrow*.

Adverbial clauses may be divided into eight classes.

(1) **Final** Clauses denoting **purpose.**
(2) **Temporal** Clauses denoting **time when.**
(3) **Local** Clauses denoting **place where.**
(4) **Causal** Clauses denoting **cause.**
(5) **Consecutive** Clauses denoting **consequence.**
(6) **Conditional** Clauses denoting **supposition.**
(7) **Concessive** or **Adversative** Clauses denoting **contrast.**
(8) **Comparative** Clauses denoting **comparison.**

Examples of Adverbial Clauses

(1) He ran *that he might get home soon*.
(2) He ran *when he got on the road*.
(3) He ran *where the road was level*.
(4) He ran *because he was late*.
(5) He ran *so that he got home soon*.
(6) He ran *if he was late*.
(7) He ran *although he was early*.
(8) He ran *as he was accustomed to do*.

The names given to the various kinds of **Adverbial Clauses** in the above list are names commonly given to them in Grammars. They are given here for that reason, and not because they have anything to recommend them in themselves. Some of the names are pedantic and obscure, and it is much better to speak of the clauses of classes 1, 2, 3, 5, as clauses denoting Purpose, Time, Place, and Consequence, respectively.

A Participle may be used to express some kinds of Adverbial Clauses. Care is often needed to distinguish such participles from those which take the place of Adjectival Clauses (see 10 above).

If the participle can be resolved into a clause consisting of a conjunction and a finite verb it is used in place of an Adverbial Clause, but if it can be resolved into a clause introduced by a relative pronoun it is used in place of an Adjectival Clause.

Example (1): Knowing this, I returned home.

Here *knowing this* obviously means *since I knew this* and is therefore an **adverbial clause** denoting cause.

Example (2): I saw a man clinging to a spar half a mile from shore.

Here *clinging to a spar* might be replaced by *who was clinging to a spar*. This is a clause introduced by a relative pronoun and *clinging to a spar* must therefore be described as an **adjectival clause**.

Example (3): Seeing the man running away, I went after him.
This might be equally well expressed as follows:
Since I saw the man who was running away, I went after him.
When the sentence is put in this form there is no difficulty in analysing it.

Even Relative Clauses are sometimes adverbial if they express cause or purpose.

Example (1). We disliked our master *who seemed to take a pleasure in punishing us*. Here *who seemed* is equivalent to *because he seemed*, and is an **adverbial clause** of cause.

Example (2). They sent men *who should spy out the land*.

Here *who should spy out the land* is equivalent to *in order to spy out the land*, and is an **adverbial clause** of purpose.

In analysing complex sentences pay very little heed to the FORM, but be sure to find out what the MEANING of the clauses is by putting them into other words if necessary.

12. PREPARATORY *IT* AND *THERE*

This construction is so common in English that it seems to require special mention.

The subject is nearly always put before the verb in English; indeed, as English nouns have no case endings to distinguish the subject from the object, the order of words in a sentence is the only way in which the subject can be distinguished from the object.

But in certain cases, especially where the subject of the sentence is in the infinitive mood, the subject is placed after the verb.

Then the pronoun *it* is placed before the verb to act as a preparatory subject and to show that the real subject is coming.

Example: It is good to walk in the way of righteousness.

Here the real subject is *to walk in the way of righteousness*, and *is good* is the predicate.

It is the preparatory subject, or the grammatical subject as it is sometimes called.

The adverb *there* is used in the same way especially when the verb in the sentence is part of the verb *to be*.

Example: There was once a boy who lived on an island.

In this sentence the subject is *a boy*. *There* should be parsed as a preparatory adverb.

Neither of these constructions exist in Latin or Greek.

The Latin or Greek for the examples given above are as follows:

Bonum est ambulare in via justitiae.
καλόν ἐστι περιπατεῖν ἐν τῇ ὁδῷ τῆς δικαιοσύνης.

Olim fuit puer qui insulam habitabat.
ἦν ποτε παῖς ὃς κατῴκει νῆσον.

LESSON I

THE ALPHABET

The Greek Alphabet consists of 24 letters, a good many of which are identical with the corresponding letters of the Latin alphabet which we still employ. Both alphabets were derived from the Phoenician alphabet, from which the Hebrew alphabet also took its origin.

The letters given in the second column are now used only as capital letters in printed Greek books; but originally letters like these were used in all Greek writing. They are generally called Uncial letters, and all the earliest manuscripts of the New Testament are called Uncial Manuscripts, because they are written throughout in these letters.

About the 9th century A.D. another style of writing more resembling the letters in the third column came into general use. These were called Cursive or running letters, because they could be written without raising the pen from the paper, like our modern handwriting.

This type of writing has remained in use ever since, both in manuscripts and printed books, with certain modifications.

The student should learn the list of the names of the letters down the column thoroughly in order that he may be able to find the words in his Dictionary as quickly as possible.

He should make sure of the letters both by reading aloud and by writing, as much time will afterwards be saved if he is able to read accurately and quickly, and to grasp the sound of a word as soon as he sees it written. It will be noticed that there are two letters to represent the English letter "e," and two to represent the letter "o."

One of these represents the short sound of the letter, and the other the long sound. The mark – written over a letter denotes that it is to be pronounced long, and the mark ⌣ that it is to be pronounced short. This distinction in the length of the sound denoted by the letters must be carefully observed in pronunciation.

THE ALPHABET

Name of the letter	Capital letters	Small letters	English equivalent	Pronunciation
Alpha	A	α	ă	When long like *a* in "father," when short like *a* in "cat."
Bēta	B	β	b	Like English *b*.
Gămma	Γ	γ	g	Always hard like *g* in "get."
Delta	Δ	δ	d	Like English *d*.
Epsĭlon	E	ε	ĕ	Like *e* in "met."
Zēta	Z	ζ	z	Like English *z* or *ds*.
Ēta	H	η	ē	Like *a* in "fate."
Thēta	Θ	θ	th	Like *th* in "thin."
Iōta	I	ι	i	When long like *ee* in "queen," when short like *i* in "hit."
Kappa	K	κ	k	Like English *k*.
Lambda	Λ	λ	l	Like English *l*.
Mu	M	μ	m	Like English *m*.
Nu	N	ν	n	Like English *n*.
Xī	Ξ	ξ	x	Like English *x*.
Ōmĭcron	O	ο	ŏ	Like *o* in "not."
Pī	Π	π	p	Like English *p*.
Rhō	P	ρ	r	Like English *r*.
Sigma	Σ	σ, ς	s	Like English *s*.
Tau	T	τ	t	Like English *t*.
Upsĭlon	Υ	υ	u	Like French *u* in "du."
Phī	Φ	φ	ph	Like English *ph*.
Chī	X	χ	ch	Like *ch* in "chaos," or in Scotch "loch."
Psī	Ψ	ψ	ps	Like *ps* in "lips."
Ōmĕgă	Ω	ω	ō	Like *o* in "tone."

Notes on the Alphabet

The letter γ is sounded like *n* before the letters γ, κ, χ, ξ:

    ἐγγίζω   ἄγκυρα   σύγχυσις   σάλπιγξ.
    engizo   ankura   sunchusis   salpinx.

It is suggested that the Greek υ should be pronounced like *u* in the French "du" because we have no exactly equivalent sound in English. The *y* sound in such words as "sympathy" will do fairly well. "Sympathy" is a word transliterated into English from the Greek word συμπαθία. It should be noted that when a Greek word is transliterated into English, υ always becomes *y*; for examples take the words "hydropathic," "hypocrite." The form of the Greek capital letter Υ is like our letter Y, the reason being that our letter *Y* is derived from the Greek alphabet through Latin.

The universal custom used to be to pronounce Greek by giving the vowels the same sound as they generally have in English. For example

    ā was pronounced as *a* in "lathe."
    η was pronounced as *ee* in "meet."
    υ was pronounced as *u* in "duty."
    ī was pronounced as *i* in "bite."

This method of pronunciation should not be followed.

It will be noticed that two forms are given for the letter σ: the first should be used when the letter occurs at the beginning or in the middle of a word, the second when it occurs at the end.

The pronunciation of Diphthongs

Diphthongs are sounds produced by two vowels being sounded together; they should be pronounced as follows in England:

    αι to be pronounced as *ai* in "aisle."
    ει to be pronounced as *ei* in "height."
    οι to be pronounced as *oi* in "oil."
    αυ to be pronounced as *ow* in "cow."
    ου to be pronounced as *oo* in "loose."
    ευ to be pronounced as *eu* in "feud."
    υι to be pronounced as *ui* in "quit."

Classification of Consonants, for reference only

Consonants are divided into three groups:

(1) MUTES, or letters which cannot be sounded by themselves. κ, γ, χ, π, β, φ, τ, δ, θ.

(2) SEMI-VOWELS, or letters which have some sound of their own. λ, μ, ν, ρ, σ.

(3) DOUBLE LETTERS, or letters which are made up of two consonants. ξ, ζ, ψ.

The MUTES are again subdivided according to the part of the vocal organs used in producing them:

(a) GUTTURALS, or letters produced in the throat (Latin "guttur"). κ, γ, χ.

(b) LABIALS, or letters produced by the lips (Latin "labia"). π, β, φ.

(c) DENTALS, or letters produced by the teeth (Latin "dens"). τ, δ, θ.

The SEMI-VOWELS are divided into:

(a) LIQUIDS. λ, μ, ν, ρ.

(b) SPIRANT. σ.

Exercise 1

(1) Write out the English alphabet and give the Greek equivalent for each letter as far as possible.

(2) Write out the Greek alphabet with the English equivalent for each letter.

These exercises should be repeated many times until perfect.

LESSON II

BREATHINGS, ACCENTS, IOTA SUBSCRIPT

It will be noticed that there is no sign for the letter *h* in the Greek alphabet. The want of such a sign is made up by the marks called breathings, one of which is written over every vowel or diphthong that begins a word. The rough breathing ‘ (turned like the opening comma in inverted commas) is sounded like our letter *h*, ὁ is pronounced "ho," ἁ is pronounced "ha." The smooth breathing ’ indicates that the vowel is to be sounded without the rough *h* sound. If the word begins with a diphthong, the breathing is placed over the second vowel, and not over the first—οὗτος not ὅυτος. ρ at the beginning of a word generally has a rough breathing.

ρρ in the middle of a word is sometimes written ῤῥ.

Accents are marks invented by Aristophanes of Byzantium about 200 B.C. in order to teach foreigners the correct pronunciation of Greek. They were not written in the ancient manuscripts. They denoted musical pitch and not stress, and no use of them is made now as a guide to correct speech. The student who is pressed for time is recommended not to trouble about the accents except in the case of verbs.

They are chiefly of use to distinguish certain words which differ only in accent. A list of these together with a brief account of the principles of accentuation is given in the appendix.

The student however must on no account neglect the breathings, but must write and pronounce them carefully.

A small ι is often written under the letters *a*, *η*, *ω* especially when one of these letters ends a word. It is called the Iota Subscript and is a relic of an ancient diphthong. It is not pronounced, but it must always be written. All the other letters in a Greek word are pronounced.

Exercise 2

Write out the following in Greek letters inserting breathings where necessary. The English letter *h* at the beginning of a word denotes a rough breathing. The vowels *e* and *o* are marked with a stroke over the line when they are long; when not marked they are short. Care must be taken to use the proper Greek letter for them.

The letter *i* in brackets denotes that ι subscript is to be written under the preceding vowel. Use small letters throughout.

en archē(i) ēn ho logos, kai ho logos ēn pros ton theon, kai theos ēn ho logos. houtos ēn en archē(i) pros ton theon. panta di autou egeneto kai chōris autou egeneto oude hen ho gegonen. en autō(i) zōē ēn, kai hē zōē ēn to phōs tōn anthrōpōn. kai to phōs en tē(i) skotia(i) phainei, kai hē skotia auto ou katelaben. egeneto anthrōpos apestalmenos para theou, onoma autō(i) iōanēs. houtos ēlthen eis marturian, hina marturēsē(i) peri tou phōtos, hina pantes pisteusōsin di autou. ouk ēn ekeinos to phōs, all hina marturēsē(i) peri tou phōtos. ēn to phōs to alēthinon ho phōtizei panta anthrōpon erchomenon eis ton kosmon. en tō(i) kosmō(i) ēn, kai ho kosmos di autou egeneto, kai ho kosmos auton ouk egnō. eis ta idia ēlthen, kai hoi idioi auton ou parelabon. hosoi de elabon auton edōken autois exousian tekna theou genesthai, tois pisteuousin eis to onoma autou, hoi ouk ex haimatōn oude ek thelēmatos sarkos oude ek thelēmatos andros all ek theou egennēthēsan. kai ho logos sarx egeneto kai eskēnōsen en hēmin, kai etheasametha tēn doxan autou, doxan hōs monogenous para patros plērēs charitos kai alētheias.

The student may correct his exercise by comparing it with the first 14 verses of the 1st chapter of St John in the Bible Society's (Nestle's) Greek Testament. This exercise should be done several times until perfect.

Write out the Greek of St John i. 19–28 in English characters.

Read as much as possible of the Greek Testament aloud, paying great attention to the breathings and the length of the vowels.

Students who are working alone and who have no one to whom they can read aloud are recommended to put portions of the Greek into English letters, and to put them back into Greek letters after an interval. It is most important to be able to read the characters accurately and quickly before proceeding further.

LESSON III

THE PRESENT INDICATIVE OF THE VERB IN THE ACTIVE VOICE

The Present Indicative Active of the verb λέγω "I say" is as follows:

1st singular	λέγω	(legō)	I say, or I am saying.
2nd "	λέγεις	(legeis)	Thou sayest, or thou art saying.
3rd "	λέγει	(legei)	He, she, or it says, or is saying.
1st plural	λέγομεν	(legŏmen)	We say, or we are saying.
2nd "	λέγετε	(legĕte)	You say, or you are saying.
3rd "	λέγουσι(ν)	(legousi)	They say, or they are saying.

Note: the ν at the end of the 3rd person is generally written when the next word begins with a vowel or at the end of a sentence.

Each of the Greek words given in the table above may be divided into two parts:

(1) a stem λεγ- which never changes, and which denotes the meaning of the verb, i.e. "say."

(2) an ending ω, εις, ει, ομεν, etc. which changes with every person.

As nearly every Greek verb has the same endings in the present tense it is easy to conjugate the present tense of any other verb by first taking off the final ω of the 1st person singular to find the stem, and then adding the endings in order to this stem.

The words in the table above, when compared with their English equivalents, furnish a good example of one of the principal differences between Greek and English, namely that one word may be sufficient to make a statement in Greek, where two or three words are necessary in English.

This is because the endings of words are changed in the Greek language to denote changes in the meaning of the words, while in English these variable endings have almost entirely disappeared.

For example, in the English present tense the only forms which retain their personal endings are the 2nd and 3rd persons singular "sayest" and "says." Consequently it is necessary to insert a personal pronoun "I," "thou," "he," etc. before the verb to avoid confusion, and to show the person and number of the subject of the verb. But in

Greek the person and number of the subject of the verb are already made sufficiently clear by the variable ending, and so there is no need to add a personal pronoun unless special emphasis is required.

It will be found that this principle applies to all forms of the verbs.

It will be noticed that two English equivalents are given for the one Greek form of the Present tense. This is because there are more tenses in English than in Greek, and one Greek tense has to do the work of two English tenses. See page xxiii.

The first form given in English above is called the Present Indefinite, or Present Simple; the second is called the Present Continuous.

The Greek Present corresponds more closely in meaning to the English Present Continuous than to the Present Simple.

In the forms of the Present Continuous tense will be noticed another difference between English and Greek, namely that in English we freely employ Auxiliary or helping verbs to form our tenses (in this case the present tense of the verb "to be" is used) while in Greek a single word is used.

In spoken English we now never use the 2nd person singular in addressing a single person, but always the 2nd person plural.

In Greek the 2nd person singular is ALWAYS used in addressing a single person, and the 2nd person plural is kept for addressing more than one person. In these exercises when "thou" is written in English the 2nd person singular must be used in Greek, and when "ye," or "you" is written the 2nd person plural must be used in Greek, unless an indication is given to the contrary.

In translating the Greek Testament it is better to use the 2nd person singular of the English verb when the 2nd person singular is used in Greek.

Exercise 3

Learn Vocabulary 1, p. 156. The words given in this and the following vocabularies are all words which occur frequently in the New Testament. The student should make a habit of carefully mastering all the words in the vocabularies as he goes along, as this will save much subsequent labour. The words given in brackets after the English meanings of the words are words derived from the Greek words. They are intended to help the learner to remember them. The Greek words are also transliterated in the first few vocabularies.

Translate into English: λέγει, λέγομεν, λέγουσι, λέγετε, λέγεις. εὑρίσκομεν, γράφει, βάλλετε, ἀποθνήσκει, βλέπεις, ἐγείρουσι, κρίνετε, βάλλομεν, ἐσθίω, ἀποστέλλουσι, ἀκούουσι, λαμβάνετε, σώζομεν, μένει.

Give the Greek for: we say, they say, thou sayest, ye say, he says, they are saying, she is saying, you say, they are dying, he dies, I am throwing, she rouses, we judge, thou art remaining, ye judge, he sends, you are writing, thou art eating, he finds, we are taking, they look, she hears.

LESSON IV

THE PRESENT INDICATIVE OF CONTRACTED VERBS IN εω[1]

When a personal ending beginning with a vowel is added to a stem ending in a vowel the vowels unite and form a diphthong or a single long vowel.

This is called "contraction."

There are many verbs whose stems end in ε, and, when the personal endings are added to such stems, contraction takes place.

ε coming before another ε becomes ει.

ε coming before ο becomes ου.

ε coming before a long vowel, or a diphthong, drops out.

The present tense of the verb φιλέω "I love" is conjugated as follows:

φιλῶ	for φιλέω	I love, or I am loving.
φιλεῖς	for φιλέεις	Thou lovest, or thou art loving.
φιλεῖ	for φιλέει	He, she, or it loves, or is loving.
φιλοῦμεν	for φιλέομεν	We love, or we are loving.
φιλεῖτε	for φιλέετε	You love, or you are loving.
φιλοῦσι	for φιλέουσι	They love, or they are loving.

[1] See Appendix, p. 186.

Exercise 4

Learn Vocabulary 2.

λαλοῦμεν, αἰτεῖς, τηροῦσι, ποιεῖτε, παρακαλεῖ, μαρτυροῦσι, ζητεῖτε, καλῶ, θεωροῦμεν, τηρεῖς.

They seek, he asks, thou callest, we bear witness, they speak, you keep safe, I exhort, she makes, you behold, we love, they call, she asks, we seek, they bear witness, he beholds.

LESSON V

NOUNS OF THE SECOND DECLENSION ENDING IN ος

Nouns of the Second Declension ending in ος in the Nominative case are declined as follows. They are nearly all Masculine.

	Name of Case	Greek	English
Singular	Nominative	λόγος	a word (subject).
	Vocative	λόγε	O word.
	Accusative	λόγον	a word (object).
	Genitive	λόγου	of a word.
	Dative	λόγῳ[1]	to or for a word.
Plural	Nominative	λόγοι	words (subject).
	Vocative	λόγοι	O words.
	Accusative	λόγους	words (object).
	Genitive	λόγων	of words.
	Dative	λόγοις	to or for words.

The declension of the noun given above brings before us again the difference between English and Greek mentioned in Lesson III, namely that it is often necessary to employ two or more words in English where one suffices in Greek. The various modifications of meaning which are expressed in Greek by adding case endings to the noun are expressed in English by placing a preposition before the noun, or by altering the order of the words in the sentence. The only noun

[1] The Iota Subscript is always written under the ω of the Dative Singular of the second declension : it is not sounded.

NOMINATIVE AND ACCUSATIVE

endings which remain in English are the 's and s' of the Possessive case, and the s or other ending added to make the plural.

For example, if we want to show that a word is the subject of a sentence, we nearly always put it before the verb, while the word which is the object of the sentence is placed after the verb.

If we invert the order of the words, we invert the meaning of the sentence.

In the sentence "An angel finds a man," the word "angel" is the subject of the sentence, and the word "man" the object.

On the other hand in the sentence "A man finds an angel" "man" is the subject of the sentence, and "angel" the object.

We have inverted the order of the words, and, in so doing, we have also inverted the meaning of the sentence.

In Greek the first sentence should be written:

$$\ddot{\alpha}\gamma\gamma\epsilon\lambda os \; \epsilon\dot{\upsilon}\rho\acute{\iota}\sigma\kappa\epsilon\iota \; \ddot{\alpha}\nu\theta\rho\omega\pi o\nu.$$

We show that ἄγγελος is the subject by putting it in the Nominative case, and that ἄνθρωπον is the object by putting it in the Accusative case.

In Greek the meaning of the sentence is still the same if we invert the order of the words and write ἄνθρωπον εὑρίσκει ἄγγελος, because in Greek it is not the order of the words, but the case form, which decides which word is the subject or object.

RULES

(1) **The subject of a Finite**[1] **verb is in the Nominative case.**

(2) **The direct object of a Transitive verb is in the Accusative case.**

Before translating an English sentence into Greek it is necessary to know which word is the subject of the verb, and which is its direct object, if it has one.

The subject can always be found by putting "who?" or "what?" before the verb.

In the first sentence given above: "An angel finds a man," we ask "Who finds?" The answer is "an angel." "An angel" is therefore the subject of the sentence.

In the same way we can easily see that "a man" is the subject of the second sentence.

[1] A Finite verb is a verb in any mood but the Infinitive.

We can find the direct Object by placing "whom?" or "what?" after the verb. In the case of the first sentence we say "an angel finds whom?" Answer "a man." Therefore "a man" is the object of the sentence.

Many verbs such as the verb "I remain" cannot have a direct object. Verbs which cannot have a direct object are called Intransitive verbs, because the action which they denote does not pass over to some other person or thing (Latin "transire").

Verbs which can have a direct object are called Transitive verbs, because the action which they denote passes over to another person or thing.

It is easy to find which English verbs are Transitive and which are Intransitive by making a sentence containing the verb and seeing if a direct object can be put after it, or not.

(3) **Finite verbs agree with their subject in number and person.**
All nouns are in the third person unless they are in the Vocative case.

If the subject of the verb is a noun in the singular number (not in the Vocative case), the verb will be in the third person singular; if the subject of the verb is a noun in the plural number, or two or more nouns joined together by "and," the verb will be in the third person plural, with the exception noted above.

Examples:
ἄνθρωπος ἐσθίει ἄρτον. A man eats bread.
ἄνθρωποι ἐσθίουσιν ἄρτον. Men eat bread.
ἄνθρωπος καὶ δοῦλος ἐσθίουσιν ἄρτον. A man and a slave eat bread.
The English Indefinite Article "a" is not translated into Greek.

Learn Vocabulary 3. **Exercise 5**

1. ἄνθρωπος ἔχει δούλους. 2. ἄγγελος λαὸν σώζει. 3. κύριος λόγους γράφει. 4. ἐγείρεις δοῦλον. 5. ἄνθρωποι ὁδὸν εὑρίσκουσι. 6. δοῦλος βλέπει οἴκους. 7. ἄνθρωπος ἀποστέλλει ἀδελφούς. 8. λαμβάνετε οἶκον. 9. δοῦλος ἔχει κύριον. 10. εὑρίσκομεν ὁδόν. 11. τηρεῖτε νόμους. 12. ἄνθρωρος καὶ δοῦλος εὑρίσκουσιν ἀδελφούς.

1. A man hears an angel. 2. An angel rouses a man. 3. Slaves find a way. 4. A brother has a house. 5. Lords send slaves. 6. They are writing words. 7. You find an angel. 8. A lord judges men. 9. We rouse slaves. 10. Thou keepest laws. 11. A man and an angel see a way. 12. Thou beholdest death.

LESSON VI

USE OF THE GENITIVE AND DATIVE CASES. THE DEFINITE ARTICLE

The **Genitive Case** can generally be translated into English by the use of the Preposition "OF," or by the Possessive Case, formed by adding 's to the noun.

Example: οἶκος ἀνθρώπου means, "a house of a man," or "a man's house."

The commonest use of the **Dative Case** is to denote the person TO or FOR whom anything is done. It is used to express the indirect object after verbs meaning "to give" and other verbs which will be noted in the vocabularies.

Examples: He writes laws for a people.
γράφει νόμους λαῷ.
He gives a house to a man.
δίδωσιν οἶκον ἀνθρώπῳ.

In the last sentence οἶκον is called the direct object, and ἀνθρώπῳ the indirect object, because it is not directly affected by the action of the verb.

The Definite Article

The Definite Article which corresponds to the English "the" is declined in Greek like a noun. The forms that go with words in the Masculine gender are as follows:

Singular. N. ὁ   Plural. N. οἱ
A. τόν   A. τούς
G. τοῦ   G. τῶν
D. τῷ   D. τοῖς

It will be noticed that the endings except the Nominative Singular are the same as the endings of λόγος.

The definite article is always in the same case and number and gender as the noun to which it is joined.

Examples: Of the man, τοῦ ἀνθρώπου.   To the men, τοῖς ἀνθρώποις.
"The man's house" is sometimes written in the following order: ὁ τοῦ ἀνθρώπου οἶκος.

Exercise 6

Revise Vocabularies 1, 2, 3.

1. οἱ δοῦλοι ποιοῦσιν ὁδὸν τῷ κυρίῳ. 2. οἱ ἄνθρωποι ζητοῦσιν τοὺς ἀγγέλους. 3. γράφει τὸν νόμον τοῦ Κυρίου[1]. 4. ὁ ἀδελφὸς τοῦ δούλου βλέπει τὸν οἶκον. 5. γράφομεν τοὺς νόμους τῷ λαῷ. 6. ὁ[2] θεὸς φιλεῖ τοὺς ἀδελφούς. 7. ζητεῖτε τὸν τῶν ἀνθρώπων ἀδελφόν. 8. τηροῦσιν τὸν λόγον τοῦ θεοῦ. 9. οἱ δοῦλοι εὑρίσκουσιν ὁδὸν τοῖς κυρίοις. 10. λαμβάνομεν τὸν νόμον τῷ κόσμῳ. 11. λαλῶ τοὺς λόγους τῷ λαῷ, καὶ ὁ λαὸς πιστεύει.

1. The angel finds the men. 2. They are writing the laws for the people. 3. We are seeking the brothers of the slave. 4. The lord's slaves are making a way. 5. The slave remains. 6. You behold the house of God[2]. 7. We keep the law of the Lord. 8. They write words for the slaves. 9. We find a way for the people. 10. The man saves the slave's brother. 11. The man and the slave are making bread. 12. The brethren believe. 13. The angel writes laws for the world.

LESSON VII

NEUTER NOUNS OF THE SECOND DECLENSION

In English all nouns denoting men or male animals are in the Masculine gender; all nouns denoting women or female animals are in the Feminine gender; all other nouns are Neuter.

But in Greek the rule is not so simple.

Nearly all nouns denoting men or male animals are Masculine, and nearly all those denoting women or female animals are Feminine: but other nouns may be either Masculine, Feminine, or Neuter. The gender is generally to be inferred from the ending.

---

[1] When Κύριος is written with a capital letter it means "The LORD"; it sometimes has the definite article and sometimes not. It is the word used in the Greek Version of the Old Testament to denote the sacred name Jehovah.

[2] Θεός generally has the definite article in Greek, but not in English.

GENDER AND TERMINATIONS

In the Second Declension nearly all nouns ending in ος in the Nominative singular are Masculine; ὁδός "a way," ἔρημος "a desert," παρθένος "a maiden," which are Feminine, are some of the few exceptions to this rule.

All nouns ending in ον in the Nominative singular are Neuter. The declension of these neuter nouns is given below.

Note that the Nominative, Vocative and Accusative cases have the same ending. The Nominative, Vocative and Accusative Plural of all neuter nouns end in α, as in Latin.

Declension of ἔργον "a work."

Singular. N. ἔργον   Plural. N. ἔργα
V. ἔργον   V. ἔργα
A. ἔργον   A. ἔργα
G. ἔργου   G. ἔργων
D. ἔργῳ   D. ἔργοις

The Definite Article that goes with neuter nouns is declined as follows:

Singular. N. τό   Plural. N. τά
A. τό   A. τά
G. τοῦ   G. τῶν
D. τῷ   D. τοῖς

A noun in the neuter plural which stands as the subject of a sentence is nearly always followed by a verb in the singular and is thus an exception to the principle stated in the rule on p. 12.

Example: τὰ παιδία εὑρίσκει τὰ βιβλία.
The children find the books.

Exercise 7

Learn Vocabulary 4.

1. ὁ δοῦλος βλέπει τὰ δένδρα τῶν ἀνθρώπων. 2. ὁ Κύριος ποιεῖ τὰ ἔργα τῷ κόσμῳ. 3. εὑρίσκομεν τὸ ἱερὸν τοῦ θεοῦ. 4. τὰ πρόβατα θεωρεῖ τὰ δένδρα. 5. ἀκούουσι τὸ εὐαγγέλιον. 6. τηρεῖς τὰ βιβλία. 7. δαιμόνιον ἔχεις. 8. λαμβάνετε τὰ πλοῖα. 9. θεωροῦμεν τὸ πρόσωπον τοῦ Κυρίου. 10. ἀποστέλλουσι τὰ παιδία τοῦ δούλου. 11. τηροῦμεν τὰ σάββατα τοῦ Κυρίου. 12. σώζετε τὰ τέκνα. 13. τὰ παιδία ἔχει τὰ βιβλία.

1. They take the garments of the men. 2. We send the brother's children. 3. The angel receives the books for the people. 4. The children have the garments. 5. He beholds the face of God. 6. Thou hast the sheep. 7 You find the trees. 8. The Lord judges the works of men. 9. We seek the temple. 10. God works miracles (does signs) for the people. 11. The man seeks the young child. 12. The children eat the loaves. 13. Thou keepest the money safe.

LESSON VIII

FEMININE NOUNS OF THE FIRST DECLENSION

Nouns of the First Declension ending in a or η in the Nominative singular are declined as follows. They are all feminine.

ἀρχή a beginning.   ἡμέρα a day.

	Singular	Plural	Singular	Plural
N. V.	ἀρχή	ἀρχαί	ἡμέρα	ἡμέραι
A.	ἀρχήν	ἀρχάς	ἡμέραν	ἡμέρας
G.	ἀρχῆς	ἀρχῶν	ἡμέρας	ἡμερῶν
D.	ἀρχῇ	ἀρχαῖς	ἡμέρᾳ	ἡμέραις

Observe the ι subscript in the Dative singular.

The article which goes with these nouns is declined as follows:

Singular.	N.	ἡ	Plural.	N.	αἱ
	A.	τήν		A.	τάς
	G.	τῆς		G.	τῶν
	D.	τῇ		D.	ταῖς

We have now had examples of nouns of all the three genders, and of the forms of the article which go with them.

The full declension of the definite article is as follows:

	Singular		
	Masc.	Fem.	Neut.
N.	ὁ	ἡ	τό
A.	τόν	τήν	τό
G.	τοῦ	τῆς	τοῦ
D.	τῷ	τῇ	τῷ

THE DEFINITE ARTICLE

	Masc.	Plural Fem.	Neut.
N.	οἱ	αἱ	τά
A.	τούς	τάς	τά
G.	τῶν	τῶν	τῶν
D.	τοῖς	ταῖς	τοῖς

RULE

The definite article agrees with the noun with which it is connected in number, gender, and case.

Exercise 8

Learn Vocabulary 5.

1. ἡ ἀγάπη μένει. 2. λαμβάνομεν τὴν[1] δικαιοσύνην. 3. παρακαλοῦσι τὴν ἐκκλησίαν. 4. ὁ Κύριος κρίνει τὰς ψυχὰς τῶν[1] ἀνθρώπων. 5. βλέπετε τὴν συναγωγὴν τῶν ἀδελφῶν. 6. ζητοῦμεν τὴν βασιλείαν τοῦ θεοῦ. 7. ἔχεις τὴν[1] σοφίαν καὶ τὴν[1] χαράν. 8. τηρεῖτε τὰς ἐντολὰς τῶν ἀγγέλων. 9. οἱ ἀδελφοὶ ἀποστέλλουσιν τὰς γραφάς.

1. We receive the promises of God. 2. They have the Lord's commands. 3. The sins of the world remain. 4. Thou hearest the voice of the Lord. 5. We bear witness to the truth (dat.). 6. You exhort the church. 7. He has righteousness, peace and joy. 8. The brethren are writing the Scriptures. 9. The Lord keeps the souls of men. 10. Ye are seeking wisdom.

LESSON IX

MASCULINE NOUNS OF THE FIRST DECLENSION. FEMININE NOUNS ENDING IN α PRECEDED BY A CONSONANT

Nouns of the First Declension ending in ης or ας in the Nominative singular are masculine. They are declined as follows:

[1] Abstract nouns generally have a definite article before them in Greek and so have also words like ἄνθρωπος when they denote a whole class. This article is not translated into English.

For the article before θεός, see p. 14.

NOUNS OF THE FIRST DECLENSION

προφήτης a prophet.

	Singular	Plural
N.	προφήτης	προφῆται
V.	προφῆτα	προφῆται
A.	προφήτην	προφήτας
G.	προφήτου	προφητῶν
D.	προφήτῃ	προφήταις

νεανίας a young man.

	Singular	Plural
N.	νεανίας	νεανίαι
V.	νεανία	νεανίαι
A.	νεανίαν	νεανίας
G.	νεανίου	νεανιῶν
D.	νεανίᾳ	νεανίαις

Nouns of the First Declension ending in α in the Nominative singular not preceded by a vowel or the letter ρ are declined as follows:

δόξα glory.

	Singular. N. V.	A.	G.	D.
	δόξα	δόξαν	δόξης	δόξῃ

	Plural.			
	δόξαι	δόξας	δοξῶν	δόξαις

Note that all nouns of the 1st Declension have the same endings in the plural.

Exercise 9

Learn Vocabulary 6. The conjunctions δέ, γάρ, οὖν never stand as the first word of a sentence. The prepositions ἐν, σύν, ἀπό, ἐκ, πρό, εἰς are always followed by a noun or pronoun in the proper case, as mentioned in the vocabulary.

1. οὐ καλοῦσι τοὺς προφήτας εἰς τὴν συναγωγήν. 2. ὁ γὰρ Κύριος γράφει τὰς ἐπαγγελίας ἐν ταῖς καρδίαις τῶν ἀδελφῶν. 3. παρακαλοῦσι τοὺς[1] προφήτας σὺν τοῖς[1] μαθηταῖς. 4. τὰ δὲ πλοῖα οὐ μένει ἐν τῇ θαλάσσῃ. 5. ἐν ἀρχῇ ὁ θεὸς ἀποστέλλει τοὺς προφήτας. 6. οὐχ εὑρίσκουσι τὰ τέκνα ἐν τῇ ὁδῷ. 7. οἱ μαθηταὶ μένουσιν ἐν τῇ ἐξουσίᾳ τοῦ δεσπότου. 8. ὁ νεανίας λαμβάνει τὸ ἱμάτιον ἀπὸ τῆς κεφαλῆς τοῦ παιδίου. 9. ἡ[1] παρθένος εὑρίσκει τὰ βιβλία.

1. We do not see the boats on the lake. 2. The master sends the children with the slaves from the synagogue. 3. Thou remainest before the house of the Lord. 4. The prophets exhort the brethren and the people. 5. Therefore the sin of the world remains. 6. They behold the glory of the Lord in the temple. 7. The Baptist remains in the synagogue with the disciples. 8. They send the prophet from

[1] See the rule on p. 17.

the lake with the Baptist. 9. You send the children out of the house. 10. For the church does not hear the commandments and the promises of the prophet. 11. They call the disciples to the assembly. 12. For God writes the commandments in the hearts of the disciples. 13. The young men hear the parables of the kingdom.

LESSON X

ADJECTIVES OF THE SECOND DECLENSION. THE PRESENT TENSE OF THE VERB "TO BE"

Adjectives of the Second Declension are declined as follows:

ἀγαθός "good."

		Masculine	Feminine	Neuter
Sing.	N.	ἀγαθός	ἀγαθή	ἀγαθόν
	V.	ἀγαθέ	ἀγαθή	ἀγαθόν
	A.	ἀγαθόν	ἀγαθήν	ἀγαθόν
	G.	ἀγαθοῦ	ἀγαθῆς	ἀγαθοῦ
	D.	ἀγαθῷ	ἀγαθῇ	ἀγαθῷ
Plur.	N. V.	ἀγαθοί	ἀγαθαί	ἀγαθά
	A.	ἀγαθούς	ἀγαθάς	ἀγαθά
	G.	ἀγαθῶν	ἀγαθῶν	ἀγαθῶν
	D.	ἀγαθοῖς	ἀγαθαῖς	ἀγαθοῖς

Note that the Masculine endings are the same as those of 2nd Declension nouns in ος. The Feminine endings are the same as those of 1st Declension nouns in η. The Neuter endings are the same as those of 2nd Declension nouns in ον.

If a vowel or the letter ρ comes immediately before the endings of an adjective, the endings in the Feminine are the same as those of ἡμέρα.

Example: ἅγιος "holy."

	Masculine	Feminine	Neuter
N.	ἅγιος	ἁγία	ἅγιον
V.	ἅγιε	ἁγία	ἅγιον
A.	ἅγιον	ἁγίαν	ἅγιον
G.	ἁγίου	ἁγίας	ἁγίου
D.	ἁγίῳ	ἁγίᾳ	ἁγίῳ

RULE

Adjectives agree with the noun which they qualify in number, gender, and case.

Note. An adjective preceded by an article is practically equivalent to a noun. ὁ πρῶτος "the first" (man); τὰ ἔσχατα "the last things"; αἱ ἀγαθαί "the good" (women); οἱ ἅγιοι "the holy" (men) or "the saints."

The Present Indicative of the verb "to be" is as follows:

	Singular		Plural
[1]1st	εἰμί	I am	ἐσμέν we are
2nd	εἶ	thou art	ἐστέ you are
3rd	ἐστί(ν)	he, she, or it is	εἰσί(ν) they are

The verb "to be" belongs to a class of verbs called "Copulative Verbs" because they serve to couple or link together two nouns or a noun and an adjective. Such verbs cannot make a statement by themselves, but must be followed by a noun or an adjective to make a complete predicate. This noun or adjective is called a predicative noun or adjective, or the complement. These predicative nouns or adjectives are not put in the Accusative case like the object of a transitive verb, because they are not objects. They must always be in the same case as the subject of the verb, and, in the case of predicative adjectives, they must agree with the subject in number and gender as well as case.

This rule is sometimes stated in this form:

RULE

The verb "to be" takes the same case after it as before it.

Examples:

Subject	Verb	Predicative noun or adjective
The man	is	a prophet
ὁ ἄνθρωπός	ἐστι	προφήτης
God	is	good
ὁ θεός	ἐστιν	ἀγαθός
We	are	slaves
	δοῦλοί ἐσμεν	

[1] For the accentuation of these words see p. 142.

IMPERFECT INDICATIVE

You	are	just
	δίκαιοί ἐστε	
The tongue	is	evil
ἡ γλῶσσά	ἐστι	κακή

Note. The various parts of the verb "to be" given above should not be placed as the first words in a sentence.

Exercise 10

Learn Vocabulary 7.

1. ἡ ἐκκλησία πιστή ἐστιν. 2. οἱ ἄνθρωποι προφῆταί εἰσιν. 3. ἡ βασιλεία ἐστὶ κακή. 4. ἡ ἐντολὴ τοῦ αἰωνίου θεοῦ δικαία ἐστίν. 5. λαμβάνουσι τὰ ἴδια ἱμάτια. 6. ἕτεροι ἄνθρωποι μένουσιν ἐν τῷ πρώτῳ πλοίῳ. 7. τέκνα ἀγαπητά ἐσμεν τοῦ θεοῦ. 8. ὁ πρῶτός ἐστιν ἔσχατος, καὶ ὁ ἔσχατος πρῶτος. 9. οἱ ἅγιοι τηροῦσιν τὰ ἅγια σάββατα τοῦ θεοῦ. 10. ἡ γλῶσσα πονηρά ἐστιν. 11. αἱ πισταὶ μένουσιν ἐν τῷ ἱερῷ. 12. μαθηταί ἐστε τοῦ Κυρίου. 13. ἅγιος εἶ, Κύριε. 14. καλοῦμεν τοὺς ἑτέρους νεανίας.

1. The brethren are disciples. 2. We are prophets. 3. Thou art good, O master. 4. The writings of the Apostles are holy. 5. A different man is in the last boat. 6. We remain in the evil world. 7. He makes his own garments. 8. The man is just and good. 9. Therefore the Baptist exhorts the evil men. 10. The saints remain before the house of God. 11. God keeps the souls of the saints. 12. Ye exhort the disciples.

LESSON XI

THE IMPERFECT INDICATIVE ACTIVE.
ACCENTUATION OF VERBS

All past tenses of the Indicative mood are preceded by the letter ε which is called the Augment. If the verb begins with a consonant the Augment is simply placed before the verb: Present, λέγω; Imperfect ἔλεγον. If the verb begins with a vowel the Augment combines with it.

ε before α becomes η,
ε before ε becomes η (except in the verb ἔχω),
ι, ο, υ are lengthened into ῑ, ω, ῡ.

THE AUGMENT

A diphthong lengthens its first vowel:

αι becomes ῃ, ει becomes ῃ,
οι becomes ῳ, αυ and ευ become ηυ.

Examples:

Present	Imperfect
ἀκούω	ἤκουον
ἐγείρω	ἤγειρον
ὁμολογέω	ὡμολόγουν
αἰτέω	ᾔτουν
οἰκέω	ᾤκουν
αὐξάνω	ηὔξανον
εὑρίσκω	ηὕρισκον
but ἔχω	εἶχον

As these changes take place at the beginning of the words they must be carefully noticed, or it will not be possible to find the words in a dictionary where verbs are generally given under the Present tense.

When a verb is compounded with a preposition[1] (compare the English verbs "to out-number," "to under-take") the Augment comes between the preposition and the verb. The last vowel of the preposition generally drops out[2]; ἐκ becomes ἐξ.

Examples:

Present	Imperfect
ἀποθνήσκω	ἀπέθνησκον
παρακαλέω	παρεκάλουν
ἐκβάλλω	ἐξέβαλλον
ὑπάγω	ὑπῆγον
but περιπατέω	περιεπάτουν
προπέμπω	προέπεμπον

The conjugation of the Imperfect Indicative Active of ordinary and contracted verbs in εω is given below.

Singular
1. ἔλεγον   I was saying, or I used to say.
2. ἔλεγες   Thou wast saying, or thou usedst to say.
3. ἔλεγε(ν) He was saying, or he used to say.

Plural
1. ἐλέγομεν We were saying, or we used to say.
2. ἐλέγετε You were saying, or you used to say.
3. ἔλεγον   They were saying, or they used to say.

[1] Verbs compounded with a preposition are marked with an asterisk (*) in the earlier vocabularies.
[2] The exceptions to this rule are περί, πρό, ἀμφί.

ἐφίλουν   for ἐφίλεον   I was loving, or I used to love.
ἐφίλεις   for ἐφίλεες   Thou wast loving, or thou usedst to love.
ἐφίλει   for ἐφίλεε   He was loving, or he used to love.
ἐφιλοῦμεν for ἐφιλέομεν   We were loving, or we used to love.
ἐφιλεῖτε for ἐφιλέετε   You were loving, or you used to love.
ἐφίλουν   for ἐφίλεον   They were loving, or they used to love.

The meaning of the Imperfect. Strictly speaking, the Imperfect denotes continuous action in past time, or action often repeated in past time, and is represented by the English Past Continuous forms given in the tables above. But a simple Past tense ("I said," "I loved" etc.) may sometimes be a sufficient translation for a Greek Imperfect tense. The Greek tense which most nearly resembles the English simple Past tense is postponed on account of its difficulty. In the next seven exercises the Greek Imperfects should be translated by the English Past Continuous forms, even if they are sometimes rather clumsy.

The Accentuation of Verbs

The accentuation of verbs is so simple, and, in many respects, so important that the student is recommended to make himself familiar with its principles, and to accent the verbs which he writes.

If the last syllable of a verb is long (i.e. if it contains a long vowel or a diphthong, with the exception of αι or οι[1]) the accent falls on the last syllable but one, with certain exceptions to be mentioned later.

If the last syllable of a verb is short (i.e. if it contains a short vowel) the accent falls on the last syllable but two.

N.B. For purposes of accentuation αι and οι are considered as short vowels[1].

The accent resembles the acute accent ′ used in French.

All syllables other than those having the written accent are supposed to have an accent sloping the other way called the grave accent. This is never written, and it is only of importance in connection with the accentuation of contracted verbs.

It will be noticed that contracted verbs have sometimes an acute accent, and sometimes a circumflex accent ˜.

The principle on which the accentuation of these verbs is determined is as follows: if when the uncontracted form of the verb is written

---

[1] Except in the Optative Mood.

with all its accents an acute and a grave come together on the two syllables that are contracted in such a way that the grave follows the acute '' the two combine and form a circumflex.

But, if the grave comes before the acute on the syllables which contract '', the acute remains alone. Examples: φιλέομεν = φιλοῦμεν, φιλέει = φιλεῖ. But ἐφιλέε = ἐφίλει, φιλεέτω = φιλείτω.

Exercise 11

Learn Vocabulary 8.

1. ἀπεκτείνετε τοὺς προφήτας τοῦ Κυρίου. 2. ὁ θεὸς ἔπεμπε τοὺς ἀγγέλους εἰς τὸν κόσμον. 3. ἦγε[1] τοὺς μαθητὰς ἀπὸ τῆς θαλάσσης. 4. οἱ νεανίαι ἔχαιρον. 5. τὰ πρόβατα ὑπῆγον[2] ἐκ τῆς ἐρήμου. 6. ὁ βαπτιστὴς βαπτίζει τὰς παρθένους. 7. ὁ ἄγγελος ἀπέλυε τὸν ἀπόστολον. 8. οἱ μαθηταὶ ἐδόξαζον τὸν Κύριον. 9. οἱ ἀγαθοὶ δοῦλοι ἔφερον τὰ πρόβατα. 10. Ἰωάνης ὁ βαπτιστὴς ἔκραζε ἐν τῇ ἐρήμῳ. 11. ἐδίδασκες τὰ παιδία σὺν τοῖς δούλοις. 12. ἐκηρύσσομεν τὸ εὐαγγέλιον τῷ λαῷ. 13. ἔπειθον οὖν τοὺς ἀνθρώπους. 14. περιεπατοῦμεν ἐν τῷ ἱερῷ. 15. ἐξέβαλλες τὰ δαιμόνια.

1. They were proclaiming the Gospel to the disciples. 2. The maidens were departing from the house. 3. They were dragging (ἄγω) the slave's boat to the sea. 4. The prophets used to teach the children in the houses. 5. Ye were glorifying the Lord, O angels. 6. Thou wast teaching the people. 7. They were driving the sheep together to the trees. 8. The child was reading the scriptures in the temple. 9. We were departing from the lake. 10. John the Baptist does not work[3] signs. 11. The Lord walked about in the wilderness. 12. Therefore you were persuading the people. 13. The saints were rejoicing. 14. He was casting out devils. 15. We were carrying the boat. 16. You were loosing the slaves.

[1] If the accent falls on the last syllable but one of any word in which the last syllable but one is long, and the last syllable short, the accent is always circumflex.

[2] The accent never goes back beyond the augment.

[3] ποιέω.

LESSON XII

THE IMPERFECT OF THE VERB "TO BE."
DEMONSTRATIVE PRONOUNS. αὐτός

The Imperfect tense of the verb "to be" is as follows:

Singular		Plural	
1. ἤμην	I was	1. ἦμεν	we were
2. ἦς (ἦσθα)	thou wast	2. ἦτε	you were
3. ἦν	he was	3. ἦσαν	they were

The Demonstrative Pronouns οὗτος "this" and ἐκεῖνος "that" are declined as follows:

		Masculine	Feminine	Neuter
Sing.	N. V.	οὗτος	αὕτη	τοῦτο
	A.	τοῦτον	ταύτην	τοῦτο
	G.	τούτου	ταύτης	τούτου
	D.	τούτῳ	ταύτῃ	τούτῳ
Plur.	N. V.	οὗτοι	αὗται	ταῦτα
	A.	τούτους	ταύτας	ταῦτα
	G.	τούτων	τούτων	τούτων
	D.	τούτοις	ταύταις	τούτοις
Sing.	N. V.	ἐκεῖνος	ἐκείνη	ἐκεῖνο
	A.	ἐκεῖνον	ἐκείνην	ἐκεῖνο
	G.	ἐκείνου	ἐκείνης	ἐκείνου
	D.	ἐκείνῳ	ἐκείνῃ	ἐκείνῳ
Plur.	N. V.	ἐκεῖνοι	ἐκεῖναι	ἐκεῖνα
	A.	ἐκείνους	ἐκείνας	ἐκεῖνα
	G.	ἐκείνων	ἐκείνων	ἐκείνων
	D.	ἐκείνοις	ἐκείναις	ἐκείνοις

It will be noticed that when there is an *o* or *ω* in the endings of οὗτος the vowel of the first syllable is *ου*, when there is an *η* or *α* it is *αυ*.

οὗτος, ἐκεῖνος, αὐτός

οὗτος and ἐκεῖνος agree with the nouns which they qualify in number, gender, and case just like adjectives. When they qualify a noun the noun always has the article.

Examples:

This man, οὗτος ὁ ἄνθρωπος, or ὁ ἄνθρωπος οὗτος.
Those sheep, ἐκεῖνα τὰ πρόβατα, or τὰ πρόβατα ἐκεῖνα.
That commandment, ἐκείνη ἡ ἐντολή, or ἡ ἐντολὴ ἐκείνη.

When οὗτος stands by itself without any word expressed for it to agree with it means "this man," αὕτη means "this woman," τοῦτο means "this thing," ταῦτα means "these things."

The same is the case with ἐκεῖνος.

αὐτός, αὐτή, αὐτό is declined like ἐκεῖνος. In the New Testament it is the ordinary word for "he, she, it" etc.

Examples:

For he saves the people.
αὐτὸς γὰρ σώζει τὸν λαόν.
They were leading him to the sea.
ἦγον αὐτὸν εἰς τὴν θάλασσαν.
He was sending her from the temple.
ἔπεμπεν αὐτὴν ἀπὸ τοῦ ἱεροῦ.
This is his slave.
οὗτός ἐστιν ὁ δοῦλος αὐτοῦ[1].
These are her houses.
οὗτοί εἰσιν οἱ οἶκοι αὐτῆς[1].

αὐτός also means "himself, herself, itself" when connected with a noun.

Example: Jesus himself taught them.
Ἰησοῦς αὐτὸς ἐδίδασκεν αὐτούς.

[1] For a fuller treatment of these pronouns see Appendix, p. 187.

EXERCISES. THE PASSIVE

Exercise 12

Revise Vocabularies 1—8.

1. οὗτοι οἱ ἄνθρωποι ἀπέθνησκον ἐν τῇ ἐρήμῳ. 2. ἐθεωροῦμεν τοὺς οἴκους αὐτῶν. 3. οὗτος οὖν ἦν μαθητὴς Ἰωάνου τοῦ βαπτιστοῦ. 4. ἦμεν γὰρ δοῦλοι τῆς ἁμαρτίας. 5. ἐκεῖνα δὲ τὰ δένδρα ἔβαλλον εἰς τὴν θάλασσαν. 6. αὗται ἔμενον ἐν τῷ πλοίῳ. 7. ὁ γὰρ θεὸς σώζει αὐτοὺς ἀπὸ τοῦ πονηροῦ (the evil one). 8. ἦτε οὖν δεσπόται τοῦ λαοῦ. 9. οὐ γὰρ κρίνομεν ταῦτα. 10. οἱ υἱοὶ αὐτοῦ ἦσαν κακοί. 11. αὕτη γὰρ ἦν ἡ ἐντολὴ αὐτοῦ. 12. ἐκηρύσσομεν ταῦτα ἐν τῇ ἐκκλησίᾳ. 13. ἐκεῖνοι δὲ ἐξέβαλλον τὰ δαιμόνια. 14. ἐν ἐκείνῃ τῇ ἡμέρᾳ ἐδόξαζον τὴν σοφίαν τοῦ Κυρίου. 15. αἱ παρθένοι συνῆγον τὰ πρόβατα αὐτῶν εἰς τὰ δένδρα. 16. ἐν ἐκείνῃ τῇ ὥρᾳ ἐχαίρομεν. 17. ὁ Ἰησοῦς αὐτὸς οὐκ ἐβάπτιζεν ἀλλὰ οἱ μαθηταὶ αὐτοῦ. 18. ἡ ζωὴ μένει ἐν αὐτοῖς.

1. In the beginning was the word. 2. This is the love of God. 3. For the Lord saves the souls of men from the evil one. 4. Peace and truth are in the kingdom of God. 5. They were glorifying his power and wisdom. 6. For in that day we were preaching the gospel of the kingdom in the synagogue, and casting out devils. 7. You saw her sons in the house. 8. We received them into the boat. 9. Ye were in the temple in those days. 10. This is life eternal. 11. We heard the voice of the angel from the trees. 12. They were holy and beloved. 13. Their children were in the assembly. 14. Thou wast reading the scriptures to them in the synagogue. 15. The Jews used to slay his prophets. 16. The Baptist himself used to baptise his disciples.

LESSON XIII

THE PASSIVE VOICE OF THE PRESENT AND IMPERFECT INDICATIVE

A verb is said to be in the Active Voice when its subject is spoken of as acting: it is said to be in the Passive Voice when its subject is spoken of as suffering, or being acted upon.

Examples: Active "I love," "I was striking."
Passive "I am loved," "I was being struck."

THE INDICATIVE PASSIVE

N.B. Only Transitive verbs can have a Passive voice. There are certain verbs such as "I fall," "I slip," etc. which do not speak of the subject as acting, but which are regarded as Active verbs because they are Intransitive.

The Passive voice is formed in Greek, as in Latin, by the use of special endings, and not by the use of the Auxiliary verb "to be" as in English.

The Passive voice of the Present and Imperfect Indicative of λύω is given below. Note that the Imperfect Passive has the Augment.

Present Indicative Passive

Sing.
1. λύομαι — I am loosed, or I am being loosed.
2. λύῃ (λύει) — Thou art loosed, or thou art being loosed.
3. λύεται — He is loosed, or he is being loosed.

Plur.
1. λυόμεθα — We are loosed, or we are being loosed.
2. λύεσθε — You are loosed, or you are being loosed.
3. λύονται — They are loosed, or they are being loosed.

Imperfect Indicative Passive

Sing.
1. ἐλυόμην — I was being loosed.
2. ἐλύου — Thou wast being loosed.
3. ἐλύετο — He was being loosed.

Plur.
1. ἐλυόμεθα — We were being loosed.
2. ἐλύεσθε — You were being loosed.
3. ἐλύοντο — They were being loosed.

Note. As in the case of the active voice a simple Past tense "I was loosed" etc. will often sufficiently translate the Imperfect.

The Present and Imperfect Indicative Passive of verbs in εω are conjugated as follows:

Present Indicative Passive

φιλοῦμαι	for φιλέομαι	I am loved, or I am being loved.
φιλεῖ, φιλῇ	for φιλέει, φιλέῃ	etc.
φιλεῖται	for φιλέεται	
φιλούμεθα	for φιλεόμεθα	
φιλεῖσθε	for φιλέεσθε	
φιλοῦνται	for φιλέονται	

AGENT AND INSTRUMENT

Imperfect Indicative Passive

ἐφιλούμην	for ἐφιλεόμην	I was being loved.
ἐφιλοῦ	for ἐφιλέου	etc.
ἐφιλεῖτο	for ἐφιλέετο	
ἐφιλούμεθα	for ἐφιλεόμεθα	
ἐφιλεῖσθε	for ἐφιλέεσθε	
ἐφιλοῦντο	for ἐφιλέοντο	

Consider the sentences:

"The angel looses the apostle."
ὁ ἄγγελος λύει τὸν ἀπόστολον.
"The apostle is loosed by the angel."
ὁ ἀπόστολος λύεται ὑπὸ τοῦ ἀγγέλου.

Both these sentences express the same idea, but they express it in different ways. It will be noticed that when a sentence with a verb in the active voice is turned into a sentence with a verb in the passive voice, as has been done in the sentences given above, the object of the first sentence "the apostle" becomes the subject of the second, while the subject of the first sentence "the angel" is introduced in English by the preposition "by."

Consider the sentence:

"The world is kept by the wisdom of God."
ὁ κόσμος τηρεῖται τῇ σοφίᾳ τοῦ θεοῦ.

It will be seen that the form of this sentence is the same in English as that of the second sentence given above.

In Greek however the sentences are not the same in form, but the preposition ὑπό followed by a Genitive is used in the one sentence, and a simple Dative in the other.

This is because the doer of the action in the first sentence is a living person, i.e. "the angel"; but the thing that does the action in the second sentence is not a living person, but "wisdom."

In sentences similar to the first of these two sentences the doer of the action is spoken of as the AGENT, because it is a living thing.

In sentences similar to the second sentence the doer of the action is spoken of as the INSTRUMENT, because it is not a living thing.

This distinction must be carefully observed.

The same distinction exists in Latin where the Agent is expressed by "a" with the Ablative, and the Instrument by the Ablative alone.

AGENT AND INSTRUMENT. PREPOSITIONS

RULE

In Classical Greek the Agent of the action of a Passive verb is expressed by ὑπό with the Genitive: the Instrument is expressed by the Dative alone.

Active verbs may also be followed by a word denoting the instrument.

Example: He kills the apostle with a sword.

ἀποκτείνει τὸν ἀπόστολον μαχαίρᾳ.

The same verb may have both an Agent and an Instrument.

Example: The apostle is loosed by the angel by a word.

ὁ ἀπόστολος λύεται ὑπὸ τοῦ ἀγγέλου λόγῳ.

The Prepositions διά and μετά may be followed by a noun or pronoun either in the Accusative or Genitive case.

The student should here refer to the lesson on prepositions on p. 121. The preposition πρός is generally followed by an Accusative case, and the preposition ὑπό by a Genitive case. For the meanings of these prepositions see the vocabulary.

Exercise 13

Learn Vocabulary 9.

1. ἐπέμπεσθε ὑπὸ τῶν διδασκάλων πρὸς ἕτερον ὄχλον. 2. ἐν τούτῳ τῷ τόπῳ ἐθεωροῦμεν τοῖς ὀφθαλμοῖς τὸν Κύριον τῶν οὐρανῶν. 3. οὗτοι οἱ λόγοι ἐλαλοῦντο ὑπὸ τῶν ἀποστόλων πρὸς τοὺς πρεσβυτέρους. 4. εὐθὺς δὲ τὰ πρόβατα συνήγετο λίθοις ὑπὸ τῶν λῃστῶν. 5. ἀπεστελλόμεθα μετὰ τῶν προφητῶν διὰ τοῦ ὄχλου. 6. διὰ τοῦτο ἐπείθου τοῖς λόγοις τῶν κριτῶν. 7. μετὰ ταῦτα οἱ τελῶναι ἐδιδάσκοντο μετὰ τῶν νεανιῶν ὑπὸ τῶν πρεσβυτέρων. 8. οἱ υἱοὶ τοῦ οἰκοδεσπότου ἤσθιον τοὺς ἄρτους. 9. ὑποκριτά, οὐ περιπατεῖς ἐν ταῖς ὁδοῖς τοῦ Κυρίου. 10. ὁ θρόνος ἐποιεῖτο ὑπὸ τῶν ἐργατῶν τῷ οἴκῳ τοῦ Κυρίου ἐν Ἰερουσαλήμ. 11. οἱ ἐργάται ἀπέστελλον τοὺς καρποὺς τῆς γῆς πρὸς τοὺς οἰκοδεσπότας. 12. ὦ Ἱερουσαλήμ, οὐχ εὑρίσκῃ πιστή. 13. παρεκαλούμεθα τοῖς λόγοις τῶν μαθητῶν ἐν ἐκείνῳ τῷ χρόνῳ. 14. ἤγομεν τὰ τέκνα διὰ τοῦ ἱεροῦ. 15. μετ' ἐκείνας τὰς ἡμέρας οἱ λῃσταὶ ὑπῆγον πρὸς τὴν ἔρημον.

1. The word of God was being preached by the apostles. 2. These fruits were sent by the householder to the elders. 3. On this account the judges were being persuaded by the faithful teachers. 4. Thou wast leading the people through the wilderness to Jerusalem. 5. After

this they were being sought for by the crowd. 6. They were wicked in the eyes of the Lord. 7. The throne was being carried by the workmen to another place through the house. 8. Immediately the elders were walking with the prophets through Jerusalem. 9. The world was being made through the Son of God. 10. O thou hypocrite, thou dost not keep the commandments of the Lord. 11. The young men were being taught by their own teachers. 12. Thou art not sent by the sons of the prophets. 13. Therefore immediately after these things we used to preach the word of God to the disciples. 14. Ye were being roused by the words of the householder.

LESSON XIV

DEPONENT VERBS. THE PRESENT IMPERATIVE. THE RELATIVE PRONOUN

Deponent verbs are verbs which have the form of the Passive voice in Greek, but which are translated by a verb in the Active voice in English. They are called "Deponent" because the old grammarians considered that they had "laid aside" (Latin "deponere") a Passive sense, and assumed an Active.

Examples:
- ἀποκρίνομαι — I answer.
- ἄρχομαι — I begin.
- ἔρχομαι — I go, or come.
- δέχομαι — I receive.

The Imperative Mood. Moods are forms which verbs assume to show the way in which the action or state denoted by the verb is to be regarded, i.e. if it is to be regarded as a statement of fact, a command, a wish, or a thought.

All the forms of verbs, which have been given so far, have been in the Indicative mood, that is the mood which is generally used in making statements, or asking questions.

The Imperative mood, the forms of which are given below, is used to express commands, exhortations and entreaties.

The forms given in this section are those of the Present tense of the Imperative mood.

Present Imperative Active
Sing. 2. λῦε — loose (thou).
      3. λυέτω — let him loose.

Present Imperative Passive
2. λύου — be loosed (thou).
3. λυέσθω — let him be loosed.

THE PRESENT IMPERATIVE

Present Imperative Active
Plur. 2. λύετε   loose (ye).
3. λυέτωσαν   let them loose.

Present Imperative Passive
2. λύεσθε   be loosed (ye).
3. λυέσθωσαν let them be loosed.

The Present Imperative of verbs in εω is as follows:

Present Imperative Active

φίλει   for φίλεε   love (thou)
φιλείτω   for φιλεέτω   etc.
φιλεῖτε   for φιλέετε
φιλείτωσαν   for φιλεέτωσαν

Present Imperative Passive

φιλοῦ   for φιλέου   be loved (thou)
φιλείσθω   for φιλεέσθω   etc.
φιλεῖσθε   for φιλέεσθε
φιλείσθωσαν   for φιλεέσθωσαν

The meaning of the Present Imperative. The Present tense in Greek in moods other than the Indicative denotes CONTINUOUS action, action IN PROGRESS, or REPEATED action rather than action in present time.

Just as the Imperfect tense denotes a continued or repeated action in past time so the Present Imperative denotes a command or entreaty to continue to do an action, or to do it repeatedly.

It is not always possible to bring this out in translating a Present Imperative into English, as we have no convenient form of expression which is equivalent to it. An attempt to express in full the force of the Greek Present Imperative is made in the translation of the examples given below. This subject will be treated more fully when we come to deal with the Aorist Imperative.

A verb in the Imperative mood is negatived by μή, and not by οὐ.

Examples of the use of the Present Imperative:

Keep on throwing the stones.
βάλλετε τοὺς λίθους.
Do not keep on answering the master.
μὴ ἀποκρίνεσθε τῷ διδασκάλῳ.

Let him continue to keep the commandments.
τηρείτω τὰς ἐντολάς.

Do not walk in the ways of wickedness any longer.
μὴ πορεύου ἐν ταῖς ὁδοῖς τῆς ἀδικίας.

The Relative Pronoun

The Relative Pronoun is declined as follows:

Singular

	Masc.	Fem.	Neut.	Masc. Fem.	Neut.
N.	ὅς	ἥ	ὅ	who, or that	which
A.	ὅν	ἥν	ὅ	whom, or that	which
G.	οὗ	ἧς	οὗ	whose, or of whom	of which
D.	ᾧ	ᾗ	ᾧ	to whom	to which

Plural

	Masc.	Fem.	Neut.	Masc. Fem.	Neut.
N.	οἵ	αἵ	ἅ	who, or that	which
A.	οὕς	ἅς	ἅ	whom, or that	which
G.	ὧν	ὧν	ὧν	whose, or of whom	of which
D.	οἷς	αἷς	οἷς	to whom	to which

Notice that the Relative Pronoun is almost the same in form as the endings of the 2nd and 1st declensions with rough breathings added.

The accentuation should be noticed and learnt and compared with that of the Article.

Note the difference between ὅ the Nom. and Acc. Sing. Neut. of the Relative and ὁ the Nom. Sing. Masc. of the Article.

Compare also
ἥ and ἡ
οἵ and οἱ
αἵ and αἱ

The Relative Pronoun always refers back to some noun or pronoun, expressed or implied, in another clause which is called its Antecedent.

In Greek Relative Pronouns agree with their antecedent in number and gender, but NOT in case.

The case of a Relative Pronoun depends on the function which it performs in the clause in which it stands, which is sometimes called a Relative Clause.

Examples:
1. I see the men who are coming.
βλέπω τοὺς ἀνθρώπους οἳ ἔρχονται.
2. The men that you are sending are going away.
οἱ ἄνθρωποι οὓς στέλλετε ἀπέρχονται.
3. This is the writing that is kept in the synagogue.
αὕτη ἐστὶν ἡ γραφὴ ἣ τηρεῖται ἐν τῇ συναγωγῇ.
4. This is the writing which the apostle used to have.
αὕτη ἐστὶν ἡ γραφὴ ἣν εἶχεν ὁ ἀπόστολος.
5. The children whom I was teaching are going away.
τὰ παιδία ἃ ἐδίδασκον ἀπέρχεται.
6. The prophet whose books thou art reading is holy.
ὁ προφήτης οὗ ἀναγινώσκεις τὰ βιβλία ἅγιός ἐστιν.
7. The men for whom I am doing this are slaves.
οἱ ἄνθρωποι οἷς ποιῶ ταῦτα δοῦλοί εἰσιν.

In example 1 ἀνθρώπους is in the Accusative case because it is the object of the clause in which it stands. οἵ is in the Nominative case because it is the subject of the clause in which it stands.

The student should carefully consider the reason for the cases of the Relative Pronouns in the other examples in the same way.

Sections 8 and 10 in the Introduction on English Grammar should be read in connexion with this lesson.

The Relative clauses in the examples given above are all ADJECTIVAL clauses, because they qualify and explain their antecedents just like adjectives.

Exercise 14

Learn Vocabulary 10.

1. ἐπορευόμεθα πρὸς τὴν θάλασσαν μετὰ τῶν μαθητῶν. 2. ἠρνοῦντο τὸν Κύριον τῆς δόξης ὃς τηρεῖ αὐτοὺς ἀπὸ τοῦ πονηροῦ. 3. ἐδέχεσθε τοὺς ἀγροὺς οὓς εἶχεν ὁ λαὸς Ἰσραήλ. 4. μὴ ἀποκρίνου τῷ δεσπότῃ. 5. ἀπήρχοντο πρὸς τὴν ἔρημον ἐν ᾗ ὁ Ἰωάνης ἐβάπτιζε. 6. ἀπεκρινόμην τοῖς ἀγγέλοις οἳ ἤρχοντο ἀπὸ τῶν πρεσβυτέρων. 7. μὴ ἐργάζεσθε τὴν ἀδικίαν. 8. οὗτος δέχεται τοὺς ἁμαρτωλοὺς οἳ ἔρχονται πρὸς αὐτὸν καὶ ἐσθίει μετ' αὐτῶν. 9. ἅπτου τῶν κεφαλῶν τῶν παιδίων ἃ πέμπω. 10. οἱ δοῦλοι οὓς ἐδέχετο ἐργάζονται ἐν τοῖς ἀγροῖς. 11. ἀποστέλλωσαν

PRESENT INFINITIVES

τὰ ἱμάτια ἃ λαμβάνουσιν εἰς τὸν οἶκον. 12. δεχέσθω τὸ βιβλίον ὃ γράφει ὁ ἀπόστολος. 13. διηρχόμεθα οὖν τοὺς ἀγροὺς αὐτῶν μετὰ τῶν τελωνῶν. 14. κακοὶ καὶ πονηροὶ δοῦλοι ἦτε. 15. ἁπτέσθωσαν τῶν λίθων τοῦ ἱεροῦ ὃ ᾠκοδομεῖτο τῷ Κυρίῳ.

1. Let the love of the brethren remain in their hearts. 2. Keep the holy commandments which you receive from the teachers. 3. Do not deny the Lord of glory who saves you[1] from the evil world. 4. Let the elders whom they send receive the law for the people. 5. We were going through the fields in which the slaves were working. 6. After these things they were building a temple to the God of Israel. 7. Do not walk (pl.) in the way of sinners. 8. Let him receive the messengers who proclaim the kingdom of heaven. 9. The disciples whom John was baptising remained in the wilderness. 10. Let them work the works of the Lord of glory. 11. For the prophet receives the sinners who are sent to him and eats with them. 12. Do not answer the teacher. 13. After those days they were going away into the place in which the young men were remaining with the sheep. 14. This is the elder whose children were reading the books of the law which the prophet was writing.

LESSON XV

THE PRESENT INFINITIVE.
PERSONAL AND POSSESSIVE PRONOUNS

The Present Infinitives are as follows:

Present Infinitive Active		Present Infinitive Passive	
λύειν	to loose	λύεσθαι	to be loosed
φιλεῖν	to love	φιλεῖσθαι	to be loved
	εἶναι	to be	

The so-called Infinitive Mood is really, both in Greek and English, the Dative case of a verbal noun. In many of its uses however its Dative sense is quite forgotten, and it is treated exactly as if it were an indeclinable verbal noun. It is always neuter. The Infinitive partakes of the nature both of a verb and a noun. As a verb it has a subject expressed or understood, and it may have an object; it is qualified by adverbs, and has tense and voice. As a noun it may stand as the subject or object of another verb.

[1] ὑμᾶς.

THE INFINITIVE

Infinitive used as a Subject. The Infinitive is especially common as the subject of an Impersonal verb or of ἐστί. As it is a verbal noun and therefore partakes of the nature of a verb, it may have a subject of its own. If this subject is expressed it is put in the ACCUSATIVE case.

Examples:
To err is human.
παραβαίνειν ἀνθρώπινόν ἐστι.
It is lawful to heal on the Sabbath.
ἔξεστι θεραπεύειν ἐν τῷ σαββάτῳ.
It was necessary for him to pass through Samaria.
ἔδει αὐτὸν διέρχεσθαι διὰ τῆς Σαμαρίας.
It is good for us to be here.
καλόν ἐστιν ἡμᾶς εἶναι ὧδε.

Notice that in the English of the last three examples the word "it" is placed first as a sort of preparatory subject, the real subjects of the three sentences are however the Noun Clauses "to heal on the Sabbath," etc., as will be seen if the sentences are written in the following form:

To heal on the Sabbath is lawful.
To pass through Samaria was necessary for him.
To be here is good for us.

In the last two examples the subjects of the Infinitives αὐτόν and ἡμᾶς are expressed in Greek in the Accusative case.

Note that in English these words are in the Dative.

The verb ἔξεστι is however followed by a noun or pronoun in the Dative case to express the person to whom the action is lawful.

Example:
It is lawful for us to heal on the Sabbath.
ἔξεστιν ἡμῖν θεραπεύειν ἐν τῷ σαββάτῳ.

Infinitive used as Object. After verbs meaning "to entreat," "to exhort," "to command," a verb in the Infinitive mood is used as the direct object, while a noun or pronoun in an Accusative, Genitive, or Dative case is used with it as the secondary object of the main verb.

Examples:
He commands them to bring Paul.
κελεύει αὐτοὺς ἄγειν τὸν Παῦλον.
I beseech thee to heal my son.
δέομαί σου θεραπεύειν τὸν υἱόν μου.

IN FINAL CLAUSES

He used to charge them not to depart from Jerusalem.

παρήγγελλεν αὐτοῖς μὴ ὑπάγειν ἀπὸ Ἱεροσολύμων.

If the subject of the Infinitive is expressed it is in the ACCUSATIVE case[1].

He commands Paul to be brought.

κελεύει τὸν Παῦλον ἄγεσθαι.

All clauses which stand as the subject or object of a verb are called Substantival Clauses.

The Infinitive with Modal Verbs. The Infinitive is used to complete the meaning of certain verbs which are called "Modal Verbs" because they give the verb the power of expressing itself in new moods or ways. Modal verbs in Greek generally correspond in meaning to those verbs which are used as Modal verbs in English.

Examples: They wish to remain.
βούλονται καταμένειν.
We are willing to hear.
θέλομεν ἀκούειν.
I am able to do this.
δύναμαι τοῦτο ποιεῖν.
They begin to build.
ἄρχονται οἰκοδομεῖν.

The Infinitive used in Final clauses. As has been already stated the Infinitive is really the DATIVE case of a verbal noun.

It may therefore be used not only as the verb in a Substantival Clause but also as the verb in an Adverbial Clause expressing Purpose.

Such clauses are called FINAL CLAUSES.

The Infinitive is used in Final clauses on the same principle that a noun in the Dative case is used in English to express purpose.

Example: He went to the market for corn.

And so both in Greek and English the Infinitive is used to express PURPOSE.

Examples:

He sends his slaves to call the prophets.

ἀποστέλλει τοὺς δούλους καλεῖν τοὺς προφήτας.

John used to go to the Jordan to baptise the disciples.

ὁ Ἰωάνης ἤρχετο πρὸς τὸν Ἰορδάνην βαπτίζειν τοὺς μαθητάς.

[1] Syntax 159.

The negative used with the Infinitive in the New Testament is always μή.

Summary. The Infinitive is used in SUBSTANTIVAL CLAUSES as being a VERBAL NOUN.

The Infinitive is used in FINAL CLAUSES as being the DATIVE CASE of a verbal noun.

Personal and Possessive Pronouns

The Personal Pronouns of the 1st and 2nd persons are as follows:

Singular

	1st person			2nd person	
[1]N.	ἐγώ	I	N. V.	σύ	thou
A.	ἐμέ, μέ	me	A.	σέ	thee
G.	ἐμοῦ, μοῦ	of me, my	G.	σοῦ	of thee, thy
D.	ἐμοί, μοί	to me	D.	σοί	to thee

Plural

N.	ἡμεῖς	we	N. V.	ὑμεῖς	you
A.	ἡμᾶς	us	A.	ὑμᾶς	you
G.	ἡμῶν	of us, our	G.	ὑμῶν	of you, your
D.	ἡμῖν	to us	D.	ὑμῖν	to you

As has been already mentioned, all cases of αὐτός are used in the New Testament as the Personal Pronoun of the 3rd person "he, she, it," etc. οὗτος and ἐκεῖνος are also sometimes used as Personal Pronouns.

Examples: He is the way, the truth and the life.
οὗτός ἐστιν ἡ ὁδός, ἡ ἀλήθεια καὶ ἡ ζωή.
But he was teaching in the temple.
ἐκεῖνος δὲ ἐδίδασκεν ἐν τῷ ἱερῷ.

The Nominative case of the Article followed by μέν and δέ is used as a Personal Pronoun of the 3rd person. This construction is frequent in the Classics but not in the N.T.

Examples: But he was sending him away.
ὁ δὲ ἀπέστελλεν αὐτόν.
But they depart into the wilderness.
οἱ δὲ ὑπάγουσι εἰς τὴν ἔρημον.

ὁ μέν followed by ὁ δέ must be translated by "One...another."

[1] The longer forms ἐμέ, etc. are used with prepositions.

POSSESSIVE PRONOUNS

οἱ μέν followed by οἱ δέ must be translated "Some...others."

Example: Some remained, but others were going away.
οἱ μὲν ἔμενον, οἱ δὲ ἀπήρχοντο.

As the personal ending of the verb is generally sufficient to show what person and number the subject is, the Nominative case of the Personal Pronouns is not used except for emphasis.

Example: Thou art a slave, but I am free.
σὺ μὲν εἶ δοῦλος, ἐγὼ δὲ ἐλεύθερος.

The Possessive Pronouns are.

ἐμός	my, or mine
σός	thy, or thine
ἡμέτερος	our, or ours
ὑμέτερος	your, or yours

They are generally equivalent to the possessive Genitive of the Personal Pronoun.

Examples: My lord, ὁ ἐμὸς κύριος, ὁ κύριός μου.
Our lord, ὁ ἡμέτερος κύριος, ὁ κύριος ἡμῶν.

Note that when a noun is qualified by a Possessive Pronoun, or the Genitive of a Personal Pronoun, it generally has an Article before it.

The Genitive singular of αὐτός is used in the place of a Possessive Pronoun of the third person singular to translate "his, hers, its"; and the Genitive plural of the same word is used to translate "their."

Exercise 15

Learn Vocabulary 11.

1. ἐβούλοντο ἀκούειν τοὺς λόγους οὓς ἐλάλει ὁ Ἰησοῦς. 2. διδάσκαλε, καλόν ἐστιν ἡμᾶς ὧδε εἶναι. 3. ἐδέοντο οὖν αὐτοῦ θεραπεύειν τοὺς υἱοὺς αὐτῶν. 4. οὗτος ἄρχεται οἰκοδομεῖν, ἀλλ' οὐ δύναται ποιεῖν τὸ ἔργον. 5. δεῖ ὑμᾶς ἀποκρίνεσθαι τοῖς πρεσβυτέροις. 6. κελεύω σε ἐξέρχεσθαι ἐκ τῆς οἰκίας. 7. ἔξεστιν ἡμῖν κηρύσσειν τὴν βασιλείαν τῶν οὐρανῶν. 8. ἔπεμπε τοὺς δούλους αὐτοῦ καλεῖν τοὺς πτωχοὺς καὶ τοὺς τυφλοὺς εἰς τὸν γάμον. 9. παρήγγελλεν αὐτοῖς ἄγειν τὸν Παῦλον. 10. ὁ γὰρ θεὸς πέμπει τὸν υἱὸν αὐτοῦ σώζειν τὸν κόσμον. 11. παρεκάλουν αὐτοὺς οἱ προφῆται μένειν ἐν τῇ ἀληθείᾳ. 12. οὐ γὰρ θέλετε ἔρχεσθαι πρός με. 13. ὁ οὖν Ἰησοῦς ἤγετο εἰς τὴν ἔρημον πειράζεσθαι ὑπὸ τοῦ διαβόλου. 14. οἱ μαθηταὶ ἤρχοντο πρὸς τὸν Ἰορδάνην ὁμολογεῖν τὰς ἁμαρτίας αὐτῶν

τῷ Ἰωάνῃ. 15. ἐκελεύομεν τοὺς ἀγγέλους πέμπεσθαι. 16. ὁ δὲ οὐκ ἤθελεν πορεύεσθαι ἐν ταῖς ὁδοῖς τοῦ Κυρίου. 17. ἐγώ σε κελεύω ἐκεῖ μένειν, σὺ δὲ οὐχ ὑπακούεις. 18. οἱ μὲν ἦσαν δοῦλοι οἱ δὲ ἐλεύθεροι. 19. παρεκαλοῦμεν τὸν λαὸν ὑπακούειν τοῖς προφήταις.

1. We must not deny the Lord of glory (use δεῖ). 2. They were not willing to obey the elders[1]. 3. It is lawful for them to receive the money from the publicans. 4. I am a man, but you are children. 5. We wish to see the temple of the God of Israel. 6. We are sending the slaves to call the blind and the poor to the marriage. 7. It is bad for them to be there. 8. It was necessary for Jesus to pass through Samaria to proclaim the Gospel to the people. 9. We were commanding the prophet to be brought. 10. I besought him to heal my child, but he would not. 11. Jesus was commanding them to send the blind man. 12. I am not able to exhort them to remain in Jerusalem. 13. They were confessing their sins to us. 14. Some were going to their houses and others to the temple. 15. We are free, but you are slaves. 16. Jesus is led into the desert to be tempted by the devil. 17. We were coming to John to be baptized by him in the Jordan. 18. They are not able to do this. 19. I was sending the messenger to you, but he was not willing to depart. 20. They wish to read the books which thou hast.

LESSON XVI

THE FUTURE INDICATIVE ACTIVE AND MIDDLE. THE MIDDLE VOICE

The Active voice of the Future tense is generally formed by inserting the letter σ between the Verbal Stem (see next exercise) and the endings of the Present Active.

The Future Middle voice is generally formed by inserting the letter σ between the Verbal Stem and the endings of the Present Passive.

The meaning of the Middle voice is explained on page 42.

[1] Dat. case.

ACTIVE AND MIDDLE

The Future Active and the Middle of λύω "I loose" are as follows:

Active		Middle	
λύσω	I shall loose, etc.	λύσομαι	I shall loose (for my own benefit), etc.
λύσεις		λύσῃ (λύσει)	
λύσει		λύσεται	
λύσομεν		λυσόμεθα	
λύσετε		λύσεσθε	
λύσουσι		λύσονται	

Future Infinitive Active		Future Infinitive Middle	
λύσειν	To be about to loose	λύσεσθαι	To be about to loose (for one's own benefit)

Note that each of these forms is made up of the stem of the verb, the σ, and the appropriate ending of the Present tense.

If the stem of the verb ends in a consonant, this consonant combines with the σ which is added to it to form the endings of the Future in the manner shown below.

If the stem of the verb ends in a guttural letter κ, γ, χ, it joins with the σ and makes ξ.

Examples:

Present		Future Act.	Future Mid.
διώκω	I pursue	διώξω	διώξομαι
ἀνοίγω	I open	ἀνοίξω	ἀνοίξομαι
ἄρχω	Act. I rule	ἄρξω	ἄρξομαι
	Mid. I begin		
ἔχω	I have	ἕξω (but observe the rough breathing)	

If the stem of the verb ends in a labial letter π, β, φ, it joins with the σ and makes ψ.

Examples:

Present		Future Act.	Future Mid.
βλέπω	I see	βλέψω	βλέψομαι
γράφω	I write	γράψω	γράψομαι
πέμπω	I send	πέμψω	πέμψομαι

If the stem of the verb ends in a dental letter τ, δ, θ, it is dropped before the σ of the Future.

Examples:

Present		Future Act.	Future Mid.
πείθω	I persuade	πείσω	πείσομαι

For further information as to the formation of Futures see Appendix, p. 188.

Verbs in εω lengthen the ε to η before adding the endings of the Future Tense, with the exception of καλέω, ἐπαινέω and τελέω.

Examples:

Present		Future Act.	Future Mid.
αἰτέω	I ask	αἰτήσω	αἰτήσομαι
καλέω	I call	καλέσω	καλέσομαι

The Future tense of εἰμί is as follows:

Indicative: ἔσομαι   I shall be, etc.
ἔσῃ (ἔσει)
ἔσται   Infinitive: ἔσεσθαι
ἐσόμεθα
ἔσεσθε
ἔσονται

The Middle voice. The Middle voice generally denotes that the subject is acting upon himself, or in some way that concerns himself, but often it is not distinguished from the Active voice in meaning.

Some verbs are only found in the middle forms in certain tenses, especially in the Future tense. These forms may have an active meaning and are then called Middle Deponent forms, because the old grammarians thought they had "laid aside" their active forms and assumed middle forms.

The Middle voice of the Present tense is the same in form as the Passive voice.

Exercise 16

Learn Vocabulary 12.

1. οὐκ ἀδικήσουσι τὰ τέκνα. 2. οἱ δὲ ἐνδύσουσι τὰ ἱμάτια. 3. ἀνοίξει τοὺς ὀφθαλμοὺς τῶν τυφλῶν οἱ συνάγονται ἐν τῇ συναγωγῇ. 4. πείσομεν τοὺς ἐργάτας ἐργάζεσθαι ἐν τοῖς ἀγροῖς. 5. πέμψω πρὸς αὐτοὺς σοφοὺς καὶ προφήτας, ἀλλ' οὐκ ἀκούσουσιν αὐτοὺς οἱ υἱοὶ Ἰσραήλ. 6. ἐκεῖνος ἔσται ἅγιος τῷ Κυρίῳ. 7. ἄρξετε τῶν Ἰουδαίων οἱ κατοικοῦσι ἐκείνην τὴν γῆν. 8. προφητεύσεις τῷ λαῷ τούτῳ καὶ ὑπακούσουσί σοι. 9. διακονήσετε τοῖς ἐχθροῖς ὑμῶν ὅτι οὐκ ἠθέλετε ὑπακούειν μοι, ἀλλ' ἐγὼ ἐλεήσω ὑμᾶς ἐν ἐκείνῃ τῇ ἡμέρᾳ. 10. κατοικήσομεν τοὺς ἀγροὺς τῶν ἐχθρῶν οἷς διηκονοῦμεν ὅτι οὐκ ἠκούομεν τὸν λόγον τοῦ Κυρίου. 11. οἱ διάκονοι τῆς συναγωγῆς οὐ διώξουσι τοὺς λῃστὰς ἐν τῷ σαββάτῳ. 12. εὐλογείτωσαν τὴν δόξαν τοῦ θεοῦ Ἰσραήλ. 13. πέμψομεν τοὺς νεανίας κατοικεῖν τὴν γῆν. 14. οἱ πρεσβύτεροι ἕξουσι τὰ πρόβατα ἃ σώζεται ἀπὸ τῶν ἐχθρῶν. 15. ἀρξόμεθα εὐλογεῖν τοὺς υἱοὺς τῶν προφητῶν.

1. I will open the books which are in the synagogue. 2. They shall be just and faithful in that day, and I will bless them because they hear my voice. 3. We shall behold the face of the Lord in the temple which is built in Jerusalem. 4. The Lord will have mercy upon them because they dwell in the land of their enemies, and he will lead them into their own land. 5. Jesus therefore was sending the apostles to proclaim the Gospel to the house of Israel. 6. We will send the slaves to pursue the robbers[1]. 7. Peace and truth shall dwell in our land because we obey the commandments of the Lord. 8. He will speak these things to the multitudes in parables. 9. I shall be first, but thou wilt be last. 10. Do not praise the wicked, for the wicked shall not dwell in our land.

LESSON XVII

THE TWO STEMS OF VERBS.
THE REFLEXIVE PRONOUN. QUESTIONS

Greek verbs are not divided into conjugations with different endings like Latin verbs.

All the verbs in ω have the same endings: the differences between them are caused by variations in the stem.

The verbs which are given as examples in the last exercise (except πείθω) and also those in the vocabulary have but one stem: but many verbs have at least two stems:—

(1) The Verbal stem from which all the tenses with the exception of the Present and Imperfect are generally formed.

(2) The Present stem from which the Present and Imperfect tenses are formed.

The fact that the meanings of verbs are given in dictionaries under the form of the Present Indicative tends to fix attention upon it, and to produce the impression that it is the original and most important form of the verb. This is however not the case. The present stem is really derived from the verbal stem, and is generally a lengthened form of the verbal stem.

The verbal stem is the most important part of the verb; nouns

---

[1] Use πέμπω.

and adjectives of kindred meaning are formed from it, and not from the present stem.

Examples:

Verbal stem	Present	Derived word	
κηρυκ	κηρύσσω	κῆρυξ	a herald
μαθ	μανθάνω	μαθητής	a disciple
φυγ	φεύγω	φυγή	flight

Some of the ways in which the verbal stem is modified so as to form the present stem are classified below.

(1) Verbs which add τ to the verbal stem in order to form the present stem:

Examples:

Stem	Present	Future	Meaning
καλυπ	ἀποκαλύπτω	ἀποκαλύψω	I reveal
κοπ	ἐκκόπτω	ἐκκόψω	I cut down
κρυπ	κρύπτω	κρύψω	I hide

(2) Verbs in which the verbal stem ends in a guttural which is softened to σσ to form the present stem.

Examples:

Stem	Present	Future	Meaning
κηρυκ	κηρύσσω	κηρύξω	I proclaim
πραγ	πράσσω	πράξω	I do
ταγ	τάσσω	τάξω	I set in order
φυλακ	φυλάσσω	φυλάξω	I guard

(3) Verbs ending in ζω in the Present: these are formed from stems ending in δ or γ. The former make their Futures in σω and the latter in ξω.

Examples:

Stem	Present	Future	Meaning
ἐλπιδ	ἐλπίζω	ἐλπίσω	I hope
κραγ	κράζω	κράξω	I cry

The majority of verbs in ζω form their futures like ἐλπίζω. The following are some of the most important:

ἁγιάζω	I sanctify	ἑτοιμάζω	I make ready
ἀγοράζω	I buy	θαυμάζω	I wonder
βαπτίζω	I baptise	καθαρίζω	I cleanse

REFLEXIVE PRONOUNS. αὐτός

βαστάζω	I carry	πειράζω	I try or tempt
δοξάζω	I glorify	σκανδαλίζω	I cause to stumble
ἐγγίζω	I draw near	σώζω	I save
	ἐργάζομαι	I work	

Observe that in all the verbs given above the Future is formed from the verbal stem in accordance with the rules given on p. 41.

Reflexive Pronouns are used when the subject and object of a sentence or clause refer to the same person or thing.

ἐμαυτόν	myself
σεαυτόν	thyself
ἑαυτόν	himself
ἑαυτήν	herself
ἑαυτό	itself
ἑαυτούς	ourselves, yourselves, themselves

The contracted forms αὑτοῦ, αὑτῆς are sometimes found for ἑαυτοῦ, ἑαυτῆς. Various case forms of ἑαυτόν are found as reflexive pronouns of the 1st and 2nd persons where no ambiguity is thereby caused. ἀφ' ἑαυτοῦ σὺ τοῦτο λέγεις; Dost thou say this thing of thyself? (Jn xviii. 34).

As we have already seen, αὐτός, αὐτή, αὐτό means "he, she, it" generally in cases other than the Nominative and can also mean "himself", etc., especially when joined to a noun or pronoun.

When αὐτός agrees with, and immediately follows, an article it means "the same."

Distinguish carefully between

The same man.
ὁ αὐτὸς ἄνθρωπος.

and

The man himself.
ὁ ἄνθρωπος αὐτός.

Note the mistranslation of Mt. iii. 4 in the R.V.

Distinguish also between this last use of αὐτός and the use of the Reflexive pronoun:

The man himself says this.
ὁ ἄνθρωπος αὐτὸς λέγει τοῦτο.

The man casts himself into the sea.
ὁ ἄνθρωπος βάλλει αὐτὸν εἰς τὴν θάλασσαν.

τὰ αὐτά contracted to ταὐτά means "the same things" (1 Thess. vi. 14).

Various forms of ἑαυτόν can be used in a reciprocal sense, i.e. they must be translated "one another." Example: "Saying one to another," λέγοντες πρὸς ἑαυτούς, Mk. x. 26, xvi. 3.

Questions

Questions are expressed in Greek not by altering the order of the words in the sentence, but by placing the question mark ; at the end of the sentence. It will be noticed that this question mark is like an English semi-colon. The Greek colon is a single dot above the line

Examples:

They are doing this.
ποιοῦσι τοῦτο.
Are they doing this?
ποιοῦσι τοῦτο;

Exercise 17

Learn Vocabulary 13.

1. κρύψομεν τὸ παιδίον ἐν τῇ οἰκίᾳ; 2. οὐχ ἁγιάσουσι τὰ σάββατά μου. 3. οἱ αὐτοὶ ἄγγελοι ἑτοιμάσουσιν ἑαυτοὺς πορεύεσθαι. 4. καθαρίζετε ἑαυτούς, ὑποκριταί. 5. ἀποκαλύψεις αὐτοῖς τὴν δόξαν τῆς σοφίας. 6. ἕξετε ζωὴν ἐν ἑαυτοῖς. 7. σὺ γὰρ πράξεις τὰ αὐτά. 8. Ἰησοῦς αὐτὸς ἤγγιζε τοῖς αὐτοῖς μαθηταῖς. 9. τάξουσι τοὺς αὐτοὺς ἀνθρώπους ἐν τοῖς ἀγροῖς. 10. σκανδαλίσετε τοὺς ἁγίους; 11. ἅψεται τοῦ ἱματίου τοῦ προφήτου. 12. πορεύσομαι πρὸς τὴν αὐτὴν οἰκίαν; 13. ἁγιάζετε τὰς καρδίας ὑμῶν τῇ ἀγάπῃ τῆς ἀληθείας. 14. ἀπάξουσι τοὺς λεπροὺς ἀπὸ τοῦ ἱεροῦ. 15. ἐκκόψετε τὰ δένδρα ἅ ἐστιν ἐν ἐκείνῃ τῇ γῇ. 16. θαυμάσει τὴν δόξαν τοῦ Κυρίου.

1. Ye shall set the books in order in the synagogue. 2. They will hope to behold the signs of the apostles. 3. We will draw near to hear the voice of the teacher. 4. The wicked man will do wicked things. 5. Will he cleanse himself in the same lake? 6. She will make herself ready to go. 7. I will cut down the trees that are in the field. 8. We will buy the same books for our children. 9. The Lord will guard the souls of his people. 10. We will begin to sanctify our hearts. 11. The maiden will carry the loaves for the workmen. 12. They will hide themselves in the trees. 13. You will begin to wonder at the power of the elders. 14. We shall not reveal ourselves to them. 15. Art thou willing to behold peace and righteousness in the kingdom of God? 16. Shall we command them to read the Scriptures to the brethren?

LESSON XVIII
THE FIRST AORIST ACTIVE

The First Aorist is so called to distinguish it from the Second Aorist, a tense which is formed in a different way, but which practically always has the same meaning. Very few verbs have both Aorists.

The two Aorists may be compared, in this respect, with the strong and weak forms of the Past tense in English. Very few verbs in English have both strong and weak Past tense forms; if they have, the meaning of the forms is identical.

Example: Present: Crow Strong Past: Crew Weak Past: Crowed

The word Aorist means unbounded or unlimited. It was given to this tense by grammarians to denote that the action spoken of is to be regarded simply as an event, without any regard being taken of the time at which it occurs or of the length of time during which it has been going on. This statement must be qualified with respect to the Indicative mood of this tense. It has an augment and is generally used of events which are spoken of as occurring in PAST time. It is the most suitable Greek tense to use to translate the English Past Simple tense. But the other moods of this tense have no augment and are not necessarily regarded as referring to Past time, or indeed to any particular time.

The student who knows Latin must beware of thinking that the Aorist Subjunctive corresponds to the Imperfect or Perfect Subjunctive in Latin.

Whatever is said here about the First Aorist applies equally to the Second Aorist forms.

The forms of the 1st Aorist of the verb λύειν are as follows:

1st Aor. Ind. Act.		1st Aor. Imper. Act.	
ἔλυσα	I loosed.		
ἔλυσας	thou loosedst.	λῦσον	loose (thou).
ἔλυσε	he loosed.	λυσάτω	let him loose.
ἐλύσαμεν	we loosed.		
ἐλύσατε	you loosed.	λύσατε	loose (you).
ἔλυσαν	they loosed.	λυσάτωσαν	let them loose.
		λυσάντων	

1st Aorist Infinitive Act.: λῦσαι, to loose.

THE FIRST AORIST ACTIVE

As in the Future σ is inserted between the stem of the verb and the endings. The characteristic vowel of the tense is a.

The σ which is inserted before the endings of the 1st Aorist produces consonantal changes similar to those produced by the σ inserted before the endings of the Future.

Examples:

Present	Future	1st Aorist
διώκω	διώξω	ἐδίωξα
ἀνοίγω	ἀνοίξω	ἀνέῳξα
κηρύσσω	κηρύξω	ἐκήρυξα
κράζω	κράξω	ἔκραξα
βλέπω	βλέψω	ἔβλεψα
γράφω	γράψω	ἔγραψα
κρύπτω	κρύψω	ἔκρυψα
πείθω	πείσω	ἔπεισα
ἐλπίζω	ἐλπίσω	ἤλπισα
ἁγιάζω	ἁγιάσω	ἡγίασα

Contracted verbs in εω lengthen ε to η before the endings are added.

1st Aor. Ind. Act. ᾔτησα, ᾔτησας, ᾔτησε(ν), etc.
1st Aor. Imp. Act. αἴτησον, αἰτησάτω, etc.
1st Aor. Inf. Act. αἰτῆσαι, to ask.

But the ε is not lengthened in καλέω, τελέω, and ἐπαινέω: ἐκάλεσα, ἐκάλεσας, etc. θέλω forms its Future and 1st Aorist as if it were a contracted verb (θελήσω, ἠθέλησα, etc.). The η in the augmented form comes from another form of the verb—ἐθέλω—which is not found in the N.T.

The meaning of the Aorist Imperative

The Aorist Imperative has no augment because it is not regarded as a past tense. The difference in meaning between it and the Present Imperative is that while the Present Imperative denotes a command or entreaty to CONTINUE to do an action, to do it HABITUALLY, the Aorist Imperative denotes a command or entreaty simply to do an action WITHOUT ANY REGARD to its continuance or frequency.

This difference of meaning is well seen in the parallel versions of a petition in the Lord's Prayer given in two of the Gospels.

The verb used in the first is the Present Imperative of the verb δίδωμι "I give," an irregular verb explained in lesson XXXIII, the verb used in the second is the Aorist Imperative of the same verb.

IMPERATIVES. AORIST INFINITIVE

Give us (keep on giving us) day by day our daily bread.
τὸν ἄρτον ἡμῶν τὸν ἐπιούσιον δίδου ἡμῖν τὸ καθ' ἡμέραν.
Lk. xi. 3.

Give to us this day our daily bread.
τὸν ἄρτον ἡμῶν τὸν ἐπιούσιον δὸς ἡμῖν σήμερον.
Mt. vi. 11.

The Present Imperative denotes a continuous act of giving—day after day. The Aorist Imperative denotes a single act of giving—for to-day.

Another good example is found in Jn ii. 16:

Take these things hence (single action), do not continue to make my Father's house a house of merchandise.

ἄρατε[1] ταῦτα ἐντεῦθεν, μὴ ποιεῖτε τὸν οἶκον τοῦ πατρός μου οἶκον ἐμπορίου.

The Aorist Infinitive

The Aorist Infinitive differs in meaning from the Present Infinitive just in the same way as the Aorist Imperative differs in meaning from the Present Imperative.

Its use denotes that the action denoted by the verb is to be regarded simply as an action happening at some time not defined, without any regard to its continuance or frequency.

The use of the Present Infinitive denotes that the action denoted by the verb is to be regarded as continuous or repeated.

The Aorist Infinitive is consequently used more frequently than the Present Infinitive in Greek: and the student should always use it unless there is some good reason to the contrary.

It is NOT confined to expressing action in past time like the Latin Perfect Infinitive, it has therefore no augment since it is not regarded as a past tense.

Examples:

To keep on writing the same things is good for you.
γράφειν τὰ αὐτὰ καλόν ἐστιν ὑμῖν. (Pres. Inf.)
I hope to write to you soon.
ἐλπίζω γράψαι ὑμῖν ταχέως. (Aor. Inf.)

---

[1] ἄρατε is an Aorist Imperative. Its form will be explained in the next lesson but one.

Exercise 18

Revise Vocabularies 9–13.

1. ἐδίωξαν τοὺς λῃστὰς οἳ ἀπῆγον τὰ πρόβατα. 2. οἱ δὲ λεπροὶ ἐπίστευσαν[1] τῷ λόγῳ τοῦ Ἰησοῦ. 3. ἔπεμψας τοὺς τελώνας ἀγοράσαι τὰ ἱμάτια. 4. σῶσον τὸ ἀργύριον ἀπὸ τῶν λῃστῶν. 5. σῶζε τὸν λαόν σου ἀπὸ τοῦ πονηροῦ. 6. ταξάτωσαν τὰ βιβλία ἐν τῷ ἱερῷ. 7. μετὰ ταῦτα ἐπείσαμεν αὐτοὺς κρύψαι τὰ παιδία. 8. ἐκαθαρίσαμεν ἑαυτοὺς ἐν τῷ ποταμῷ. 9. ὁ διδάσκαλος αὐτὸς ἐθαύμασε τὴν σοφίαν τῶν μαθητῶν. 10. ἐπορεύετο διὰ τῆς γῆς ἐκκόψαι τὰ δένδρα. 11. διὰ τοῦτο οὐ δεῖ σκανδαλίζειν τοὺς πιστούς. 12. βάστασον τὸ πλοῖον ἀπὸ τῆς θαλάσσης. 13. ἁγιάσατε ἑαυτούς, ἐγγίζει γὰρ ἡ ἡμέρα τοῦ Κυρίου. 14. ἐκέλευσεν τὸν λεπρὸν ὁ προφήτης καθαρίσαι ἑαυτὸν ἐν τῷ Ἰορδάνῃ ποταμῷ. 15. ἡ φωνὴ τοῦ Ἰωάνου ἔκραξε ἐν τῇ ἐρήμῳ 'ἑτοιμάσατε τὴν ὁδὸν τῷ Κυρίῳ.' 16. ἐτηρήσαμεν τὰς ἐντολὰς ἃς ἠκούομεν ἀπὸ τῶν ἁγίων ἀποστόλων. 17. καλόν ἐστιν ἡμᾶς πράσσειν τὴν δικαιοσύνην. 18. ἐδέοντο[2] αὐτοῦ μὴ πρᾶξαι ἑαυτῷ κακόν. 19. μετὰ τοῦτο οὖν ἀνέῳξεν τοὺς ὀφθαλμοὺς τοῦ τυφλοῦ. 20. ἐλπίζεις θεωρεῖν τὴν δόξαν τῶν ἀγγέλων. 21. ἡ εἰρήνη κατοικείτω τὰς καρδίας ὑμῶν. 22. ταῦτα γὰρ ἠθέλησαν βλέψαι οἱ ἄγγελοι.

1. They baptised the publicans in the river. 2. You were going through the land to behold the houses and the people. 3. Hide the stones in the field. 4. Do not continue to offend the brethren (use the Pres. Imper.). 5. Let them set the men in order. 6. You revealed the commandments and promises to the church. 7. Shall we begin to read the books? 8. Cleanse your hearts, ye sinners, and confess your sins to the church. 9. Is it lawful to heal on the Sabbath? 10. Save thy people, O Lord, from the wickedness of this world. 11. Make ready therefore to hide yourselves and your children in Jerusalem. 12. Let love and righteousness dwell in your hearts. 13. He commanded me to write these words in a book. 14. It is good for them to keep on reading the same things. 15. After this I will reveal my power to the children of Israel. 16. He wished to call the publicans to the marriage.

[1] πιστεύω is often followed by a Dative.
[2] This verb is not contracted.

LESSON XIX

THE SECOND AORIST ACTIVE. OBJECT CLAUSES AFTER VERBS OF SAYING, OR THINKING

The ENDINGS of the Second Aorist Indicative Active are the SAME as those of the Imperfect Indicative Active. The ENDINGS of the 2nd Aorist Imperative Active are the SAME as those of the Present Imperative Active. The ENDINGS of the 2nd Aorist Infinitive Active are the SAME as those of the Present Infinitive Active.

The 2nd Aorist can only be distinguished from the Imperfect and the Present Imperative and Infinitive by the STEM.

The Imperfect and the Present Imperative and Infinitive are formed from the present stem. The 2nd Aorist Indicative, Imperative and Infinitive are formed from the verbal stem (see p. 43).

There is no difference in meaning between a 1st and a 2nd Aorist[1]; few verbs have both.

Take for example the verb βάλλω "I throw."

Verbal Stem βαλ.   Present Stem βαλλ.

2nd Aor. Ind.	2nd Aor. Imperative	Imperfect Ind.	Present Imperative
ἔβαλον		ἔβαλλον	
ἔβαλες	βάλε	ἔβαλλες	βάλλε
ἔβαλε	βαλέτω	ἔβαλλε	βαλλέτω
ἐβάλομεν		ἐβάλλομεν	
ἐβάλετε	βάλετε	ἐβάλλετε	βάλλετε
ἔβαλον	βαλέτωσαν	ἔβαλλον	βαλλέτωσαν
	βαλόντων		βαλλόντων

2nd Aorist Infinitive βαλεῖν.

Present Infinitive βάλλειν.

The 2nd Aorist Infinitive always has a circumflex accent on the last syllable.

Examples of verbs with 2nd Aorists:

Present		Verbal Stem	2nd Aor. Ind.
ἁμαρτάνω	I sin	ἁμαρτ	ἥμαρτον
λαμβάνω	I take	λαβ	ἔλαβον

[1] Except in the case of ἵστημι, which will be given later.

THE SECOND AORIST ACTIVE

Present		Verbal Stem	2nd Aor. Ind.
μανθάνω	I learn	μαθ	ἔμαθον
πίνω	I drink	πι	ἔπιον
ἀποθνήσκω	I die	θαν	ἀπέθανον
εὑρίσκω	I find	εὑρ	εὗρον
πίπτω	I fall	πεσ	ἔπεσον
τίκτω	I bring forth	τεκ	ἔτεκον
καταλείπω	I abandon	λιπ	κατέλιπον
φεύγω	I flee	φυγ	ἔφυγον
ἄγω	I lead, or drive	ἀγ	ἤγαγον[1]
γινώσκω	I know	γνο	ἔγνων
βαίνω	I go	βα	ἔβην

The 2nd Aorist of γινώσκω and βαίνω are conjugated as follows:

2nd Aor. Ind.	2nd Aor. Imper.	Infin.	2nd Aor. Ind.	2nd Aor. Imper.	Infin.
ἔγνων		γνῶναι	ἔβην		βῆναι
ἔγνως	γνῶθι		ἔβης	βῆθι (βά)	
ἔγνω	γνώτω		ἔβη	βήτω	
ἔγνωμεν			ἔβημεν		
ἔγνωτε	γνῶτε		ἔβητε	βῆτε	
ἔγνωσαν	γνώτωσαν		ἔβησαν	βήτωσαν	

No present tenses are formed from the stems from which the following 2nd Aorists are made. In grammars and dictionaries, however, they are always connected with certain Present tenses of similar meaning and they are said to be the 2nd Aorist tenses of these Presents.

This is an unfortunate arrangement, but it must be taken as it is found, and the meanings of these Aorists looked for in dictionaries under the Present tenses with which they have been connected.

All these 2nd Aorists are of most frequent occurrence and must be carefully learnt.

Stem	2nd Aor. Ind.		Present with which these words are connected in dictionaries
ἰδ	εἶδον	I saw	ὁράω
ἐπ	εἶπον[2]	I said	λέγω
σεχ	ἔσχον	I held	ἔχω
φαγ	ἔφαγον	I ate	ἐσθίω

[1] ἤγαγον is an exception to the usual formation of the 2nd Aorist, the stem is "reduplicated" or repeated twice in the 2nd Aorist.

[2] See Appendix, p. 189.

OBJECT CLAUSES

παθ	ἔπαθον	I suffered	πάσχω
ἐλθ	ἦλθον	I came	ἔρχομαι
ἐνεγκ	ἤνεγκον	I carried	φέρω

The Imperative of εἶδον is ἰδέ, that of εἶπον is εἰπέ, that of ἔσχον is σχές, that of ἦλθον is ἐλθέ. The infinitives of these verbs are ἰδεῖν, εἰπεῖν, σχεῖν, ἐλθεῖν. The middle form ἰδού is often used instead of ἴδε.

Object clauses after verbs of saying or thinking

Object clauses after verbs meaning "to say" or "to think" are sometimes expressed in Greek, as they nearly always are in English, by a clause introduced by ὅτι, "that[1]", with a verb in the Indicative mood.

Examples: They say that they hear the voice.
λέγουσιν ὅτι ἀκούουσι τὴν φωνήν.
We believe that we beheld the temple.
πιστεύομεν ὅτι ἐβλέψαμεν τὸ ἱερόν.

In Greek however the TENSE of the verb which was used by the original speaker or thinker when he uttered the words or framed the thought is always retained, and the verb in the object clause is not put into a past tense as it is in English when the verb in the principal clause is in a past tense. In English we say "The man said that he heard the voice." The words that the man actually uttered were "I hear the voice." In Greek this present tense is retained and we write

ὁ ἄνθρωπος εἶπεν ὅτι ἀκούει τὴν φωνήν.

Again, in the sentence "The men believed that the slave was there," the thought that the men framed in their minds was "the slave is there," consequently we translate this sentence into Greek as follows:

οἱ ἄνθρωποι ἐπίστευσαν ὅτι ὁ δοῦλός ἐστιν ἐκεῖ.

So in the following sentences:

He said that he had seen the boats. (I saw the boats.)
εἶπεν ὅτι εἶδε τὰ πλοῖα.
They thought that they had seen a vision. (We saw a vision.)
ἐνόμισαν ὅτι εἶδον ὀπτασίαν.

[1] N.B. ὅτι also means "because," as has been already mentioned.

OBJECT CLAUSES. EXERCISES

In English the tense of the verb in the object clause is put one stage further into the past: the Past is used instead of the Present, and the Pluperfect instead of the Past. But in Greek the tense used by the original speaker or thinker is always retained.

The student should always ask himself what were the original words uttered, or the original thought framed, before trying to translate such sentences as these.

Exercise 19

Learn Vocabulary 14.

1. μετὰ ταῦτα ἀπέθανεν ὁ πτωχός. 2. ἔβημεν εἰς τὸ ἱερὸν ἐν ἐκείνῃ τῇ ὥρᾳ. 3. ἔμαθες ὅτι ἔρχεται ὁ κριτής. 4. ὦ Κύριε, ἥμαρτον εἰς σέ. 5. εἴδομεν ὅτι ὁ τελώνης φέρει τὸ ἀργύριον ἐκ τῆς οἰκίας. 6. ἰδὲ τοὺς δεσπότας τῆς γῆς. 7. γινώσκομεν ὅτι ὁ υἱὸς τοῦ θεοῦ ἦλθεν εἰς τὸν κόσμον σώζειν τοὺς ἁμαρτωλούς. 8. εἶπεν ὅτι πίνουσι τὸν οἶνον καὶ ἐσθίουσι τὸν ἄρτον. 9. ἠνέγκομεν τοὺς λίθους ἀπὸ τῆς θαλάσσης. 10. τὰ δένδρα ἔπεσε εἰς τὸν ἀγρόν. 11. οἱ λῃσταὶ ἔφευγον ἀπὸ τῶν νεανίων. 12. οἱ δὲ προφῆται ἔφυγον εἰς τὴν ἔρημον. 13. ἐν τούτῳ γινώσκομεν τὴν ἀγάπην τοῦ θεοῦ ὅτι ἔπεμψεν τὸν υἱὸν αὐτοῦ τὸν ἀγαπητὸν εἰς τὸν κόσμον. 14. βῆθι εἰς τοὺς ἀγροὺς καὶ λάβε τὸν καρπὸν ἀπὸ τῶν ἐργάτων. 15. ἔγνων ὅτι ὁ Κύριος ἔπεμψε τὸν ἄγγελον αὐτοῦ σώζειν με. 16. ἐλθέτω τὰ παιδία πρός με. 17. εἴπομεν ὅτι δεῖ παθεῖν αὐτοὺς πολλά. 18. εἶδον ὅτι ἠγάγομεν τὸν ὄχλον εἰς τὴν συναγωγήν. 19. ἔσχεν τὰ βιβλία τοῦ ἀδελφοῦ μου. 20. ἔγνωμεν ὅτι πολλὰ ἔμαθον οἱ μαθηταὶ ἀπὸ τῶν ἀποστόλων.

1. We cast ourselves into the river. 2. You received the garments which the elders sent for the poor. 3. They fled from the face of the judges. 4. After this the disciples knew that they had sinned (their thought was "we sinned"). 5. This is the stone that fell from heaven. 6. The virgin brought forth a son, and they called him Jesus.[1] 7. Ye follow[2] me, not because ye saw signs, but because ye ate the loaves. 8. The Son of man must suffer many things. 9. After these days we went to Samaria. 10. Behold the Lamb of God. 11. He said that he had learnt many things from the prophet. 12. We know that we must suffer many things. 13. On this account they left the sheep in the fields and fled. 14. He commanded the multitude to eat the bread and drink the wine which the young men brought. 15. The prophet

[1] Accusative case.   [2] See Vocabulary 30.

LIQUID VERBS, FUTURE AND AORIST 55

who had the book died in the wilderness. 16. We saw that the slaves were carrying the boat to the lake (the thought was "they are carrying"). 17. They said that the children had eaten the fruit (the words used were "the children ate the fruit"). 18. They knew that the maidens were in the house. 19. I heard that the apostles were going to Jerusalem.

LESSON XX

THE FUTURE AND AORIST ACTIVE OF LIQUID VERBS. TEMPORAL CLAUSES

The Future and Aorist of verbs whose stems end in a liquid letter λ, μ, ν, ρ present some peculiarities.

(1) The present stem is longer than the verbal stem: (*a*) it has a long vowel or a diphthong where the verbal stem has a short vowel, or (*b*) it ends in λλ where the verbal stem ends in λ (except in the case of ὀφείλω).

(2) The Future Active and Middle instead of inserting σ before their endings have endings like those of the Present of contracted verbs in εω.

(3) The 1st Aor. Act. generally has a long vowel or diphthong in the stem, and does not insert σ before its endings, but adds them direct to the lengthened stem.

The following verbs of this class are important.

Present	Verbal stem	Future	1st or 2nd Aor. Act.	Meaning
ἀγγέλλω	ἀγγελ	ἀγγελῶ	ἤγγειλα	I announce
αἴρω	ἀρ	ἀρῶ	ἦρα	I raise, or take up
ἀποθνήσκω	θαν	ἀποθανοῦμαι	ἀπέθανον	I die
ἀποκτείνω	κτεν	ἀποκτενῶ	ἀπέκτεινα	I kill
ἀποστέλλω	στελ	ἀποστελῶ	ἀπέστειλα	I send
βάλλω	βαλ	βαλῶ	ἔβαλον	I throw
ἐγείρω	ἐγερ	ἐγερῶ	ἤγειρα	I rouse
κρίνω	κριν	κρινῶ	ἔκρινα	I judge
μένω	μεν	μενῶ	ἔμεινα	I remain
ὀφείλω	ὀφελ	ὀφελῶ	ὤφειλα	I owe, foll. by Inf. I ought

| σπείρω | σπερ | σπερῶ | ἔσπειρα | I sow |
| φθείρω | φθερ | φθερῶ | ἔφθειρα | I destroy |

The compound forms of these verbs such as παραγγέλλω, ἐπαίρω, ἐκβάλλω, κατακρίνω form their tenses in exactly the same way as the uncompounded forms given above. The Future of ἀγγέλλω is conjugated as follows : ἀγγελῶ, ἀγγελεῖς, ἀγγελεῖ, ἀγγελοῦμεν, ἀγγελεῖτε, ἀγγελοῦσ

The 1st Aor. Imperat. is ἄγγειλον and the Infinitive is ἀγγεῖλαι.

The other verbs are all conjugated in the same way.

Temporal Clauses, or clauses denoting time

A Temporal Clause denotes the time of the action of the verb in the clause on which it depends.

Temporal clauses are introduced by ὅτε or ὥς meaning "when," ἕως meaning "while" or "until."

When a temporal clause refers to a single definite event its verb is in the Indicative mood, just as in English.

N.B. Distinguish carefully between ὅτε "when," and ὅτι "that," or "because."

Examples :

When he came to the sea he saw the ships.
ὅτε ἦλθε πρὸς τὴν θάλασσαν εἶδε τὰ πλοῖα.
While he read the books he remained in the house.
ἕως ἀνεγίγνωσκε τὰ βιβλία κατέμεινεν ἐν τῇ οἰκίᾳ.
He remained in the house until the slave came.
κατέμεινεν ἐν τῇ οἰκίᾳ ἕως ἦλθεν ὁ δοῦλος.

The Preposition παρά

The root meaning of this preposition is BESIDE.

It is used with a noun or pronoun in the accusative, genitive, or dative case.

When used with the **Accusative** case it denotes generally motion to beside or motion along side of places.

Examples :

ὁ δὲ σπόρος ἔπεσεν παρὰ τὴν ὁδόν.
But the seed fell by the roadside.
ὁ δὲ Ἰησοῦς ἦλθεν παρὰ τὴν θάλασσαν τῆς Γαλιλαίας.
But Jesus went along the side of the sea of Galilee.

παρά. EXERCISES

When used with the **Genitive** case it denotes motion from beside of persons.

Example : καὶ ἔγνωσαν ὅτι παρὰ σοῦ ἐξῆλθον.

And they knew that I came forth from Thee.

When used with the **Dative** it denotes rest beside and may be translated "near," or "by," or "with," or "at the house of."

Example : ἔμειναν παρ' αὐτῷ τὴν ἡμέραν ἐκείνην.

They remained with him that day.

See Lesson XXXVIII.

Exercise 20

Learn Vocabulary 15.

1. ὅτε δὲ οἱ στρατιῶται ἦλθον εἰς τὴν οἰκίαν ἀπήγγειλαν ὅτι ἀπέστειλεν αὐτοὺς ὁ[1] Κορνήλιος. 2. κατακρινοῦσι τὰς χήρας καὶ ἀποκτενοῦσι τὰ τέκνα αὐτῶν μαχαίρᾳ. 3. οὐ μενεῖτε ἐν τῷ τόπῳ τούτῳ ἀλλ' ἀποθανεῖσθε ἐν τῇ γῇ τῶν ἐχθρῶν ὑμῶν. 4. οἱ ἀπόστολοι ἔσπειραν τὸν λόγον ἐν ταῖς καρδίαις τῶν μαθητῶν. 5. ᾖρεν οὖν τὸν σταυρὸν καὶ ἦλθεν ὀπίσω τοῦ Ἰησοῦ. 6. ἐν ἐκείνῳ τῷ καιρῷ οἱ κριταὶ ἔκριναν τὰς φυλὰς Ἰσραήλ. 7. ἐφθείραμεν τὰς κώμας αἳ ἦσαν παρὰ τὴν θάλασσαν. 8. ἔμεινα ἐκεῖ ἕως ἀνέγνω τὸ βιβλίον. 9. ὅτε δὲ ἀπέκτεινεν ὁ Ἡρώδης τὰ παιδία ἐν Βηθλεὲμ κατέφυγεν ὁ[1] Ἰωσὴφ εἰς Αἴγυπτον σὺν Μαρίᾳ. 10. δύνασθε πιεῖν τὸ ποτήριον ὃ δεῖ με πιεῖν; 11. φθερῶ τὴν γῆν αὐτῶν μαχαίρᾳ ὅτι οὐχ ὑπήκουόν μοι. 12. ἐμείναμεν ἐν τῷ ἱερῷ ἕως ᾠκοδόμουν οἱ ἐργάται τὸν θρόνον. 13. ὡς δὲ ἤκουσαν ταῦτα παρὰ τῆς χήρας ἔμειναν παρ' αὐτῇ. 14. ὤφειλες ἀργύριον τοῖς τελώναις. 15. ὁ δὲ Ἰησοῦς εἶπεν τῷ παραλυτικῷ Ἔγειρε, ἆρον τὴν κλίνην σου καὶ ὕπαγε εἰς τὸν οἶκόν σου, ὡς δὲ ἤκουσεν ταῦτα ἦρεν τὴν κλίνην καὶ ὑπῆγεν. 16. ἀπεστείλαμεν τοὺς ἀγγέλους ἑτοιμάσαι τὴν ὁδόν. 17. ὁ προφήτης εἶπεν ὅτι πάντα δυνατά ἐστι παρὰ τῷ θεῷ[2]. 18. παρηγγείλατε αὐτοῖς μὴ φθεῖραι τὰ πλοῖα. 19. ἠθέλησας ἄγειν τὰ πρόβατα παρὰ τὰ δένδρα. 20. παρὰ τοῖς ἀνθρώποις ἀδύνατόν ἐστιν ἀλλ' οὐ παρὰ τῷ θεῷ, πάντα γὰρ δυνατὰ παρὰ τῷ θεῷ. 21. καὶ τοῦτο ἠκούσαμεν παρ' αὐτοῦ ὅτι δεῖ φιλεῖν τοὺς ἀδελφοὺς ἡμῶν. 22. οἱ Φαρισαῖοι ἔλεγον ὅτι ἐσθίει παρὰ ἁμαρτωλῷ.

1. Send the young men to rouse the soldiers. 2. Joseph took the Child and Mary and departed into Egypt. 3. They shall not die in

[1] Proper nouns in Greek are often preceded by the article; this article must not be translated into English.

[2] παρὰ τῷ θεῷ etc. "near God"; translate "with God," or "to God."

the wilderness, for the soldiers will save them. 4. I will judge my people in that day, saith the Lord. 5. The Pharisees went to eat bread at the house of the prophet[1]. 6. This is impossible with men, but it is possible with God. 7. When Herod heard these words he sent his servants to destroy the children in Bethlehem with the sword. 8. They remained in the house while the paralytic took up his bed. 9. We announced that the apostle was staying (use μένω) in the house of Cornelius. 10. Take up thy cross and carry it after me. 11. You ought not to condemn these widows. 12. I shall cast the sword into the lake. 13. When the disciples came to the village they sowed the word in the hearts of the people. 14. The Son of man (insert the article before "of man") must suffer many things. 15. I heard this from (παρά) the prophet who lives (μένω) at the house of the widow in Bethlehem. 16. Wilt thou not slay the wicked, O Lord? 17. They wished to throw the stones beside the temple. 18. The Pharisees said that the disciples of John did not eat with publicans and sinners (use παρά).

[1] Use παρά with the dat. for "at the house of."

LESSON XXI

THE THIRD DECLENSION

The third declension contains all nouns which do not belong to the first or second declension.

The stems of third declension nouns end (1) in a consonant, (2) in a vowel, generally ι, υ or ευ.

(1) **Third Declension nouns with stems ending in a consonant.**

The endings of these nouns when masculine or feminine are as follows:

	Singular	Plural
Nom.	Various	ες
Voc.	Same as Nom., or same as stem	ες
Acc.	α	ας
Gen.	ος	ων
Dat.	ι	σι (ν)

The letter ν is written after the ending of the Dat. Pl. if the next word begins with a vowel or at the end of a sentence.

THIRD DECLENSION, EXAMPLES

These endings are added to the stem. The stem is found by taking away the ending of the Genitive Singular.

Examples:	Nominative		Genitive	Stem
	νύξ	night	νυκτός	νυκτ
	παῖς	boy	παιδός	παιδ
	ἄρχων	ruler	ἄρχοντος	ἀρχοντ

The following are examples of the declension of nouns of the third declension.

Stems ending in a mute letter

	(ὁ) φύλαξ a guard	(ἡ) σαλπίγξ a trumpet	(ὁ) ὀδούς a tooth	(ἡ) ἐλπίς hope
Stem	φυλακ	σαλπιγγ	ὀδοντ	ἐλπιδ

Singular

Nom.	φύλαξ	σάλπιγξ	ὀδούς	ἐλπίς
Voc.	φύλαξ	σάλπιγξ	ὀδούς	ἐλπί
Acc.	φύλακα	σάλπιγγα	ὀδόντα	ἐλπίδα
Gen.	φύλακος	σάλπιγγος	ὀδόντος	ἐλπίδος
Dat.	φύλακι	σάλπιγγι	ὀδόντι	ἐλπίδι

Plural

Nom.	φύλακες	σάλπιγγες	ὀδόντες	ἐλπίδες
Voc.	φύλακες	σάλπιγγες	ὀδόντες	ἐλπίδες
Acc.	φύλακας	σάλπιγγας	ὀδόντας	ἐλπίδας
Gen.	φυλάκων	σαλπίγγων	ὀδόντων	ἐλπίδων
Dat.	φύλαξι	σάλπιγξι	ὀδοῦσι	ἐλπίσι

Stems ending in a liquid letter

	(ὁ) ποιμήν a shepherd	(ὁ) αἰών an age	(ὁ) ἡγεμών a leader	(ὁ) σωτήρ a saviour
Stem	ποιμεν	αἰων	ἡγεμον	σωτερ

Singular

Nom.	ποιμήν	αἰών	ἡγεμών	σωτήρ
Voc.	ποιμήν	αἰών	ἡγεμών	σῶτερ
Acc.	ποιμένα	αἰῶνα	ἡγεμόνα	σωτῆρα
Gen.	ποιμένος	αἰῶνος	ἡγεμόνος	σωτῆρος
Dat.	ποιμένι	αἰῶνι	ἡγεμόνι	σωτῆρι

THIRD DECLENSION, CONSONANT ENDINGS

Plural

Nom.	ποιμένες	αἰῶνες	ἡγεμόνες	σωτῆρες
Voc.	ποιμένες	αἰῶνες	ἡγεμόνες	σωτῆρες
Acc.	ποιμένας	αἰῶνας	ἡγεμόνας	σωτῆρας
Gen.	ποιμένων	αἰώνων	ἡγεμόνων	σωτήρων
Dat.	ποιμέσι	αἰῶσι	ἡγεμόσι	σωτῆρσι

Note on the Formation of the Vocative Singular and Dative Plural

The Vocative is the same as the Nominative in nouns with stems ending in a mute letter such as φύλαξ, and in nouns with stems ending in a liquid letter which are accented on the last syllable such as ποιμήν. Nouns not accented on the last syllable have the Vocative like the stem, as δαίμων, Vocative δαῖμον.

Exceptions. Nouns with stems in ιδ such as ἐλπίς have the Vocative like the stem without the final consonant. σωτήρ has the Vocative σῶτερ.

All other nouns have the Vocative the same as the stem.

When σι is added to the stem to form the Dative plural, the same consonantal changes take place as take place in forming the Future of verbs:

- gutturals followed by σ form ξ,
- labials followed by σ form ψ,
- dentals and ν followed by σ drop out.

Examples:

Nominative	Meaning	Stem	Dative plural
φύλαξ	a guard	φυλακ	φύλαξι
φλέψ	a vein	φλεβ	φλέψι
ἐλπίς	hope	ἐλπιδ	ἐλπίσι
ποιμήν	a shepherd	ποιμεν	ποιμέσι

The best way to learn 3rd declension nouns is to learn the Nom. Sing., Gen. Sing., and gender all at once.

The gender of nouns is generally indicated in dictionaries by adding the proper gender of the article to the noun, thus χάρις ἡ means that χάρις is feminine, πῦρ τό means that πῦρ is neuter.

The following are some of the most common 3rd declension nouns in the New Testament.

Nominative	Genitive	Gender	Meaning
ἀλέκτωρ	ἀλέκτορος	ὁ	a cock
ἀμπελών	ἀμπελῶνος	ὁ	a vineyard

THIRD DECLENSION. EXERCISES

ἄρχων	ἄρχοντος	ὁ	a ruler
ἀστήρ	ἀστέρος Dat. pl. ἄστρασι	ὁ	a star
εἰκών	εἰκόνος	ἡ	an image
λαμπάς	λαμπάδος	ἡ	a lamp
μήν	μηνός	ὁ	a month
νύξ	νυκτός	ἡ	a night
παῖς	παιδός	ὁ	a child
σάρξ	σαρκός	ἡ	flesh
χάρις[1]	χάριτος	ἡ	favour or grace

Exercise 21

Learn Vocabulary 16.

1. ἐγείρεσθε τῇ φωνῇ τῆς σάλπιγγος. 2. φυλασσέσθωσαν αἱ θύραι ὑπὸ τῶν φυλάκων. 3. ἀπέστειλαν τοὺς ποιμένας συνάγειν τὰ πρόβατα νυκτός[2]. 4. οἱ παῖδες ἦραν τὴν εἰκόνα. 5. μενοῦσι ἐν τῇ γῇ αὐτῶν εἰς[3] τὸν αἰῶνα. 6. ὅτε δὲ ἐξῆλθεν ὁ Πέτρος εὐθὺς ἐφώνησεν ὁ ἀλέκτωρ. 7. ἔλαβες τὸν καρπὸν τοῦ ἀμπελῶνος τοῖς ποιμέσι. 8. ἐποίησα τοῦτον τὸν χιτῶνα τῷ παιδί. 9. αἱ δὲ παρθένοι ἔλαβον τὰς λαμπάδας καὶ ἐξῆλθον ἰδεῖν τὸν νυμφίον. 10. σωζόμεθα γὰρ ἐλπίδι καὶ τῇ χάριτι τοῦ θεοῦ. 11. ἰδὲ τοὺς ἀστέρας ἐν τῷ οὐρανῷ. 12. ἐκάλουν αὐτὸν τὸν σωτῆρα τοῦ κόσμου. 13. εἰ μή[4] ἐσθίετε τὴν σάρκα τοῦ υἱοῦ τοῦ ἀνθρώπου οὐκ ἔχετε ζωὴν ἐν ἑαυτοῖς. 14. πέμπομαι ὑπὸ τῶν ἡγεμόνων ἀπαγγεῖλαι ὑμῖν ταῦτα. 15. ἄκουσον ἡμῶν[5], σῶτερ τοῦ Ἰσραήλ. 16. ταύτην τὴν χάριν ἔλαβον παρὰ τοῦ Κυρίου. 17. μετὰ δὲ τρεῖς μῆνας οἱ ἄρχοντες εἰσῆλθον εἰς τὸ ἱερὸν νυκτός[2].

1. We destroyed the images which we saw in the temple. 2. Peter went out of the door, and immediately the cock crew. 3. The master sent the labourers into his vineyard. 4. After three months we beheld the star in the heavens. 5. When the bridegroom came by night they took their lamps and went out to see him. 6. You were being roused by the trumpets. 7. We announced to you that he was the Saviour of the world. 8. Receive the grace of God. 9. The garments were

[1] Note that the Acc. Sing. of χάρις is χάριν.
[2] νυκτός "by night," the Genitive case is used in Greek to express the time within which anything is done.
[3] εἰς τὸν αἰῶνα "until the age," a Hebrew expression generally translated "for ever."
[4] εἰ μή "unless," or "except."
[5] ἀκούω is sometimes followed by a Genitive.

being sent for the children by the widows. 10. The shepherds called their own sheep, and they came after them. 11. Unless we eat the flesh of the Son of man we shall have no life in ourselves. 12. Here will I dwell for ever, saith the Lord.

LESSON XXII

NOUNS WITH STEMS ENDING IN A VOWEL, ETC. NEUTER NOUNS OF THE THIRD DECLENSION.

(2) **Nouns of the Third Declension with stems ending in a vowel.**

These nouns have stems ending in $ι$, $υ$, or $ευ$.

Examples:

	(ἡ) πόλις a city	(ὁ) ἰχθύς a fish	(ὁ) βασιλεύς a king
Stem	πολι	ἰχθυ	βασιλευ

Singular

Nom.	πόλις	ἰχθύς	βασιλεύς
Voc.	πόλι	ἰχθύ	βασιλεῦ
Acc.	πόλιν	ἰχθύν	βασιλέα
Gen.	πόλεως	ἰχθύος	βασιλέως
Dat.	πόλει	ἰχθύι	βασιλεῖ

Plural

Nom.	πόλεις	ἰχθύες	βασιλεῖς
Voc.	πόλεις	ἰχθύες	βασιλεῖς
Acc.	πόλεις	ἰχθύας	βασιλεῖς, βασιλέας
Gen.	πόλεων	ἰχθύων	βασιλέων
Dat.	πόλεσι	ἰχθύσι	βασιλεῦσι

The nouns of this class which occur most frequently in the N. T. are given in the vocabularies.

Neuter nouns of the 3rd declension are declined as follows:

	Singular		Plural
Nom. Voc. Acc.	γράμμα	a letter	γράμματα
Gen.	γράμματος		γραμμάτων
Dat.	**γράμματι**		**γράμμασι**

THIRD DECLENSION, NEUTER AND IRREGULAR

Notice that as in the case of neuter nouns of the 2nd declension the Nominative, Vocative, and Accusative cases have the same endings, and the Nominative, Vocative, and Accusative Plural end in *a*.

Decline like γράμμα the words given in the vocabulary, and also πῦρ, πυρός, fire; τέρας, τέρατος, a wonder; φῶς, φωτός, light; which are all neuter.

Neuter Nouns with Stems Ending in ες

The final ς of the stem appears only in the Nominative singular, and there the ες is changed to ος.

In the other cases ς is dropped and the two vowels thus brought together are contracted.

Example: Stem γενες with Genitive ending added becomes γενεσος, when the ς is omitted it becomes γενεος, and this is contracted to γένους. The same takes place in the other cases.

	Singular	Plural
Nom. Voc. Acc.	γένος a race	γένη
Gen.	γένους	γενέων or γενῶν
Dat.	γένει	γένεσι

The nouns of this class which occur most frequently in the N.T. are given in the vocabularies. They must be carefully distinguished from nouns of 2nd declension ending in ος which are nearly all masculine.

Irregular nouns of the Third Declension

The declension of the following nouns should be noted: they are contracted in the Dat. and Gen. Sing. and Dat. Pl. and have the Voc. Sing. the same as the stem.

πατήρ ὁ father,   θυγάτηρ ἡ daughter
μήτηρ ἡ mother

They are declined as follows:

	Singular	Plural
Nom.	πατήρ	πατέρες
Voc.	πάτερ	πατέρες
Acc.	πατέρα	πατέρας
Gen.	πατρός	πατέρων
Dat.	πατρί	πατράσι

THIRD DECLENSION, IRREGULAR

The following is the declension of ἀνήρ, a man.

	Singular	Plural
Nom.	ἀνήρ	ἄνδρες
Voc.	ἄνερ	ἄνδρες
Acc.	ἄνδρα	ἄνδρας
Gen.	ἀνδρός	ἀνδρῶν
Dat.	ἀνδρί	ἀνδράσι

The following nouns should also be specially noticed:

Nominative		Genitive Sing.		Dative Pl.
γόνυ	a knee	γόνατος	τό	γόνασι
γυνή	a woman Voc. γύναι	γυναικός	ἡ	γυναιξί
θρίξ	a hair	τριχός	ἡ	θριξί
κύων	a dog	κύνος	ὁ	κύσι
οὖς	an ear	ὠτός	τό	ὠσί
πούς	a foot	ποδός	ὁ	ποσί
ὕδωρ	water	ὕδατος	τό	ὕδασι
χείρ	a hand	χειρός	ἡ	χερσί

Exercise 22

Learn Vocabulary 17.

1. ἦλθεν ὁ Ἰωάνης εἰς τὸν Ἰορδάνην ποταμὸν καὶ ἐκήρυσσε τὸ βάπτισμα μετανοίας εἰς ἄφεσιν ἁμαρτιῶν. 2. ἴδετε πηλίκοις[1] γράμμασι ὑμῖν ἔγραψα τῇ ἐμῇ χειρί. 3. εἶπεν ὅτι οὐκ ἔστιν αὐτὸς τὸ φῶς, ἀλλ' ἔρχεται μαρτυρῆσαι περὶ τοῦ φωτός. 4. οἱ ἐχθροὶ ἔφθειραν τὰς πόλεις ἡμῶν πυρί. 5. μὴ ποιεῖτε τὸν οἶκον τοῦ πατρός μου οἶκον ἐμπορίου[2]. 6. ζητῇ ὑπὸ τῆς μητρὸς καὶ τῶν ἀδελφῶν σου. 7. οὐ δεῖ λαβεῖν τὸν ἄρτον τῶν παίδων καὶ βαλεῖν αὐτὸν τοῖς κυσί. 8. οἱ ἄνδρες περιεπάτουν τοὺς ἀγροὺς σὺν ταῖς γυναιξὶν αὐτῶν. 9. ἐκέλευσα τοὺς ἄνδρας ἑτοιμάζειν τὴν ὁδὸν τῷ βασιλεῖ. 10. ἐγὼ μὲν βαπτίζω ὑμᾶς ὕδατι, ἐκεῖνος δὲ βαπτίσει ὑμᾶς πνεύματι ἁγίῳ καὶ πυρί. 11. ἔχομεν γὰρ τὴν ἄφεσιν τῶν ἁμαρτιῶν ἡμῶν διὰ τοῦ αἵματος αὐτοῦ. 12. ποιήσει σημεῖα καὶ τέρατα τῷ γένει τούτῳ. 13. οἱ παῖδες ἔλαβον τὸν ἰχθὺν ἐκ τοῦ ὕδατος. 14. ἀνοίξει τὰ ὦτα τῶν κωφῶν. 15. καὶ μετὰ ταῦτα ἦλθον οἱ μαθηταὶ αὐτοῦ καὶ ἐθαύμαζον ὅτι μετὰ γυναικὸς ἐλάλει. 16. ἔγραψα πάντα ταῦτα τῇ χειρὶ τῆς θυγατρός μου. 17. ἐγὼ γὰρ οὐκ ἦλθον ποιῆσαι τὸ θέλημά μου, ἀλλὰ τὸ θέλημα τοῦ πατρὸς ὃς ἀπέστειλέ με. 18. οἱ γραμματεῖς εἶπον ὅτι εἶδον τὴν θυγατέρα τοῦ βασιλέως.

---

[1] πηλίκος "how large."   [2] ἐμπόριον "merchandise."

1. This man did signs and wonders in the city. 2. Behold my hands and my feet. 3. Ye are the light of the world. 4. The woman was wiping (ἐξέμασσε) the feet of Jesus with her hair. 5. Our fathers did eat the manna (τὸ μάννα) in the wilderness. 6. He touched[1] the ear of the deaf man with his hand. 7. The king sent this woman to bring her father from the city. 8. He was seeking his mother and his daughter. 9. The Holy Spirit shall remain with them for ever. 10. Thou sayest that thou knowest the will of God. 11. The dogs ate the fish which I took out of the water. 12. In that year my father went through your city. 13. The scribes would not receive baptism for[2] the remission of their sins. 14. I read the letters which he wrote by the hand of his wife. 15. Your cities are destroyed with fire. 16. We bowed (ἐκάμψαμεν) our knees to the king. 17. O woman, depart in peace, for I will heal thy daughter.

LESSON XXIII

ADJECTIVES OF THE THIRD DECLENSION, IRREGULAR ADJECTIVES

Adjectives of the third declension have only two terminations, because the feminine is the same as the masculine.

The two principal forms of these adjectives are declined as follows:

ἀληθής[3] true

Stem ἀληθες

	Singular		Plural	
	Masc. Fem.	Neut.	Masc. Fem.	Neut.
Nom.	ἀληθής	ἀληθές	ἀληθεῖς	ἀληθῆ
Voc.	ἀληθές	ἀληθές	ἀληθεῖς	ἀληθῆ
Acc.	ἀληθῆ	ἀληθές	ἀληθεῖς	ἀληθῆ
Gen.	ἀληθοῦς	ἀληθοῦς	ἀληθῶν	ἀληθῶν
Dat.	ἀληθεῖ	ἀληθεῖ	ἀληθέσι	ἀληθέσι

[1] ἥψατο. [2] "for" εἰς.
[3] For the contractions in the endings, see p. 63.

IRREGULAR ADJECTIVES

ἄφρων foolish
Stem ἀφρον

	Singular			Plural	
	Masc. Fem.	Neut.		Masc. Fem.	Neut.
Nom.	ἄφρων	ἄφρον		ἄφρονες	ἄφρονα
Voc.	ἄφρον	ἄφρον		ἄφρονες	ἄφρονα
Acc.	ἄφρονα	ἄφρον		ἄφρονας	ἄφρονα
Gen.	ἄφρονος	ἄφρονος		ἀφρόνων	ἀφρόνων
Dat.	ἄφρονι	ἄφρονι		ἄφροσι	ἄφροσι

Some adjectives have the masculine and neuter of the 3rd declension and the feminine of the 1st declension.

Example: πᾶς, πᾶσα, πᾶν all.

	Singular			Plural		
	Masc.	Fem.	Neut.	Masc.	Fem.	Neut.
Nom.	πᾶς	πᾶσα	πᾶν	πάντες	πᾶσαι	πάντα
Voc.	πᾶς	πᾶσα	πᾶν	πάντες	πᾶσαι	πάντα
Acc.	πάντα	πᾶσαν	πᾶν	πάντας	πάσας	πάντα
Gen.	παντός	πάσης	παντός	πάντων	πασῶν	πάντων
Dat.	παντί	πάσῃ	παντί	πᾶσι	πάσαις	πᾶσι

The following irregular adjectives occur frequently.

πολύς, πολλή, πολύ much or great, Plural many.
μέγας, μεγάλη, μέγα great or large.

	Singular			Plural		
	Masc.	Fem.	Neut.	Masc.	Fem.	Neut.
Nom.	πολύς	πολλή	πολύ	πολλοί	πολλαί	πολλά
Voc.				πολλοί	πολλαί	πολλά
Acc.	πολύν	πολλήν	πολύ	πολλούς	πολλάς	πολλά
Gen.	πολλοῦ	πολλῆς	πολλοῦ	πολλῶν	πολλῶν	πολλῶν
Dat.	πολλῷ	πολλῇ	πολλῷ	πολλοῖς	πολλαῖς	πολλοῖς
Nom.	μέγας	μεγάλη	μέγα	μεγάλοι	μεγάλαι	μεγάλα
Voc.	μέγας	μεγάλη	μέγα	μεγάλοι	μεγάλαι	μεγάλα
Acc.	μέγαν	μεγάλην	μέγα	μεγάλους	μεγάλας	μεγάλα
Gen.	μεγάλου	μεγάλης	μεγάλου	μεγάλων	μεγάλων	μεγάλων
Dat.	μεγάλῳ	μεγάλῃ	μεγάλῳ	μεγάλοις	μεγάλαις	μεγάλοις

The declension of εἷς "one" and of the derived words οὐδείς and μηδείς "no one, nothing" should be noticed.

IRREGULAR ADJECTIVES

Great care must be taken to distinguish εἷς "one" (masc.) from εἰς "to," and ἕν "one" (neuter) from ἐν "in."

	Masc.	Fem.	Neut.
Nom.	εἷς	μία	ἕν
Acc.	ἕνα	μίαν	ἕν
Gen.	ἑνός	μιᾶς	ἑνός
Dat.	ἑνί	μιᾷ	ἑνί

	Masc.	Fem.	Neut.	Masc.	Fem.	Neut.
Nom.	οὐδείς	οὐδεμία	οὐδέν	μηδείς	μηδεμία	μηδέν
Acc.	οὐδένα	οὐδεμίαν	οὐδέν	μηδένα	μηδεμίαν	μηδέν
Gen.	οὐδενός	οὐδεμιᾶς	οὐδενός	μηδενός	μηδεμιᾶς	μηδενός
Dat.	οὐδενί	οὐδεμιᾷ	οὐδενί	μηδενί	μηδεμιᾷ	μηδενί

οὐδείς is used when the verb with which it is connected is in the Indicative mood, μηδείς is used when the verb with which it is connected is in the Subjunctive, Imperative, or Infinitive mood, or a Participle.

οὐδείς and μηδείς are used even when the verb already has a negative.

Examples:

No one told me this.
οὐδεὶς εἶπέ μοι τοῦτο.

Do not hurt any one.
μὴ βλάπτε μηδένα.

They said nothing to any one.
οὐδὲν οὐδενὶ εἶπον.

I am not able to see any one.
οὐ δύναμαι ἰδεῖν μηδένα.

Exercise 23

Learn Vocabulary 18.

1. ἴδε ὑγιὴ ἐποίησά σε, μηκέτι ἁμάρτανε. 2. οἱ λῃσταὶ ἔφυγον εἰς τὰ ὄρη. 3. οὐδεὶς θέλει πιεῖν τὸν οἶνον τοῦτον. 4. τὸ ὄνομά μου μέγα ἔσται ἐν πᾶσι τοῖς ἔθνεσι. 5. οἱ ἱερεῖς ἦλθον νυκτὸς καὶ ἦραν τὸ σῶμα τοῦ προφήτου. 6. εἰ οὖν τὸ φῶς τὸ ἐν σοὶ σκότος ἐστίν, τὸ σκότος πόσον[1, 2]. 7. ὦ γύναι, μεγάλη[2] σου ἡ πίστις. 8. γινώσκομεν ὅτι τὰ ῥήματα ταῦτα ἀληθῆ ἐστίν, ὅτι[3] ἐλάλησεν αὐτὰ ὁ Κύριος διὰ στόματος Δαυεὶδ τοῦ προφήτου. 9. αὕτη δέ ἐστιν ἡ κρίσις ὅτι τὸ φῶς ἦλθεν εἰς τὸν κόσμον καὶ ἐφίλησαν οἱ ἄνθρωποι μᾶλλον τὸ σκότος ἢ[4] τὸ φῶς· ἦν γὰρ αὐτῶν πονηρὰ τὰ ἔργα. 10. πεμπέσθω εἷς τῶν δούλων σπείρειν τὸ σπέρμα ἐν τῷ ἀγρῷ μου. 11. συνήρχοντο δὲ πολλοὶ ἐκ τῶν κωμῶν καὶ ἔφερον αὐτῷ τοὺς ἀσθενεῖς καὶ ἔβαλον αὐτοὺς παρὰ τοὺς πόδας αὐτοῦ, καὶ ἐδέοντο αὐτοῦ θεραπεύειν

---

[1] πόσον "how great." [2] Understand ἐστί. [3] ὅτι "because."
[4] ἤ "than"; distinguish carefully from ἡ and ἥ.

FIRST AORIST PASSIVE

αὐτούς. 12. μηδεὶς σκανδαλιζέτω ἕνα τῶν παίδων τούτων. 13. οἱ δὲ γονεῖς αὐτοῦ οὐκ ἔγνωσαν ὅτι μένει ἐν τῇ πόλει. 14. οὐχ ἡ γραφὴ εἶπεν ὅτι ἐκ τοῦ σπέρματος Δαυείδ, καὶ ἀπὸ Βηθλεὲμ τῆς κώμης ὅπου[1] ἦν Δαυείδ, ἔρχεται ὁ Χριστός; 15. ἐν ἐκείνῃ τῇ ὥρᾳ συνάγονται αὐτῷ πολλοὶ τῶν ἀρχιερέων οἱ λέγουσιν ὅτι οὐκ ἔσται ἀνάστασις.

1. Thou shalt open my mouth, O Lord, and my tongue shall praise thy name. 2. Didst not thou sow good seed in thy field? 3. Do not carry any (use μηδείς) sick man to the synagogue on the Sabbath day. 4. If thou wilt, thou art able to heal me. 5. I came into this world for (εἰς) judgement. 6. One of the lepers, when he saw that he was being healed, cast himself at his feet. 7. The high priests knew that this saying was true. 8. All the disciples were full of faith and of the Holy Spirit, and they healed the sick, and cast out many devils. 9. None of the priests believes that there is a resurrection. 10. My parents built many houses in this city. 11. Let no one love darkness more than light. 12. When they came to the villages they preached the Gospel to all the Gentiles who dwelt there. 13. If I judge, my judgement is true. 14. When the disciples of John heard that he was dead, they came and took up his body.

LESSON XXIV

THE FIRST AND SECOND AORIST PASSIVE. THE FUTURE PASSIVE

The conjugation of the First Aorist Passive is as follows:

Indicative		Imperative	
ἐλύθην	I was loosed etc.		
ἐλύθης		λύθητι	be loosed etc.
ἐλύθη		λυθήτω	
ἐλύθημεν			
ἐλύθητε		λύθητε	
ἐλύθησαν		λυθήτωσαν	

Infinitive
λυθῆναι to be loosed

Notice that the characteristic letters of the First Aorist Passive are θη.

[1] ὅπου "where."

FUTURE AND SECOND AORIST PASSIVE

The conjugation of the Future Passive is as follows: it is formed by adding θησ to the stem of the verb and putting after it the endings of the Present Passive.

Indicative		Infinitive
λυθήσομαι	I shall be loosed etc.	λυθήσεσθαι to be about to be loosed.
λυθήσῃ (λυθήσει)		
λυθήσεται		
λυθησόμεθα		
λυθήσεσθε		
λυθήσονται		

The presence of the letter θ at the beginning of the endings of these tenses causes certain consonantal changes which may be summarised as follows:

κ, γ, χ   followed by θ become χθ,
π, β, φ   followed by θ become φθ,
τ, δ, θ, ζ followed by θ become σθ.

In the contracted verbs the short vowel is lengthened before θ.

Examples:

Present	Stem	1st Aor. Pass.	Fut. Pass.
ἄγω	ἀγ	ἤχθην	ἀχθήσομαι
πράσσω	πραγ	ἐπράχθην	πραχθήσομαι
πέμπω	πεμπ	ἐπέμφθην	πεμφθήσομαι
πείθω	πειθ	ἐπείσθην	πεισθήσομαι
φιλέω	φιλε	ἐφιλήθην	φιληθήσομαι

The Second Aorist Passive does not occur very frequently in the N.T. Its endings are practically the same as those of the First Aorist Passive with the exception that the θ is omitted. The 2nd Aor. Pass. of φαίνω is given below.

Indicative		Imperative	
ἐφάνην	I appeared etc.		
ἐφάνης		φάνηθι	appear etc.
ἐφάνη		φανήτω	
ἐφάνημεν			
ἐφάνητε		φάνητε	
ἐφάνησαν		φανήτωσαν	
		φανέντων	

Infinitive
φανῆναι to appear

AORIST AND FUTURE PASSIVES

The following are some of the Second Aorists Passive found in the N.T.

ἐγράφην	"I was written"	from γράφω
ἐκρύβην	"I was hidden"	from κρύπτω
ἐσπάρην	"I was sown"	from σπείρω
ἐστάλην	"I was sent"	from στέλλω
ἐστράφην	"I was turned"	from στρέφω
ἐφθάρην	"I was destroyed"	from φθείρω

The following important verbs have irregular forms of the 1st Aorist and Future Passive.

Present Indicative	Future Passive	1st Aorist Passive
ἀκούω	ἀκουσθήσομαι	ἠκούσθην
βάλλω	βληθήσομαι	ἐβλήθην
ἐγείρω	ἐγερθήσομαι	ἠγέρθην
καλέω	κληθήσομαι	ἐκλήθην
λαμβάνω	ληφθήσομαι	ἐλήφθην
λέγω root ἐρ		ἐρρέθην, ἐρρήθην
ὁράω root ὀπ	ὀφθήσομαι (I shall be seen, or I shall appear)	ὤφθην (I was seen, or I appeared)
φέρω root ἐνεγκ		ἠνέχθην

N.B. The Future Passive and 1st Aorists given as coming from the last three verbs are really in no way derived from them. These verbs are defective as is explained on p. 52.

Exercise 24

Revise Vocabularies 14–18.

1. ἤχθη ὁ Ἰησοῦς ὑπὸ τοῦ Πνεύματος εἰς τὰ ὄρη πειρασθῆναι ὑπὸ τοῦ διαβόλου. 2. ὁ ἀρχιερεὺς ἐκρύβη ἐν τοῖς ὄρεσι πολλὰ ἔτη[1]. 3. τὸ ὄνομά μου κηρυχθήσεται ἐν πᾶσι τοῖς ἔθνεσι. 4. τῇ γὰρ χάριτι ἐσώθημεν διὰ θελήματος θεοῦ. 5. οἱ νεκροὶ ἐγερθήσονται ἐν ἡμέρᾳ κρίσεως τῇ φωνῇ τοῦ ἀγγέλου καὶ τῇ σάλπιγγι. 6. καὶ ὅτε ἐξεβλήθη τὸ δαιμόνιον ἐθαύ-

---

[1] πολλὰ ἔτη "for many years": the Accusative case is used to express duration of time, see author's *Syntax of N.T. Greek*, 18.

EXERCISES

μαζεν ὁ ὄχλος, ἔλεγον δὲ πολλοὶ ὅτι² ταῦτα τὰ τέρατα οὐκ ἐπράχθη ἐν ταῖς ἡμέραις τῶν πατέρων ἡμῶν. 7. μετὰ ταῦτα ὤφθη πᾶσι τοῖς ἀποστόλοις. 8. ἐκέλευσε τὸν ἄνδρα ἐνεχθῆναι διὰ τῆς πόλεως. 9. ἐν ἐκείνῃ τῇ ἡμέρᾳ πᾶς ὁ λαὸς κληθήσεται ἅγιος τῷ Κυρίῳ. 10. αἱ γυναῖκες παρεκλήθησαν ὑπὸ τῶν ἀνδρῶν αὐτῶν. 11. ποιήσω τὰ ῥήματά μου ἀκουσθῆναι ὑπὸ τοῦ βασιλέως. 12. οὐδεὶς τῶν ἀγγέλων ἀκουσθήσεται. 13. πάντες οἱ ἰχθύες ἐβλήθησαν εἰς τὸ ὕδωρ. 14. ταῦτα ἐρρήθη διὰ στόματος Δαυείδ. 15. πεμφθήτω εἷς τῶν ἱερέων πείθειν τὸν βασιλέα. 16. ὅτε καρπὸν ἐποίησε τὸ καλὸν σπέρμα ἐφάνη καὶ τὰ ζιζάνια³. 17. ὦ βασιλεῦ, φιληθήσῃ ὑπὸ παντὸς τοῦ γένους. 18. τὰ σώματα τῶν ἁγίων ἐσπάρη ἐν ἀτιμίᾳ⁴, ἐγερθήσεται δὲ ἐν δόξῃ. 19. ἐκλήθητε ἄφρονες ὑπὸ τῶν σοφῶν τοῦ αἰῶνος τούτου.

1. All this nation was called righteous (neut. agreeing with γένος)⁵. 2. Many of these words were written in a book by the high priest. 3. The fish were taken by these boys. 4. We were sown in weakness (ἀσθένεια), we shall be raised in power.* 5. If the devil shall be cast out the crowd will wonder. 6. The good seed was carried to the fields. 7. I was sent by the king's servants to seek for thee. 8. We know that this Gospel shall be preached to all the Gentiles, and that many will hear. 9. In that day many bodies of the saints arose (were raised), and came into the city, and appeared⁶ to many. 10. We wish those sheep to be driven to the hills. 11. Thou shalt be saved by faith and hope, if thou wilt abide in them. 12. You commanded the stones to be cast into the water. 13. All these things shall be done in the darkness. 14. Ye have heard that it was said by our fathers "Thou shalt not make an image of the Lord thy God⁷." 15. We were called foolish⁸ by many of the rulers of the Gentiles, but we know that the words which we speak are true.

² ὅτι must not be translated, it is often used to introduce the exact words of a speaker, like our inverted commas, Syntax 158.
³ ζιζάνια "tares."
⁴ ἐν ἀτιμίᾳ "in dishonour."
⁵ Syntax 11.
⁶ Use pass. of ἐμφανίζω.
⁷ See note 2 on the Greek exercise.
⁸ "foolish," plural, Syntax 11.

* δύναμις.

LESSON XXV

PARTICIPLES

Participles are verbal adjectives sharing the characteristics both of verbs and adjectives.

As a verb a participle has a subject, and, if it is the participle of a transitive verb in the active voice, it may have an object. It has also tense and voice.

As an adjective it agrees with the noun which it qualifies, that is with its subject, in number, gender and case.

The active participles are declined with 3rd declension endings in the masculine and neuter, and 1st declension endings in the feminine. They are as follows:

	Masc.	Fem.	Neut.	Stem	Meaning
Pres. Part. Act.	λύων	λύουσα	λῦον	λυοντ	loosing
Fut. Part. Act.	λύσων	λύσουσα	λῦσον	λυσοντ	being about to loose
1st Aor. Part. Act.	λύσας	λύσασα	λῦσαν	λυσαντ	having loosed
2nd Aor. Part. Act.	βαλών	βαλοῦσα	βαλόν	βαλοντ	having thrown
Pres. Part. of εἰμί	ὤν	οὖσα	ὄν	ὀντ	being

It will be observed that (1) the future participle is the same as the present with the insertion of σ before the endings.

(2) The characteristic σα occurs in the 1st aorist participle.

(3) The endings of the 2nd aorist participle are the same as those of the present participle, but the stem and the accents differ.

The present and 1st aorist participles active are declined as follows:

Present Participle Active

	Singular				Plural		
N.V.	λύων	λύουσα	λῦον		λύοντες	λύουσαι	λύοντα
A.	λύοντα	λύουσαν	λῦον		λύοντας	λυούσας	λύοντα
G.	λύοντος	λυούσης	λύοντος		λυόντων	λυουσῶν	λυόντων
D.	λύοντι	λυούσῃ	λύοντι		λύουσι	λυούσαις	λύουσι

Note that the masc. and neut. dat. pl. is the same in form as the 3rd pl. pres. ind.

First Aorist Participle Active

	Singular			Plural		
N.V.	λύσας	λύσασα	λῦσαν	λύσαντες	λύσασαι	λύσαντα
A.	λύσαντα	λύσασαν	λῦσαν	λύσαντας	λυσάσας	λύσαντα
G.	λύσαντος	λυσάσης	λύσαντος	λυσάντων	λυσασῶν	λυσάντων
D.	λύσαντι	λυσάσῃ	λύσαντι	λύσασι	λυσάσαις	λύσασι

The present participles active of the contracted verbs in εω are declined as follows:

N.V.	φιλῶν	φιλοῦσα	φιλοῦν
A.	φιλοῦντα	φιλοῦσαν	φιλοῦν
G.	φιλοῦντος	φιλούσης	φιλοῦντος etc.

The present participle of εἰμί is declined like λύων.

N.V.	ὤν	οὖσα	ὄν
A.	ὄντα	οὖσαν	ὄν
G.	ὄντος	οὔσης	ὄντος etc.

The present participle middle and passive is declined like an adjective of the 2nd declension. The aorist participles passive are declined with 3rd declension endings in the masculine and neuter and 1st declension endings in the feminine.

Pres. Part. Mid. and Pass.	λυόμενος, η, ον	being loosed
1st Aor. Part. Pass.	λυθείς, θεῖσα, θέν	loosed, or having been loosed
2nd Aor. Part. Pass.	φανείς, εἶσα, έν	having appeared

The 1st Aor. Part. Pass. is declined as follows:

	Singular			Plural		
N.V.	λυθείς	λυθεῖσα	λυθέν	λυθέντες	λυθεῖσαι	λυθέντα
A.	λυθέντα	λυθεῖσαν	λυθέν	λυθέντας	λυθείσας	λυθέντα
G.	λυθέντος	λυθείσης	λυθέντος	λυθέντων	λυθεισῶν	λυθέντων
D.	λυθέντι	λυθείσῃ	λυθέντι	λυθεῖσι	λυθείσαις	λυθεῖσι

Participles are generally negatived with μή in the New Testament.
Participles are used much more frequently in Greek than in English. They may be used either Adjectivally or Adverbially.

74   ADJECTIVAL AND ADVERBIAL PARTICIPLES

1. The Adjectival Participle.

In this use the adjectival side of the participle is most prominent. The adjectival participle is generally preceded by an article with which it agrees. The participle preceded by an article is very common in the New Testament. It should generally be translated by a **clause introduced by a relative pronoun**, but may sometimes be translated by a **noun**.

Examples:

    οἱ πιστεύοντες   those who believe, or believers.
    ὁ σπείρων   the sower.

They that hunger and thirst after righteousness.

    οἱ πεινῶντες[1] καὶ διψῶντες[1] τὴν δικαιοσύνην.   Mt. v. 6.

This is he that was sown by the way side.

    οὗτός ἐστιν ὁ παρὰ τὴν ὁδὸν σπαρείς.   Mt. xiii. 19.

Notice that any number of qualifying words may be inserted between the article and the participle.

2. The Adverbial Participle.

In this use the verbal side of the participle is most prominent.

When a participle is used adverbially it is equivalent to an Adverbial Clause modifying some other verb in the sentence.

Such participles are best translated into English by a suitable **adverbial clause**. The context must decide what kind of adverbial clause the participle in question is equivalent to. In the New Testament an adverbial participle is generally equivalent to a Temporal[2] clause, sometimes to a Causal[2] clause, rarely to a Concessive[2] clause.

Examples: (a) A participle denoting the time of the action of the main verb, translated by a **Temporal clause** in English.

    And when he came out, he saw a great multitude.

    καὶ ἐξελθὼν εἶδεν πολὺν ὄχλον.   Mt. xiv. 14.

And when the chief priests and Pharisees had heard his parables, they knew that he spoke about them.

    καὶ ἀκούσαντες οἱ ἀρχιερεῖς καὶ οἱ Φαρισαῖοι τὰς παραβολὰς αὐτοῦ ἔγνωσαν ὅτι περὶ αὐτῶν λέγει.   Mt. xxi. 45.

(b) Participle denoting the cause of the action of the main verb translated by a **Causal clause** in English.

---
[1] For these forms see lesson 28.
[2] See Introduction on English Grammar.

ADVERBIAL PARTICIPLES

Examples:

And they were all afraid of him, because they did not believe that he was a disciple.

καὶ πάντες ἐφοβοῦντο αὐτόν, μὴ πιστεύοντες ὅτι ἐστὶν μαθητής.
Acts ix. 26.

Godliness is profitable for everything, because it has a promise for the life that is now, as well as for that which is to come.

ἡ δὲ εὐσέβεια πρὸς πάντα ὠφέλιμός ἐστιν, ἐπαγγελίαν ἔχουσα ζωῆς τῆς νῦν καὶ τῆς μελλούσης. 1 Tim. iv. 8.

The Participle often denotes the **attendant circumstances** of an action, and may be best translated into English by a **finite verb** joined to that which is the main verb in Greek by "and."

Examples:
He answered and said....
ἀποκριθεὶς εἶπεν....
Immediately the father of the child cried out and said....
εὐθὺς κράξας ὁ πατὴρ τοῦ παιδίου ἔλεγεν.... Mk ix. 24.
Take Mark and bring him with thee.
Μάρκον ἀναλαβὼν ἄγε μετὰ σεαυτοῦ. 2 Tim. iv. 11.

In some cases however it is better to translate the Greek participle by an English **participle**. The method of translation which sounds best in English must be chosen.

Examples:

In those days John the Baptist came into the wilderness of Judea preaching and saying "Repent."

ἐν δὲ ταῖς ἡμέραις ἐκείναις παραγίγνεται Ἰωάνης ὁ Βαπτιστὴς κηρύσσων ἐν τῇ ἐρήμῳ τῆς Ἰουδαίας, λέγων Μετανοεῖτε.

And they were baptised by him in the river Jordan, confessing their sins.

καὶ ἐβαπτίζοντο ὑπ' αὐτοῦ ἐν τῷ Ἰορδάνῃ ποταμῷ ἐξομολογούμενοι τὰς ἁμαρτίας αὐτῶν. Mt. iii. 6.

The Meaning of the Tense in Participles.

Generally speaking, the Present Participle denotes action taking place at the same time as the action of the main verb, and the Aorist Participle denotes action which took place before the action of the main verb.

Examples. Present Participle:

He appeared to them as they were fighting.

ὤφθην αὐτοῖς μαχομένοις. Acts vii. 26.

Aorist Participle:

And having fasted forty days and forty nights he afterwards hungered.

καὶ νηστεύσας ἡμέρας τεσσαράκοντα καὶ τεσσαράκοντα νύκτας ὕστερον ἐπείνασεν. Mt. iv. 2.

Present Participle:

He that has ears to hear let him hear.

ὁ ἔχων ὦτα ἀκούειν ἀκουέτω.

Aorist Participle:

But he that had been healed did not know who it was.

ὁ δὲ ἰαθεὶς[1] οὐκ ᾔδει[2] τίς ἐστιν. Jn v. 13.

Exercise 25

Learn Vocabulary 19.

1. καὶ παράγων παρὰ τὴν θάλασσαν τῆς Γαλιλαίας εἶδεν Σίμωνα καὶ Ἀνδρέαν τὸν ἀδελφὸν Σίμωνος ἀμφιβάλλοντας ἐν τῇ θαλάσσῃ. 2. καὶ ἦλθεν κηρύσσων εἰς τὰς συναγωγὰς αὐτῶν καὶ δαιμόνια ἐκβάλλων. 3. πῶς δυσχόλως[3] οἱ τὰ χρήματα ἔχοντες εἰς τὴν βασιλείαν τοῦ θεοῦ εἰσελεύσονται. 4. καὶ ἦσαν οἱ φαγόντες τοὺς ἄρτους πεντακισχίλιοι ἄνδρες. 5. οἱ μὲν οὖν διασπαρέντες διῆλθον εὐαγγελιζόμενοι τὸν λόγον. 6. παραγενόμενος δὲ εἰς Ἰερουσαλὴμ ἐπείραζε κολλᾶσθαι[4] τοῖς μαθηταῖς, καὶ πάντες ἐφοβοῦντο αὐτόν, μὴ πιστεύοντες ὅτι ἐστὶν μαθητής. 7. ἀκούων δὲ Ἀνανίας τοὺς λόγους τούτους πεσὼν ἐξέψυξεν[5] καὶ ἐγένετο[6] φόβος μέγας ἐπὶ[7] πάντας τοὺς ἀκούοντας. 8. καὶ σπαράξαν[8] αὐτὸν τὸ πνεῦμα τὸ ἀκάθαρτον, καὶ φωνῆσαν φωνῇ μεγάλῃ, ἐξῆλθεν ἐξ αὐτοῦ. 9. καὶ ἦν ἐν τῇ ἐρήμῳ τεσσαράκοντα ἡμέρας καὶ τεσσαράκοντα νύκτας πειραζόμενος ὑπὸ τοῦ Σατανᾶ. 10. ὑμεῖς οὖν ἀκούσατε τὴν παραβολὴν τοῦ σπείραντος. 11. καὶ ὤφθη αὐτοῖς Μωϋσῆς καὶ Ἡλείας συνλαλοῦντες μετ' αὐτοῦ.

[1] See Lesson 28. [2] See Lesson 36.
[3] δυσχόλως "with difficulty, hardly."
[4] κολλᾶσθαι "to join himself," see Lesson 28.
[5] ἐξέψυξεν "gave up the ghost," from ἐκψύχω.
[6] See page 83. [7] ἐπί "upon."
[8] σπαράξαν 1st Aor. part. from σπαράσσω.

GENITIVE ABSOLUTE

Participles should be used to translate all the words marked *, and also all the English participles.

1. Those that had preached* the word were scattered abroad.
2. And passing by the sea of Galilee the disciples taught many people.
3. Blessed[1] are those that hear* and those that believe* the words of this book.
4. Many of the publicans therefore were baptised confessing their sins.
5. But he answered* and said "How hardly[2] shall ye enter into the kingdom of heaven."
6. The sower* soweth the word.
7. And when he came forth* he saw a great multitude.
8. And all those that heard* kept these words in their hearts.
9. But we were afraid because we did not believe* that his words were true.
10. This is he that was sent* by the king.
11. While they were teaching* the people they remained in the temple.
12. And having come out of the city he went to another place.
13. But the prophet cried and said* "Behold the man that cometh* after me: him shall ye hear."
14. When the governor therefore heard* this he was afraid and all that were* with him.
15. And when they had cast* the net[3] into the sea they took many fishes.
16. And when they had come* to Bethlehem they tried to enter into the synagogue, but those that kept* it cast them out.
17. But while I was walking* through the fields I saw a great light from heaven and heard a voice speaking to me.
18. The prophet remained in the mountain forty days[4] and forty nights writing the words of this law.

LESSON XXVI

THE GENITIVE ABSOLUTE. INTERROGATIVE AND INDEFINITE PRONOUNS. CERTAIN PREPOSITIONS

A noun or pronoun and a participle may stand by themselves in the Genitive case if the noun or pronoun does not denote the same person or thing as the subject or object of the clause on which it depends.

This construction is called the Genitive Absolute.

Absolute means "loosed," from the Latin "absolutus": phrases of this kind are called "absolute" because they are loosed in construction from the rest of the sentence.

---

[1] μακάριος.   [2] δυσκόλως.   [3] τὸ δίκτυον.
[4] Days and nights, use Acc. case, Syntax 18.

INTERROGATIVE PRONOUN

The Genitive Absolute should generally be translated by an adverbial clause in English. The context must decide whether this clause is to be Temporal, Causal, or Concessive. Most of the Genitives Absolute in the New Testament may best be translated by Temporal clauses.

Examples:

And when the devil was cast out the dumb man spoke.
καὶ ἐκβληθέντος τοῦ δαιμονίου ἐλάλησεν ὁ κωφός.   Mt. ix. 33.
And while the bridegroom tarried they all slumbered and slept.
χρονίζοντος δὲ τοῦ νυμφίου ἐνύσταξαν πᾶσαι καὶ ἐκάθευδον.

Mt. xxv. 5.

The same construction is found in Latin, but the case there used is the Ablative. A similar construction is also rarely found in English, but in that language the case used is the Nominative.

Example: "This done, he went home."

N.B. The rule given above as to the noun or pronoun in a Genitive Absolute not referring to the same person or thing as the subject or object of the clause on which it depends is generally observed in Classical Greek. But it is frequently broken in New Testament Greek as the following example will show:

And as he was coming out of the temple, one of his disciples said to him...

καὶ ἐκπορευομένου αὐτοῦ ἐκ τοῦ ἱεροῦ λέγει αὐτῷ εἷς τῶν μαθητῶν αὐτοῦ...

Mk xiii. 1.

The Interrogative Pronoun τίς who? τί what? can take the place of either a noun or an adjective. τί often means "why?"

It is declined as follows:

Singular		Plural	
Masc. Fem.	Neut.	Masc. Fem.	Neut.
N. τίς	τί	τίνες	τίνα
A. τίνα	τί	τίνας	τίνα
G. τίνος	τίνος	τίνων	τίνων
D. τίνι	τίνι	τίσι	τίσι

Examples of its use:

Whom do I hear? τίνας ἀκούω;
What men do I hear? τίνας ἀνθρώπους ἀκούω;

CERTAIN PREPOSITIONS

The Indefinite Pronoun τις is generally translated by "some" or "any."

It is distinguished from τίς Interrogative by having no accent[1], and by the fact that it usually cannot stand as the first word in a sentence.

It is declined in the same way as τίς Interrogative.

Examples of its use:
   Some one says this. τοῦτο λέγει τις.
   A certain man says this. ἄνθρωπός τις τοῦτο λέγει.

The following **prepositions** present some difficulty:

κατά, root-meaning DOWN.

κατά is followed by the Accusative or Genitive case. When followed by an Accusative it means "down along, throughout, with regard to, <u>according to</u>," when followed by a Genitive it means "down from, <u>against</u>."

The meanings underlined are the commonest in the New Testament.

Examples:
   Take him and judge him according to your law.
   λάβετε αὐτὸν ὑμεῖς, καὶ κατὰ τὸν νόμον ὑμῶν κρίνατε αὐτόν.
                                                          Jn xviii. 31.

   He that is not with me is against me.
   ὁ μὴ ὢν μετ' ἐμοῦ κατ' ἐμοῦ ἐστίν.   Lk. xi. 23.

Notice the following special phrases:
   κατ' ὄναρ   in a dream.
   κατὰ καιρόν   in due season.
   καθ' ἡμέραν   daily.
   κατ' ἰδίαν   privately.

ἐπί, root-meaning UPON.

ἐπί is followed by the Accusative, Genitive or Dative case. It is difficult to draw any clear distinction between its meanings with these three cases, but with the Accusative it means "upon," "on," or "to" often with some idea of motion, with the Genitive it means "upon," "on," and occasionally "in the time of," "in the presence of," with the Dative it means "on," or "at."

Examples:
   And other fell on good ground.
   ἄλλα δὲ ἔπεσεν ἐπὶ τὴν γῆν τὴν καλήν.   Mt. xiii. 8.

---

[1] It is an "enclitic"; see page 142.

CERTAIN PREPOSITIONS

Take my yoke upon you.
ἄρατε τὸν ζυγόν μου ἐφ' ὑμᾶς.   Mt. xi. 29.
And seeing one fig tree on the road he went to it.
καὶ ἰδὼν συκῆν μίαν ἐπὶ τῆς ὁδοῦ ἦλθεν ἐπ' αὐτήν.
   Mt. xxi. 19.
I have glorified thee upon the earth.
ἐγώ σε ἐδόξασα ἐπὶ τῆς γῆς.   Jn xvii. 4.
In the time of Elisha the prophet.
ἐπὶ Ἐλισαίου τοῦ προφήτου.   Lk. iv. 27.
And they wondered at him.
καὶ ἐθαύμαζον ἐπ' αὐτῷ.   Mk xii. 17.
Know that it is near at the doors.
γινώσκετε ὅτι ἐγγύς ἐστιν ἐπὶ θύραις.   Mk xiii. 29.

πρός, root-meaning TOWARDS.

πρός is followed by the Accusative, Genitive or Dative case, but it is so rarely followed by a Genitive or Dative case in the New Testament that it will be sufficient to regard it as a preposition followed only by the Accusative case.

It means "towards, up to, to, with regard to," and in certain cases "with," it is also used after verbs meaning "to say" where a simple Dative would have been expected.

Examples:

In the fourth watch of the night he went to them walking on the sea.

τετάρτῃ δὲ φυλακῇ τῆς νυκτὸς ἦλθεν πρὸς αὐτοὺς περιπατῶν ἐπὶ τὴν θάλασσαν.   Mt. xiv. 25.

And Jesus said to Simon "Fear not."
καὶ εἶπεν πρὸς τὸν Σίμωνα Ἰησοῦς Μὴ φοβοῦ.   Lk. v. 10.
The word was with God.
ὁ λόγος ἦν πρὸς τὸν θεόν.   Jn i. 1.

See Lesson XXXVIII.

Exercise 26

A

Learn Vocabulary 20.

1. ἔτι[1] δὲ λαλοῦντος τοῦ Πέτρου τὰ ῥήματα ταῦτα, ἔπεσεν τὸ πνεῦμα τὸ ἅγιον ἐπὶ πάντας τοὺς ἀκούοντας τὸν λόγον. 2. ἡ γὰρ σὰρξ ἐπιθυμεῖ κατὰ τοῦ πνεύματος καὶ τὸ πνεῦμα κατὰ τῆς σαρκός. 3. ἐγγὺς δὲ οὔσης Λύδδας

[1] ἔτι "still."

EXERCISES

τῇ Ἰόππῃ, οἱ μαθηταὶ ἀκούσαντες ὅτι Πέτρος ἐστὶν ἐν αὐτῇ, ἀπέστειλαν δύο ἄνδρας πρὸς αὐτόν. 4. ὁ δὲ ἐπὶ τὰ πετρώδη[1] σπαρείς, οὗτός ἐστιν ὁ τὸν λόγον ἀκούων, καὶ εὐθὺς μετὰ χαρᾶς λαμβάνων αὐτόν. 5. ἀναχωρούντων δὲ αὐτῶν, ἴδε ἄγγελος Κυρίου φαίνεται κατ᾽ ὄναρ τῷ Ἰωσὴφ λέγων Παράλαβε τὸ παιδίον καὶ τὴν μητέρα αὐτοῦ, καὶ φεῦγε εἰς Αἴγυπτον. 6. ἐξεπλήσσοντο δὲ οἱ ὄχλοι ἐπὶ τῇ διδαχῇ αὐτοῦ. 7. ἀλλὰ λήμψεσθε[2] δύναμιν, ἐλθόντος τοῦ ἁγίου πνεύματος ἐφ᾽ ὑμᾶς. 8. καθ᾽ ἡμέραν δὲ προσεκαρτέρουν ὁμοθυμαδὸν[3] ἐν τῷ ἱερῷ. 9. καὶ ὄψονται[4] τὸν υἱὸν τοῦ ἀνθρώπου ἐρχόμενον ἐπὶ τῶν νεφελῶν τοῦ οὐρανοῦ. 10. τίς ἐκ τῶν δύο ἐποίησεν τὸ θέλημα τοῦ πατρός; 11. τότε προσῆλθεν αὐτῷ γυνή τις αἰτοῦσά τι παρ᾽ αὐτοῦ, ὁ δὲ εἶπεν αὐτῇ Τί θέλεις;

B

1. ἐπ᾽ ἀρχιερέως Ἄννα καὶ Καιάφα ἐγένετο* ῥῆμα Κυρίου ἐπὶ Ἰωάννην τοῦ Ζαχαρίου ἐν τῇ ἐρήμῳ. 2. ἐπὶ ταύτῃ τῇ πέτρᾳ οἰκοδομήσω μου τὴν ἐκκλησίαν. 3. οἱ δὲ ἀρχιερεῖς καὶ τὸ συνέδριον ὅλον ἐζήτουν ψευδομαρτυρίαν[5] κατὰ τοῦ Ἰησοῦ. 4. καθ᾽ ἡμέραν ἤμην πρὸς ὑμᾶς ἐν τῷ ἱερῷ καὶ οὐκ ἐκρατήσατέ με. 5. εἶδεν ὁ Ἰησοῦς πνεῦμα θεοῦ καταβαῖνον ὡσεὶ περιστερὰν[6] ἐρχόμενον ἐπ᾽ αὐτόν. 6. καὶ θαυμάσαντες ἐπὶ τῇ ἀποκρίσει αὐτοῦ ἐσίγησαν[7]. 7. ὁ μὴ ὢν μετ᾽ ἐμοῦ κατ᾽ ἐμοῦ ἐστίν. 8. καὶ ἐσπλαγχνίσθη[8] ἐπ᾽ αὐτοῖς καὶ ἐθεράπευσέν τινας αὐτῶν. 9. ὑμεῖς κατὰ τὴν σάρκα κρίνετε, ἐγὼ δὲ κρίνω οὐδένα. 10. καὶ ἀπῆλθεν καθ᾽ ὅλην τὴν πόλιν κηρύσσων ὅσα ἐποίησεν αὐτῷ ὁ Ἰησοῦς. 11. καὶ ὥρμησεν[9] ἡ ἀγέλη[10] κατὰ τοῦ κρημνοῦ[11] εἰς τὴν θάλασσαν. 12. καὶ ἀπῆλθόν τινες τῶν σὺν ἡμῖν ἐπὶ τὸ μνημεῖον. 13. κύριε, εἰ σὺ εἶ, κέλευσόν με ἐλθεῖν πρός σε ἐπὶ τὰ ὕδατα. 14. καὶ εἰσῆλθεν κατὰ τὸ εἰωθὸς αὐτῷ[12] ἐν τῇ ἡμέρᾳ τῶν σαββάτων εἰς τὴν συναγωγήν. 15. ἐπιστάτα, δι᾽ ὅλης νυκτὸς κοπιάσαντες οὐδὲν ἐλάβομεν, ἐπὶ δὲ τῷ ῥήματί σου χαλάσω[13] τὰ δίκτυα. 16. ὁ δὲ εἶπεν πρὸς αὐτούς Ἀγωνίζεσθε[14] εἰσελθεῖν διὰ τῆς στενῆς θύρας.

* This word is given in the next exercise. It is the Second Aor. Middle of γίνομαι. Translate "came."

[1] τὰ πετρώδη "the rocky ground."
[2] λήμψεσθε, future deponent from λαμβάνω.
[3] ὁμοθυμαδόν "with one accord."
[4] ὄψονται, a deponent future given as the future of ὁράω.
[5] ψευδομαρτυρίαν "false witness."
[6] ὡσεὶ περιστεράν "like a dove."
[7] ἐσίγησαν "they became silent."
[8] ἐσπλαγχνίσθη "he was moved with compassion."
[9] ὥρμησεν "rushed."
[10] ἡ ἀγέλη "the herd."
[11] τοῦ κρημνοῦ "the cliff."
[12] τὸ εἰωθὸς αὐτῷ "his custom."
[13] χαλάσω "I will let down."
[14] ἀγωνίζεσθε "strive."

The clauses marked * should be translated by a Genitive absolute.

1. And when the disciples had entered into the boat* Jesus sent the multitudes away. 2. Then a certain man came to him and said "What art thou doing here?" 3. What power shall we receive when the Holy Spirit comes upon us*? 4. The day is drawing near in which the Son of man shall come upon the clouds of heaven. 5. Take and judge these men according to your law. 6. Peter went to him, walking upon the water. 7. The disciples were preaching in the days of Caiaphas the high priest. 8. They went into the assembly on the Lord's day according to custom. 9. I was with you daily in Jerusalem. 10. The high priest therefore said to the disciples "Who gave[1] you authority to do these things?" 11. The Pharisees will say many things against the Son of man. 12. When the messengers of Herod had departed* the disciples told him privately all that they had done. 13. But although he sent his own son to them* they would not receive him. 14. You were astonished at his promises. 15. And when we had toiled all the night* Jesus came to us walking on the sea. 16. And while he was holding my hand* I received power to walk. 17. Who is able to endure these things? 18. And while they were drawing near to the city* the whole multitude was rejoicing saying "Blessed[2] is he that cometh in the name of the Lord." 19. In the days of Herod the king Joseph went down[3] into Egypt taking with him the child Jesus and Mary his mother.

LESSON XXVII

THE FIRST AND SECOND AORIST MIDDLE. THE COMPARISON OF ADJECTIVES. ADVERBS

The conjugation of the **First Aorist Middle** is as follows:

Indicative		Imperative	
ἐλυσάμην	I loosed (for my own benefit) etc.		
ἐλύσω		λῦσαι	loose (for thy own benefit) etc.
ἐλύσατο		λυσάσθω	
ἐλυσάμεθα			
ἐλύσασθε		λύσασθε	
ἐλύσαντο		λυσάσθωσαν	
		λυσάσθων	

[1] ἔδωκεν.   [2] εὐλογημένος.   [3] κατέβη.

SECOND AORIST MIDDLE

Infinitive		Participle	
λύσασθαι	to loose (for one's own benefit)	λυσάμενος, η, ον	having loosed (for one's own benefit)

Notice the presence of the σα, the distinguishing mark of the First Aorist.

The endings of the **Second Aorist Indicative Middle** are the same as those of the Imperfect Passive. The endings of the other moods are the same as the corresponding moods of the Present Passive. The endings are however not added to the present stem, but to the verbal stem, as explained on page 43.

The Second Aor. Mid. of γίνομαι "I come into being" is as follows:

Indicative		Imperative	
ἐγενόμην	I came into being or I was		
ἐγένου		γενοῦ	come into being or be, etc.
ἐγένετο		γενέσθω	
ἐγενόμεθα			
ἐγένεσθε		γένεσθε	
ἐγένοντο		γενέσθωσαν	

Infinitive		Participle	
γενέσθαι	to come into being, to be, to come to pass	γενόμενος, η, ον	coming into being, being, coming to pass, happening

This word is especially common in the New Testament: it is an example of a verb which is deponent in the Middle voice.

The form which occurs most frequently is ἐγένετο "it came to pass."

Most of the Middle forms which are found in the N.T. are deponent, and must therefore be translated by an active verb in English.

In a few cases verbs are found in the Middle voice which denote that the subject is acting upon himself, or in some way that concerns himself, or is allowing something to be done to himself.

Examples are found in sentences 8, 13, 14 in the following exercise A.

The comparison of Adjectives

There are three degrees of comparison:

The **Positive** degree which denotes simply that the person or thing denoted by the noun which the adjective qualifies possesses the quality expressed by the adjective.

COMPARISON OF ADJECTIVES

The **Comparative** degree which denotes that the person or thing possesses this quality in a higher degree than some other person or thing.

The **Superlative** degree which denotes that the person or thing possesses this quality in the highest degree, or in a very high degree.

Examples:

Positive degree.	He is a tall man.
Comparative degree.	He is taller than his brother.
Superlative degree.	He is the tallest man in the town.

The Comparative and Superlative degrees of comparison are expressed in Greek by adding τερος and τατος to the stem of adjectives of the 2nd dec., and to the stem of those ending in ης in the 3rd dec.

When the last vowel but one of the adjective is short the final ο of the stem is lengthened to ω.

Examples:

Positive	Comparative	Superlative
δίκαιος	(δικαιότερος, η, ον)	(δικαιότατος, η, ον)
ἰσχυρός	ἰσχυρότερος, α, ον	(ἰσχυρότατος, η, ον)
σοφός	σοφώτερος, α, ον	(σοφώτατος, η, ον)
ἀληθής	(ἀληθέστερος α, ον)	(ἀληθέστατος, η, ον)

The following adjectives form their degrees of comparison irregularly.

Positive	Comparative	Superlative
ἀγαθός good	κρείσσων, κρείττων better	κράτιστος best
κακός bad	χείρων, ἥσσων, ἥττων worse	(χείριστος) worst
πολύς many	πλείων, πλέων more	πλεῖστος most
μικρός little	μικρότερος, ἐλάσσων, ἐλάττων less	(μικρότατος), ἐλάχιστος least
μέγας great	μείζων greater	μέγιστος greatest

Adjectives in the Comparative degree ending in ων are declined as follows:

	Masc. Fem.	Neut.
N.	μείζων	μεῖζον
A.	μείζονα, μείζω	μεῖζον
G.	μείζονος	μείζονος
D.	μείζονι	μείζονι

ADVERBS

	Masc. Fem.	Neut.
N.	μείζονες, μείζους	μείζονα, μεῖζω
A.	μείζονας, μείζους	μείζονα, μεῖζω
G.	μειζόνων	μειζόνων
D.	μείζοσι	μείζοσι

An adjective or adverb in the comparative degree is followed either by a noun or pronoun in the Genitive, or by ἤ "than" followed by a noun or pronoun in the same case as the noun or pronoun with which the adjective agrees.

Examples : He is wiser than his son.
σοφώτερός ἐστιν τοῦ υἱοῦ.
or σοφώτερός ἐστιν ἢ ὁ υἱός.

Adverbs

Adverbs are formed from adjectives by changing the ν of the Gen. pl. masc. to ς.

Examples :

Adjective		Adverb	
φίλος	dear	(φίλως)	dearly
σοφός	wise	(σοφῶς)	wisely
ἀληθής	true	ἀληθῶς	truly

The comparative and superlative degrees of adverbs are formed by taking the Neuter Singular of the comparative of the adjective to form the comparative of the adverb, and the Neuter Plural of the superlative of the adjective to form the superlative of the adverb.

Examples :

Positive	Comparative	Superlative
(σοφῶς)	(σοφώτερον)	(σοφώτατα)
ἀληθῶς	(ἀληθέστερον)	(ἀληθέστατα)

The following forms should be noted.

Positive	Comparative	Superlative
εὖ well	βέλτιον, κρεῖσσον better	(βέλτιστα) best
καλῶς well, beautifully	κάλλιον better, more beautifully	(κάλλιστα) best, most beautifully
κακῶς badly	ἧσσον, ἧττον worse	(ἥκιστα) worst
(μάλα)	μᾶλλον more	μάλιστα most
πολύ much	πλεῖον, πλέον more	(πλεῖστα) most
ἐγγύς near	ἐγγύτερον nearer	ἔγγιστα nearest
ταχέως, ταχύ swiftly	τάχιον more swiftly	τάχιστα most swiftly

EXERCISES

The Comparative degree of adjectives and adverbs is not much used in the New Testament. The Superlative degree is scarcely used at all: its place it taken by the Comparative degree.

Example:

Being the least of all seeds that are on the earth.

μικρότερον ὂν πάντων τῶν σπερμάτων τῶν ἐπὶ τῆς γῆς.

Mk iv. 31.

The forms enclosed in brackets in the tables above are not found in the New Testament.

Exercise 27

A

Learn Vocabulary 21.

1. τῇ δὲ ἐπαύριον[1], ὁδοιπορούντων ἐκείνων καὶ τῇ πόλει ἐγγιζόντων, ἀνέβη Πέτρος ἐπὶ τὸ δῶμα[2] προσεύξασθαι. 2. οὐχὶ ἡ ψυχὴ πλεῖόν ἐστι τῆς τροφῆς; 3. καὶ συνεβουλεύσαντο ἀποκτείνειν τὸν Παῦλον. 4. ὁ μείζων ἐν ὑμῖν γενέσθω ὡς ὁ νεώτερος. 5. κατελάβοντο ὅτι ἄνθρωποι ἀγράμματοι καὶ ἰδιῶται[3] εἰσίν. 6. νῦν γὰρ ἐγγύτερόν ἐστιν ἡ σωτηρία ἡμῶν ἢ ὅτε ἐπιστεύσαμεν. 7. ἀληθῶς οὗτος ὁ ἄνθρωπος υἱὸς θεοῦ ἦν. 8. καὶ ῥίψας τὰ ἀργύρια εἰς τὸν ναὸν ἀνεχώρησεν, καὶ ἀπελθὼν ἀπήγξατο[4]. 9. ὁ δὲ μικρότερος ἐν τῇ βασιλείᾳ τῶν οὐρανῶν μείζων αὐτοῦ ἐστίν. 10. νυνὶ δὲ μένει πίστις, ἐλπίς, ἀγάπη· τὰ τρία ταῦτα, μείζων δὲ τούτων ἡ ἀγάπη. 11. ἔρχεται ὁ ἰσχυρότερός μου ὀπίσω μου. 12. μείζονα τούτων ὄψει. 13. καὶ νῦν τί μέλλεις; βάπτισαι, καὶ ἀπόλουσαι τὰς ἁμαρτίας σου, ἐπικαλεσάμενος τὸ ὄνομα τοῦ Κυρίου. 14. πάντες οἱ πατέρες ἡμῶν ἐβαπτίσαντο εἰς τὸν Μωυσῆν ἐν τῇ νεφέλῃ καὶ ἐν τῇ θαλάσσῃ.

B

1. οἱ δὲ μεῖζον ἔκραξαν λέγοντες Κύριε, ἐλέησον ἡμᾶς. 2. σὺ Κύριε, ἀνάδειξον[5] τὸν ἄνθρωπον ὃν ἐξελέξω. 3. ἡ βασίλισσα νότου[6] ἦλθεν ἐκ τῶν περάτων[7] τῆς γῆς ἀκοῦσαι τὴν σοφίαν Σολομῶνος, καὶ ἰδοὺ πλεῖον Σολομῶνος ὧδε. 4. οὐδεὶς ἐπιβάλλει ἐπίβλημα[8] ῥάκους ἀγνάφου[9] ἐπὶ ἱματίῳ παλαιῷ·

---

[1] τῇ δὲ ἐπαύριον "And on the next day," ἐπαύριον is an adverb meaning "to-morrow," τῇ agrees with ἡμέρᾳ understood.
[2] τὸ δῶμα "the house top."
[3] ἀγράμματοι καὶ ἰδιῶται "unlettered and ignorant."
[4] ἀπήγξατο middle aorist from ἀπάγχω "I hang."
[5] ἀνάδειξον "show."
[6] ἡ βασίλισσα νότου "the queen of the south."
[7] ἐκ τῶν περάτων "from the furthest parts."
[8] ἐπίβλημα, τό, "a thing put on, a patch."
[9] ῥάκους ἀγνάφου "of undressed cloth."

CONTRACTED VERBS IN αω AND οω

αἴρει γὰρ τὸ πλήρωμα αὐτοῦ[1] ἀπὸ τοῦ ἱματίου καὶ χεῖρον σχίσμα γίνεται.
5. ἀμὴν λέγω ὑμῖν ἐφ᾽ ὅσον[2] ἐποιήσατε ἑνὶ[3] τούτων τῶν ἀδελφῶν μου τῶν ἐλαχίστων, ἐμοὶ ἐποιήσατε. 6. καὶ γίνεται τὰ ἔσχατα τοῦ ἀνθρώπου ἐκείνου χείρονα τῶν πρώτων. 7. ἐγὼ γάρ εἰμι ὁ ἐλάχιστος τῶν ἀποστόλων.
8. εἰ οὖν οὐδὲ ἐλάχιστον δύνασθε, τί περὶ τῶν λοιπῶν μεριμνᾶτε[4];
9. λέγω ὑμῖν μείζων ἐν γεννητοῖς[5] γυναικῶν Ἰωάνου οὐδείς ἐστιν· ὁ δὲ μικρότερος ἐν τῇ βασιλείᾳ τοῦ θεοῦ μείζων αὐτοῦ ἐστίν. 10. πειθαρχεῖν[6] δεῖ θεῷ μᾶλλον ἢ ἀνθρώποις.

1. And when Solomon had prayed he departed out of the temple.
2. The younger of the sons would not work for[7] his father. 3. The robbers hanged themselves, for those that pursued them were more than they. 4. We called upon the name of the Lord, for he is stronger than all the kings of the earth. 5. He chose Simon whom he surnamed Peter. 6. Behold, love is greater than faith. 7. Why then do ye delay to go to Jerusalem, for behold a greater than Solomon is there?
8. We ought to obey the king rather than the priest. 9. They say that these days are worse than the days of our fathers. 10. Ye took counsel together to slay the wisest of men. 11. He that is least shall become[8] the greatest. 12. But he cried out the more "Behold what things[9] I suffer at the hands of[10] my enemies." 13. Truly I perceive that there is a division among them. 14. We cannot do the least of these things. 15. Inasmuch as[2] thou hast done this thou hast done worse than all thy brethren. 16. But he answered them more wisely than his father.

LESSON XXVIII

CONTRACTED VERBS ENDING IN αω AND οω.

The rules for the contraction of the vowels in these verbs may be stated as follows:

α followed by ο or ω becomes ω.
α followed by ε or η becomes α.

---

[1] τὸ πλήρωμα αὐτοῦ "that which fills it up."
[2] ἐφ᾽ ὅσον "inasmuch as."   [3] ἑνί dat. from εἷς "one."
[4] μεριμνᾶτε "do ye take anxious thought," see the next lesson.
[5] γεννητοῖς "the offspring."
[6] πειθαρχεῖν "to obey," followed by a Dative.
[7] ὑπέρ followed by a Genitive.   [8] γενήσεται.   [9] οἷα.
[10] διά followed by a Genitive.

CONTRACTED VERBS IN αω

ι is generally written subscript except occasionally in the Present Infinitive Active.

ο followed by a long vowel becomes ω.

ο followed by a short vowel becomes ου.

ο followed by any combination with ι, whether subscript or not, becomes οι, except in the pres. inf. act.

Present Active of τιμάω "I honour"

Present Ind.
τιμῶ (τιμάω)
τιμᾷς (τιμάεις)
τιμᾷ (τιμάει)
τιμῶμεν (τιμάομεν)
τιμᾶτε (τιμάετε)
τιμῶσι (τιμάουσι)

Present Imper.

τίμα (τίμαε)
τιμάτω (τιμαέτω)

τιμᾶτε (τιμάετε)
τιμάτωσαν (τιμαέτωσαν)

Present Inf.
τιμᾷν (τιμάειν) or τιμᾶν

Pres. Participle
τιμῶν, ῶσα, ῶν
τιμῶντος etc.

Imperfect Indicative Active

ἐτίμων (ἐτίμαον)
ἐτίμας (ἐτίμαες)
ἐτίμα (ἐτίμαε)

ἐτιμῶμεν (ἐτιμάομεν)
ἐτιμᾶτε (ἐτιμάετε)
ἐτίμων (ἐτίμαον)

Present Passive

Present Ind.	Present Imper.	Present Inf.	Present Participle
τιμῶμαι		τιμᾶσθαι	τιμώμενος, η, ον
τιμᾷ	τιμῶ		
τιμᾶται	τιμάσθω		
τιμώμεθα			
τιμᾶσθε	τιμᾶσθε		
τιμῶνται	τιμάσθωσαν		

Imperfect Indicative Passive

ἐτιμώμην
ἐτιμῶ
ἐτιμᾶτο

ἐτιμώμεθα
ἐτιμᾶσθε
ἐτιμῶντο

Present Active of φανερόω "I make manifest"

Present Ind.
φανερῶ (φανερόω)
φανεροῖς (φανερόεις)
φανεροῖ (φανερόει)
φανεροῦμεν (φανερόομεν)
φανεροῦτε (φανερόετε)
φανεροῦσι (φανερόουσι)

Present Imper.
φανέρου (φανέροε)
φανερούτω (φανεροέτω)

φανεροῦτε (φανερόετε)
φανερούτωσαν (φανεροέτωσαν)

Present Inf.
φανεροῦν (φανερόειν)

Present Participle
φανερῶν, φανεροῦσα, φανεροῦν
φανεροῦντος etc.

Imperfect Indicative Active

ἐφανέρουν (ἐφανέροον)
ἐφανέρους (ἐφανέροες)
ἐφανέρου (ἐφανέροε)

ἐφανεροῦμεν (ἐφανερόομεν)
ἐφανεροῦτε (ἐφανερόετε)
ἐφανέρουν (ἐφανέροον)

Present Passive

Present Ind.	Present Imperat.	Present Inf.	Present Participle
φανεροῦμαι		φανεροῦσθαι	φανερούμενος, η, ον
φανεροῖ	φανεροῦ		
φανεροῦται	φανερούσθω		
φανερούμεθα			
φανεροῦσθε	φανεροῦσθε		
φανεροῦνται	φανερούσθωσαν		

Imperfect Indicative Passive

ἐφανερούμην   ἐφανερούμεθα
ἐφανεροῦ   ἐφανεροῦσθε
ἐφανεροῦτο   ἐφανεροῦντο

The verb ζάω has η for a in the contracted forms.
Present Ind. ζῶ ζῇς ζῇ, ζῶμεν ζῆτε ζῶσι.
Pres. Inf. ζῆν.

The Future and Aorist of verbs in αω and οω are formed by lengthening the last vowel of the stem before adding the endings.

Present.	Fut. Act.	Aor. Act.	Fut. Mid.
τιμάω	τιμήσω	ἐτίμησα	τιμήσομαι
φανερόω	φανερώσω	ἐφανέρωσα	φανερώσομαι

Fut. Pass.	Aor. Mid.	Aor. Pass.
τιμηθήσομαι	ἐτιμησάμην	ἐτιμήθην
φανερωθήσομαι	ἐφανερωσάμην	ἐφανερώθην

For forms of ἐάω see Vocabulary.

Exercise 28

Learn Vocabulary 22.

1. ἐπυνθάνετο παρ' αὐτῶν ποῦ ὁ Χριστὸς γεννᾶται. 2. θεὸς οὐκ ἔστι νεκρῶν ἀλλὰ ζώντων, πάντες γὰρ αὐτῷ ζῶσιν. 3. οὗτος ὁ λόγος οὐ φανεροῦται ἡμῖν. 4. ἔλεγον τὴν ἔξοδον αὐτοῦ ἣν ἤμελλεν[1] πληροῦν ἐν Ἰερουσαλήμ. 5. Σίμων Ἰωάνου, ἀγαπᾷς με πλέον τούτων; 6. φωνὴ βοῶντος ἐν τῇ ἐρήμῳ. 7. ἐν τῇ αὐτῇ ὥρᾳ ἠγαλλιῶντο οἱ μαθηταί. 8. ὁ γὰρ θεὸς ταπεινοῖ τοὺς ὑψοῦντας ἑαυτούς, τοὺς δὲ ταπεινοῦντας ἑαυτοὺς ὑψοῖ. 9. τότε ἐσταύρουν σὺν αὐτῷ δύο λῃστάς. 10. τί με ἐρωτᾷς περὶ τοῦ ἀγαθοῦ; 11. λέγει αὐτῷ ὁ Ἰησοῦς Πορεύου, ὁ υἱός σου ζῇ. 12. ὁ δὲ θεὸς εἴασε πάντα τὰ ἔθνη περιπατεῖν ἐν ταῖς ὁδοῖς αὐτῶν. 13. Αἰνέα[2], ἰᾶταί σε Ἰησοῦς Χριστός. 14. οὐκ εἴα Ἰησοῦς τὰ δαιμόνια λαλεῖν.

1. The disciples were making manifest the things which they had heard. 2. We did not permit them to crucify the slave. 3. The king humbled those that were exalted. 4. They are inquiring if the servant is healed. 5. Why do you allow them to live in our city? 6. Do ye desire to love the Lord your God, O ye sons of men? 7. The voice said "Cry," and he answered "What shall I cry?" 8. Now is fulfilled the word of the prophet. 9. When Jesus was born in Bethlehem wise men came to worship him asking where the king of the Jews must be born. 10. God justifies the sons of men by faith and not by works. 11. And all men rejoiced greatly that the man that had the devil was healed. 12. Rejoice greatly, for thy son liveth. 13. Humble yourselves therefore under[3] the mighty[4] hand of God, for he will exalt you in due season. 14. I manifested thy name to this people and I will manifest it to their children.

[1] ἤμελλεν a past tense with a double augment from μέλλω.
[2] A proper name, "Aeneas."
[3] "Under" ὑπό followed by an Accusative.
[4] "Mighty" κραταιός.

LESSON XXIX

THE PERFECT AND PLUPERFECT TENSES

The Perfect tense does not occur very frequently in the New Testament. Its use denotes that the action of the verb is to be regarded as brought to its appropriate conclusion at the time of speaking in such a way that its results still remain in action.

The Perfect has therefore as much to do with Present as with Past time, since it describes the present result of a past action.

The Pluperfect or Past Perfect is the past tense of the Perfect.

There is no exact equivalent to the Greek Perfect in English; the so-called English Perfect formed by the auxiliary verb "have" is the nearest equivalent that can be given, but it will not always serve to translate a Greek Perfect.

The conjugation of the Perfect and Pluperfect of λύω is as follows:

Active Voice

Perfect Ind.	Pluperfect Ind.	Perfect Inf.	Perfect Part.
λέλυκα	ἐλελύκειν	λελυκέναι	λελυκώς, λελυκυῖα, λελυκός
λέλυκας	ἐλελύκεις		
λέλυκε	ἐλελύκει		
λελύκαμεν	ἐλελύκειμεν		
λελύκατε	ἐλελύκειτε		
λελύκασι	ἐλελύκεισαν		

The Perfect Participle Active is declined as follows:

Nom. Sing.	λελυκώς	λελυκυῖα	λελυκός
Gen. Sing.	λελυκότος	λελυκυίας	λελυκότος
Dat. Pl.	λελυκόσι	λελυκυίαις	λελυκόσι

The other cases can be easily formed from these.

Middle and Passive Voice

Perf. Ind.	Plup. Ind.	Perf. Inf.	Perf. Part.
λέλυμαι	ἐλελύμην	λελύσθαι	λελυμένος, η, ον
λέλυσαι	ἐλέλυσο		
λέλυται	ἐλέλυτο		
λελύμεθα	ἐλελύμεθα		
λέλυσθε	ἐλέλυσθε		
λέλυνται	ἐλέλυντο		

PERFECT AND PLUPERFECT TENSES

There is a Perfect Imperative, but it is very seldom used in the New Testament. It is given in the complete table of verbs at the end.

Note that the Perfect participle passive always has the accent on the last syllable but one.

It will be noticed that in all moods of the Perfect tense and also in the Pluperfect tense the first consonant of the verb followed by the letter ε is placed before the verb.

This is called REDUPLICATION.

The Pluperfect has an augment in addition, although this is often omitted in the New Testament.

Verbs beginning with a vowel, two consonants (except a mute and a liquid) or a double consonant, have no reduplication, but have an augment instead.

Verbs beginning with a rough mute (φ, χ, θ) have the corresponding smooth mute (π, κ, τ) in the reduplication.

Examples:

Present	Perfect
ἁμαρτάνω	ἡμάρτηκα
στέλλω	ἔσταλκα
πληρόω	πεπλήρωκα
ψάλλω	ἔψαλκα
φιλέω	πεφίληκα
θεάομαι	τεθέαμαι

Note that the characteristic consonant of the Perfect active is κ.

The Second, or Strong, Perfect

Some Perfects are formed by adding the endings direct to the stem without κ, these are called Strong Perfects, or Second Perfects.

The following are examples:

Present	Perfect
ἀκούω	ἀκήκοα
γίνομαι	γέγονα
γράφω	γέγραφα
ἔρχομαι	ἐλήλυθα (from stem ἐλθ)
κράζω	κέκραγα
κρύπτω	κέκρυφα
πάσχω	πέπονθα
πείθω	πέποιθα

The verb λαμβάνω and the stem ἐρ (generally given under λέγω) begin their Perfect tenses with εἰ instead of a reduplication.

Present	Perfect Active	Perfect Passive
λαμβάνω	εἴληφα	εἴλημμαι
Stem ἐρ	εἴρηκα	εἴρημαι

Examples of the use of the Perfect from the New Testament

Perfect Indicative

Ye have filled Jerusalem with your teaching.
πεπληρώκατε τὴν Ἰερουσαλὴμ τῆς διδαχῆς ὑμῶν.
Acts v. 28.

I have fought the good fight, I have finished my course, I have kept the faith.
τὸν καλὸν ἀγῶνα ἠγώνισμαι, τὸν δρόμον τετέλεκα, τὴν πίστιν τετήρηκα.
2 Tim. iv. 7.

Pluperfect

For it had been founded on the rock.
τεθεμελίωτο γὰρ ἐπὶ τὴν πέτραν.   Mt. vii. 25.

Participle

Having been filled with all knowledge.
πεπληρωμένοι πάσης τῆς γνώσεως.   Rom. xv. 14.
To all that have loved his appearing.
πᾶσι τοῖς ἠγαπηκόσι τὴν ἐπιφάνειαν αὐτοῦ.
2 Tim. iv. 8.

Note that in all these examples stress is laid on the completeness and permanence of the action described.

A good example of the exact meaning of the Perfect participle will be found in sentence 9 in the following exercise.

This should be contrasted with the meaning of the Present participle of the same verb which is used in sentence 10.

Another good example is found in sentence 14 where ἐσταυρωμένον denotes a permanent quality—"one who has been crucified."

It is impossible to render this meaning exactly in English, as has been said above. If the Aorist participle σταυρωθείς had been used in this sentence it would simply have denoted the historical fact that Christ was crucified.

The tenses of the Greek Verb have now all been given. To repeat the first person singular of the Indicative mood of each of these tenses is called giving the parts of the verb. A list of the parts of the verbs occurring most commonly in the New Testament is given at the end. The student should now begin to learn those which are given at the head of each exercise.

Exercise 29

Learn Vocabulary 23.

Before doing this exercise the parts of the following Verbs should be learnt: βάλλω (34), γίνομαι (41), ἔρχομαι (67), λαμβάνω (50), λέγω (70), ὁράω (71).

1. Ἕλληνας εἰσήγαγεν εἰς τὸ ἱερόν, καὶ κεκοίνωκεν τὸν ἅγιον τόπον. 2. πτωχὸς δέ τις ὀνόματι Λάζαρος ἐβέβλητο πρὸς τὸν πυλῶνα[1] αὐτοῦ. 3. παιδία, ἐσχάτη ὥρα ἐστίν, καὶ καθὼς ἠκούσατε ὅτι ἀντίχριστος[2] ἔρχεται καὶ νῦν ἀντίχριστοι πολλοὶ γεγόνασιν. 4. λέγει αὐτῷ ὁ Ἰησοῦς, Ὅτι ἑώρακάς με πεπίστευκας; μακάριοι οἱ μὴ ἰδόντες καὶ πιστεύσαντες. 5. ὅτε δὲ γέγονα ἀνήρ, κατήργηκα[3] τὰ τοῦ νηπίου[4]. 6. καὶ ἀπελθοῦσα εἰς τὸν οἶκον αὐτῆς εὗρεν τὸ παιδίον βεβλημένον ἐπὶ τὴν κλίνην καὶ τὸ δαιμόνιον ἐξεληλυθός. 7. πεπλήρωται ὁ καιρὸς καὶ ἤγγικεν ἡ βασιλεία τοῦ θεοῦ. 8. ἔρχεται πρὸς αὐτὸν Μαρία ἡ καλουμένη Μαγδαληνή, ἀφ' ἧς δαιμόνια ἑπτὰ ἐξεληλύθει. 9. καὶ πολλὰ σώματα τῶν κεκοιμημένων ἁγίων ἠγέρθησαν. 10. οἱ μαθηταὶ αὐτοῦ νυκτὸς ἐλθόντες ἔκλεψαν αὐτόν, ἡμῶν κοιμωμένων. 11. Ἰουδαίους οὐδὲν ἠδίκηκα ὡς καὶ σὺ κάλλιον ἐπιγιγνώσκεις. 12. πειρασμὸς ὑμᾶς οὐκ εἴληφεν εἰ μὴ ἀνθρώπινος[5]. 13. ὁ γὰρ θεὸς εἴρηκε τοῦτο διὰ στόματος πάντων τῶν προφητῶν. 14. ἡμεῖς δὲ κηρύσσομεν Χριστὸν ἐσταυρωμένον.

1. The days of the kingdom of heaven have been fulfilled. 2. He has not injured thee nor thy friends. 3. We have seen and testified that this is the prophet spoken of by Moses. 4. Then the young men were astonished, for great fear had taken hold upon them. 5. The

---

[1] πυλών, ῶνος, ὁ "a door."
[2] ἀντίχριστος, ου, ὁ "Antichrist."
[3] κατήργηκα perf. from καταργέω "I bring to nought, I put away."
[4] τὰ τοῦ νηπίου "childish things."
[5] ἀνθρώπινος "proper to a man, such as a man can bear."

Lord hath spoken evil concerning thee. 6. They have defiled the house of the Lord with dead bodies. 7. Thou must proclaim the things which thou hast seen and heard. 8. The governor asks what the slaves have done. 9. Ye have suffered many things at the hands* of the Jews. 10. Then Pilate[1] answered saying "What I have written, I have written." 11. But when I became king I walked in the ways of my fathers. 12. The poor and the blind are cast[2] at the doors of the rich[3]. 13. O Lord, in thee have we trusted. 14. They found that the devils had gone out. 15. I have told you the words of the kingdom, but ye have not believed me. 16. Those that have kept the faith shall receive the crown[4] of life which the Lord promised to those that love him. 17. They beheld the temple filled with the glory of the Lord.

LESSON XXX

THE SUBJUNCTIVE MOOD

The forms of the Subjunctive Mood are as follows:

Pres. Sub. Act.	1st Aor. Sub. Act.	2nd Aor. Sub. Act.
λύω	λύσω	βάλω
λύῃς	λύσῃς	βάλῃς
λύῃ	λύσῃ	βάλῃ
λύωμεν	λύσωμεν	βάλωμεν
λύητε	λύσητε	βάλητε
λύωσι	λύσωσι	βάλωσι

It will be seen that the endings of the Subjunctive are the same in all these tenses, but that in the 1st Aorist the letter σ is placed between the ending and the stem, and in the 2nd Aorist the endings are added to the verbal, and not to the present stem. The endings are the same as those of the Present Indicative Active with the exception that the vowels are lengthened and ι is written subscript.

There is no Future Subjunctive.

Pres. Sub. Pass. or Mid.	1st Aor. Sub. Mid.	2nd Aor. Sub. Mid.
λύωμαι	λύσωμαι	βάλωμαι
λύῃ	λύσῃ	βάλῃ
λύηται	λύσηται	βάληται
λυώμεθα	λυσώμεθα	βαλώμεθα
λύησθε	λύσησθε	βάλησθε
λύωνται	λύσωνται	βάλωνται

[1] Πειλᾶτος.
[2] "Are cast," use the perfect pass.
[3] πλούσιος.
[4] στέφανος.
* "At the hands of," ὑπό + Gen.

SUBJUNCTIVE MOOD

In these tenses the endings are the same as those of the Pres. Ind. Pass. or Mid. with the exception that the vowels are lengthened.

1st Aor. Sub. Pass.	2nd Aor. Sub. Pass.
λυθῶ	φανῶ
λυθῇς	φανῇς
λυθῇ	φανῇ
λυθῶμεν	φανῶμεν
λυθῆτε	φανῆτε
λυθῶσι	φανῶσι

Note that the endings of the 1st and 2nd Aor. Subjunctive Pass. are the same as those of the Pres. Sub. **Act.**; but the characteristic θ of the 1st Aor. Pass. is inserted before the endings, and in the 2nd Aor. Pass. the endings are added to the verbal stem. In both Aorists the endings have the circumflex accent on the long vowel.

It is impossible to give any single English equivalent to the Subjunctive mood, as the use of the Greek Subjunctive is much wider than that of the English. It is better therefore not to attach any such meaning to it as "that I may loose" etc., as is done in some grammars, since this would cover only a portion of its uses.

Four of the principal uses of the Subjunctive in the N.T. are as follows:

(1) It is used in clauses which express the **purpose** of the action of the main verb. (**Final clauses.**)

Such clauses are introduced by ἵνα or ὅπως "in order that" or "that" if affirmative, and by μή or ἵνα μή "in order that not" or "lest" if negative.

Examples:

He came that he might bear witness to the light.

ἦλθεν ἵνα μαρτυρήσῃ περὶ τοῦ φωτός.

They are going away that they may not see the battle, or lest they should see the battle.

ἀπέρχονται ἵνα μή (or μή) ἴδωσι τὴν μαχήν.

He was crying with a loud voice that all might hear.

μεγάλῃ τῇ φωνῇ ἔκραζε ἵνα πάντες ἀκούωσι.

As we have already seen (page 37) clauses of this kind may also be expressed by an Infinitive.

SUBJUNCTIVE MOOD

Either the Present or the Aorist Subjunctive may be used in these clauses, the Present if a continuous or repeated action is spoken of, the Aorist if a single action is spoken of. The Aorist is used more frequently than the Present. There is no "sequence of tenses," as in Latin, and, if the verb in the main clause is in a past tense, it does not follow that the verb in the dependent clause must be in the Aorist Subjunctive.

(2) The Subjunctive is used in all clauses introduced by a relative pronoun **which does not refer to a definite person or thing**; i.e. all clauses in which the word "ever" may be introduced in English after the relative pronoun.

In these clauses the word ἄν or ἐάν is placed after the relative pronoun in Greek and the verb is in the Subjunctive.

Example:
Whoever believes on the name of the Lord shall be saved.
ὃς ἂν πιστεύσῃ εἰς τὸ ὄνομα τοῦ Κυρίου σωθήσεται.

Clauses introduced by ὅταν (ὅτε ἄν) "**whenever**" and ὅπου ἄν "**wherever**" and referring to the future also have their verb in the Subjunctive mood.

Examples:
Whenever ye depart go into the city.
ὅταν ἀπέλθητε εἰσέρχεσθε εἰς τὴν πόλιν.
Wherever the Gospel is preached many will hear.
ὅπου ἂν τὸ εὐαγγέλιον κηρύχθῃ πολλοὶ ἀκούσουσι.

Clauses introduced by ἕως depending on a verb denoting future or habitual action and referring to the future also have their verb in the Subjunctive, generally with ἄν. Such clauses may also be introduced by ἕως οὗ or ἕως ὅτου without ἄν.

Examples:
There remain until ye depart thence.
ἐκεῖ μένετε ἕως ἂν ἐξέλθητε ἐκεῖθεν.   Mk vi. 10.
And goeth after that which is lost, until he find it.
καὶ πορεύεται ἐπὶ τὸ ἀπολωλὸς ἕως εὕρῃ αὐτό.   Lk. xv. 4.
Tell the vision to no man until the Son of Man is risen from the dead.
μηδενὶ εἴπητε τὸ ὅραμα ἕως οὗ ὁ υἱὸς τοῦ ἀνθρώπου ἐκ νεκρῶν ἐγερθῇ.
   Mt. xvii. 9.

THE SUBJUNCTIVE

(3) **The Hortatory Subjunctive.** The Subjunctive is used in the 1st person plural when the speaker is exhorting others to join him in the doing of an action.

Example: Beloved, let us love one another.
ἀγαπητοί, ἀγαπῶμεν ἀλλήλους.   1 Jn iv. 7.

(4) **The Deliberative Subjunctive.** The Subjunctive is used in deliberative questions, when a person asks himself or others what he is to do.

Example: What shall we do?
τί ποιήσωμεν;   Lk. iii. 10.

Note that the Subjunctive is always negatived with μή.

Exercise 30

Before doing this exercise learn the parts of ἄγω (1), ἀκούω (2), δέχομαι (8), ἀποστέλλω (35), κρίνω (43), κηρύσσω (28).

Learn Vocabulary 24.

1. καλῶς ἀθετεῖτε τὴν ἐντολὴν τοῦ θεοῦ, ἵνα τὴν παράδοσιν ὑμῶν τηρήσητε. 2. ἄγωμεν ἀλλαχοῦ[1] εἰς τὰς ἐχομένας κωμοπόλεις[2], ἵνα καὶ ἐκεῖ κηρύξω. 3. ὃς ἂν ἓν τῶν τοιούτων παιδίων δέξηται ἐπὶ τῷ ὀνόματί μου, ἐμὲ δέχεται· καὶ ὃς ἂν ἐμὲ δέχηται, οὐκ ἐμὲ δέχεται, ἀλλὰ τὸν ἀποστείλαντά με. 4. μὴ κρίνετε ἵνα μὴ κριθῆτε. 5. ὃς γὰρ ἂν θέλῃ τὴν ψυχὴν αὐτοῦ σῶσαι ἀπολέσει αὐτήν. 6. καὶ τοὺς ὀφθαλμοὺς αὐτῶν ἐκάμμυσαν[3], μή ποτε[4] ἴδωσιν τοῖς ὀφθαλμοῖς. 7. ὃ ἐὰν δήσῃς[5] ἐπὶ τῆς γῆς ἔσται δεδεμένον ἐν τοῖς οὐρανοῖς. 8. κύριοι, τί με δεῖ ποιεῖν ἵνα σωθῶ; 9. αὐτοῦ ἀκούσεσθε κατὰ πάντα ὅσα ἂν λαλήσῃ πρὸς ὑμᾶς. 10. λέγωμεν ἆρα[6] Ποιήσωμεν τὰ κακά, ἵνα ἔλθῃ τὰ ἀγαθά; 11. πάντοτε γὰρ τοὺς πτωχοὺς ἔχετε μεθ' ἑαυτῶν, καὶ ὅταν θέλητε δύνασθε αὐτοῖς εὖ ποιῆσαι. 12. φεῦγε εἰς Αἴγυπτον καὶ ἴσθι[7] ἐκεῖ ἕως ἂν εἴπω σοι. 13. ὁμοία ἐστὶν ἡ βασιλεία τῶν οὐρανῶν ζύμῃ[8] ἣν λαβοῦσα γυνὴ ἐνέκρυψεν εἰς ἀλεύρου σάτα τρία[9] ἕως οὗ ἐζυμώθη[10] ὅλον.

1. The Pharisees disregarded the commandment of God that they might keep their own tradition. 2. Whatever I say to you privately[11] that proclaim to all the people. 3. What shall we do then? shall we

[1] ἀλλαχοῦ "elsewhere."   [2] ἐχομένας κωμοπόλεις "the next villages."
[3] καμμύω "I close."   [4] ποτε "ever."   [5] δήσῃς from δέω.
[6] ἆρα, "then," in questions denoting surprise.
[7] ἴσθι, 2nd pers. sing. imp. from εἶναι "to be."
[8] ζύμη -ης, "leaven."
[9] ἀλεύρου σάτα τρία "three measures of meal."
[10] ζυμόω "I leaven."   [11] κατ' ἰδίαν.

continue in sin that grace may abound[1]? 4. Whenever ye see the Gentiles in the Holy Place know that the end[2] of the age draweth nigh. 5. Wherever the Gospel is preached those that believe shall be saved. 6. Send away the children to the wilderness that the robbers may not kill them. 7. God sent many prophets that they might teach this people. 8. Let us eat and drink, for we must depart quickly. 9. Let us go elsewhere that we may exhort the multitudes. 10. Whenever we will we can do good to the poor. 11. Remain in the house until I call thee. 12. We have cut down all the trees that the enemy may not eat the fruit. 13. I will not drink wine lest I cause my brother to stumble. 14. I beseech thee to guard my sheep until I find that which is lost[3]. 15. Whosoever wishes to be greatest among you let him humble himself as a little child. 16. O Lord, make manifest thy power to us that thy name may be glorified. 17. Bring the garments to me that they may be carried to the widows.

LESSON XXXI

SUBJUNCTIVE OF CONTRACTED VERBS AND OF εἰμί. FURTHER USES OF THE SUBJUNCTIVE

The Present Subjunctive of the contracted verbs is as follows:

Active

φιλῶ	τιμῶ	φανερῶ
φιλῇς	τιμᾷς	φανεροῖς
φιλῇ	τιμᾷ	φανεροῖ
φιλῶμεν	τιμῶμεν	φανερῶμεν
φιλῆτε	τιμᾶτε	φανερῶτε
φιλῶσι	τιμῶσι	φανερῶσι

Passive and Middle

φιλῶμαι	τιμῶμαι	φανερῶμαι
φιλῇ	τιμᾷ	φανεροῖ
φιλῆται	τιμᾶται	φανερῶται
φιλώμεθα	τιμώμεθα	φανερώμεθα
φιλῆσθε	τιμᾶσθε	φανερῶσθε
φιλῶνται	τιμῶνται	φανερῶνται

For the rules of contraction see pp. 9, 87, 88.

[1] "I abound" περισσεύω. [2] "end" τέλος -ους, τό. [3] τὸ ἀπολλύμενον.

The subjunctive of εἰμί is as follows:

Singular	Plural
ὦ	ὦμεν
ᾖς	ἦτε
ᾖ	ὦσι

Further uses of the Subjunctive

The Subjunctive is used in all **conditional clauses** introduced by ἐάν "if" referring to the future.

Example:

If ye do not repent ye shall all perish in like manner.

ἐὰν μὴ μετανοήσητε, πάντες ὡσαύτως ἀπολεῖσθε.   Lk. xiii. 5.

The **Aorist Subjunctive** (not the Present) is used with μή in **prohibitions**.

Example: Do not get gold for your purses.

μὴ κτήσησθε χρυσὸν εἰς τὰς ζώνας ὑμῶν.   Mt. x. 9.

The **Present Imperative** (not the Aorist) with μή may also be used to express a prohibition.

The Present Imperative generally denotes a command to **cease** to do an action already begun, in accordance with the principle that the moods of the Present tense denote action in progress.

Example:

And they all wept and lamented her. But he said to them "Do not continue to weep; she is not dead, but sleepeth."

ἔκλαιον δὲ πάντες καὶ ἐκόπτοντο αὐτήν. ὁ δὲ εἶπεν Μὴ κλαίετε, οὐκ ἀπέθανεν ἀλλὰ καθεύδει.   Lk. viii. 52.

The Aorist Subjunctive generally denotes a command not to **begin** to do an action.

Example:

Whenever therefore thou doest alms, do not sound a trumpet before thee.

ὅταν οὖν ποιῇς ἐλεημοσύνην, μὴ σαλπίσῃς ἔμπροσθέν σου.

Mt. vi. 2.

In Acts xviii. 9 we have an example of both ways of expressing a prohibition in the same verse:

Do not fear, but speak and hold not thy peace.

μὴ φοβοῦ, ἀλλὰ λάλει καὶ μὴ σιωπήσῃς.

The **double negative** οὐ μή is used with the Aorist Subjunctive and

OF THE SUBJUNCTIVE

occasionally with the Future Indicative in the sense of the Future Indicative with οὐ, but with more emphasis.

Examples:
Him that cometh to me I will in no wise cast out.
τὸν ἐρχόμενον πρός με οὐ μὴ ἐκβάλω ἔξω. Jn vi. 37.
If I must die with thee, I will not deny thee.
ἐὰν δέῃ με συναποθανεῖν σοι, οὐ μή σε ἀρνήσομαι.
Mk xiv. 31.

Frequently however, especially in the Gospels, it is used simply as a negative future without any special emphasis.

Exercise 31

Learn the parts of πράσσω (29), θέλω (11), γινώσκω (55), ἐσθίω (68), πίνω (49).
Learn Vocabulary 25.

1. κύριε, ἐὰν θέλῃς δύνασαί με καθαρίσαι. 2. ἐφώνησεν δὲ Παῦλος μεγάλῃ φωνῇ λέγων Μηδὲν πράξῃς σεαυτῷ κακόν, ἅπαντες[1] γάρ ἐσμεν ἐνθάδε. 3. ἐὰν μὴ περισσεύσῃ ὑμῶν ἡ δικαιοσύνη πλεῖον τῶν γραμματέων καὶ Φαρισαίων, οὐ μὴ εἰσέλθητε εἰς τὴν βασιλείαν τῶν οὐρανῶν. 4. μὴ οὖν μεριμνήσητε εἰς τὴν αὔριον. 5. ὃς ἂν μὴ δέξηται τὴν βασιλείαν τοῦ θεοῦ ὡς παιδίον, οὐ μὴ εἰσέλθῃ εἰς αὐτήν. 6. λέγω γὰρ ὑμῖν ὅτι οὐ μὴ φάγω αὐτὸ ἕως ὅτου πληρωθῇ ἐν τῇ βασιλείᾳ τοῦ θεοῦ. 7. ἐάν τις θέλῃ τὸ θέλημα αὐτοῦ ποιεῖν, γνώσεται περὶ τῆς διδαχῆς πότερον[2] ἐκ θεοῦ ἐστίν. 8. μὴ νομίσητε ὅτι ἦλθον καταλῦσαι τὸν νόμον ἢ τοὺς προφήτας. 9. ὑμεῖς ἐστὲ τὸ ἅλας τῆς γῆς· ἐὰν δὲ τὸ ἅλας μωρανθῇ[3], ἐν τίνι ἁλισθήσεται; 10. εἶπεν δὲ ὁ Κύριος τῷ Παύλῳ Μὴ φοβοῦ, ἀλλὰ λάλει, καὶ μὴ σιωπήσῃς. 11. ἐὰν ἀγαπᾶτέ με, τὰς ἐντολὰς τὰς ἐμὰς τηρήσετε. 12. ἀμὴν λέγω ὑμῖν ὅτι εἰσίν τινες τῶν ὧδε ὄντων οἵτινες οὐ μὴ γεύσωνται[4] θανάτου ἕως ἂν ἴδωσιν τὸν υἱὸν τοῦ ἀνθρώπου ἐρχόμενον ἐν τῇ βασιλείᾳ αὐτοῦ. 13. ἐὰν γὰρ ἀγαπήσητε τοὺς ἀγαπῶντας ὑμᾶς, τίνα μισθὸν ἔχετε; 14. καὶ ἐποίησεν δώδεκα[5] ἵνα ὦσιν μετ' αὐτοῦ καὶ ἵνα ἀποστέλλῃ κηρύσσειν καὶ ἔχειν ἐξουσίαν ἐκβάλλειν τὰ δαιμόνια. 15. μὴ οὖν λέγετε Τί φάγωμεν; ἢ Τί πίωμεν; ἢ Τί περιβαλώμεθα;

1. If ye do good to them that do good to you what reward have ye? 2. Do not bring Gentiles into the temple. 3. Let us not seek the things of this age, but the things of the age that is to come[6]. 4. If ye do these things ye shall be loved by my Father. 5. Do not continue to receive the enemies of the Gospel. 6. I will in no wise allow thee

---

[1] ἅπαντες another form of πᾶς.
[2] πότερον "whether."
[3] μωρανθῇ "is corrupted."
[4] γεύσωνται "shall taste."
[5] δώδεκα "twelve."
[6] Use pres. part. of ἔρχομαι.

to eat bread in this place. 7. If we confess our sins he will have mercy upon us. 8. They went to the priest that they might ask him about the vision[1]. 9. And all the people were silent that they might hear the messengers of Caesar. 10. If we love him we shall keep his commandments. 11. The slaves brought me bread and fish that I might taste it[2]. 12. Sin no longer, lest a worse thing come upon thee. 13. If these men are wicked the Lord will destroy them and their city. 14. I will in no wise manifest myself to this generation. 15. Do not carry wine to the slaves. 16. If the enemy draw near I will set the soldiers in order. 17. How shall we buy bread that these may eat? 18. Let us love our parents that we may be loved by them.

LESSON XXXII

FURTHER USES OF THE INFINITIVE MOOD

The Infinitive mood, as has already been pointed out, is really a verbal noun, and, as such, can be used as the subject or object of a verb.

Its character as a noun can be emphasised by prefixing an article to it: it then practically becomes a declinable neuter noun.

Its case is shown by the case of the article, for the infinitive itself cannot have inflections.

The Infinitive preceded by an Article, or the Articular Infinitive, as it is sometimes called, may have a subject, object or other limiting words attached to it. These words generally come between the article and the infinitive and form with it a phrase equivalent to a noun.

The Articular Infinitive is frequently used in connexion with a Preposition. Phrases of this kind are generally best translated by an Adverbial clause in English.

Examples: εἰς or πρός followed by the Accusative of the Articular Infinitive expressing PURPOSE.

And they shall deliver him to the Gentiles to mock and to scourge and to crucify.

καὶ παραδώσουσιν αὐτὸν τοῖς ἔθνεσιν εἰς τὸ ἐμπαῖξαι καὶ μαστιγῶσαι καὶ σταυρῶσαι. Mt. xx. 19.

I sent that I might know your faith.

ἔπεμψα εἰς τὸ γνῶναι τὴν πίστιν ὑμῶν. 1 Thess. iii. 5.

---

[1] δραμα -ατος, τό.   [2] Use genitive case.

But take heed that ye do not your righteousness before men in order to be seen of them.

προσέχετε δὲ τὴν δικαιοσύνην ὑμῶν μὴ ποιεῖν ἔμπροσθεν τῶν ἀνθρώπων πρὸς τὸ θεαθῆναι αὐτοῖς. Matt. vi. 1.

ἐν followed by the Dative of the Articular Infinitive expressing the TIME DURING WHICH something takes place.

And as he sowed, some fell by the way side.

καὶ ἐν τῷ σπείρειν αὐτὸν ὃ μὲν ἔπεσεν παρὰ τὴν ὁδόν.
Lk. viii. 5.

And while men slept, his enemy came and sowed tares among the wheat.

ἐν δὲ τῷ καθεύδειν τοὺς ἀνθρώπους ἦλθεν αὐτοῦ ὁ ἐχθρὸς καὶ ἐπέσπειρεν ζιζάνια ἀνὰ μέσον τοῦ σίτου. Mt. xiii. 25.

πρό followed by the Genitive of the Articular Infinitive to be translated by BEFORE.

For your Father knoweth the things of which ye have need before ye ask him.

οἶδεν[1] γὰρ ὁ Πατὴρ ὑμῶν ὧν χρείαν ἔχετε πρὸ τοῦ ὑμᾶς αἰτῆσαι αὐτόν.
Mt. vi. 8.

μετά followed by the Accusative of the Articular Infinitive to be translated by AFTER.

But after I am raised up, I will go before you into Galilee.

ἀλλὰ μετὰ τὸ ἐγερθῆναί με προάξω ὑμᾶς εἰς τὴν Γαλιλαίαν.
Mk xiv. 28.

διά followed by an Accusative of the Articular Infinitive to express CAUSE.

And because it had no root it withered away.

καὶ διὰ τὸ μὴ ἔχειν ῥίζαν ἐξηράνθη. Mk iv. 6.

The Infinitive in Object clauses after verbs of saying or thinking

We have already seen that object clauses after verbs of saying or thinking may be expressed by a clause introduced by ὅτι with a verb in the Indicative mood. They may also be expressed by putting the verb in the **same tense** of the Infinitive as that used by the original speaker or thinker when he uttered the words, or framed the thoughts, which are reported in these object clauses. The original speaker or thinker used a verb in the Indicative, Subjunctive or Imperative mood to express his words or thoughts: when these words or thoughts are turned into an object clause the mood is altered but **not** the tense.

[1] See Exercise 86.

The subject of the Infinitive is of course put into the Accusative case, unless it denotes the same person as the subject of the verb of saying or thinking.

This construction is called the "Accusative and Infinitive" construction.

We have a similar construction in English, but it is seldom used. We prefer to use the construction which corresponds with the ὅτι construction in Greek and to introduce object clauses after verbs of saying or thinking with the conjunction "that."

Examples of the Accusative and Infinitive construction in English.

"The priests pronounced the lepers to be clean."
"We know them to be guilty."
"I perceive them to be making a mistake."

The Accusative and Infinitive construction does not occur frequently in the New Testament after verbs of saying or thinking. It is not therefore thought necessary to treat the subject at length here. For further information the student is referred to the author's *Syntax of New Testament Greek*.

The following are examples of this construction from the New Testament.

Ye say that I cast out devils by Beelzebub.
λέγετε ἐν Βεεζεβοὺλ ἐκβάλλειν με τὰ δαιμόνια.
Lk. xi. 18

How do they say that Christ is the son of David?
πῶς λέγουσιν τὸν Χριστὸν εἶναι Δαυεὶδ υἱόν; Lk. xx. 41.

The Sadducees who say that there is no resurrection.
οἱ Σαδδουκαῖοι οἱ λέγοντες μὴ εἶναι ἀνάστασιν.
Mt. xxii. 23.

The Infinitive in Consecutive clauses introduced by ὥστε

The Infinitive is often used in Consecutive clauses introduced by ὥστε to express the result of the action of the main verb.

Example:

And behold there arose a great tempest in the sea so that the boat was covered by the waves.

καὶ ἰδοὺ σεισμὸς μέγας ἐγένετο ἐν τῇ θαλάσσῃ, ὥστε τὸ πλοῖον καλύπτεσθαι ὑπὸ τῶν κυμάτων.
Mt. viii. 24.

CONSECUTIVE AND TEMPORAL CLAUSES

The Infinitive in Temporal clauses introduced by πρίν or πρὶν ἤ, "Before."

When the verb in the principal clause is affirmative the clause introduced by πρίν has the Accusative and Infinitive construction.

Example:
Before the cock crow thou shalt deny me thrice.
πρὶν ἀλέκτορα φωνῆσαι τρὶς ἀπαρνήσῃ με. Mt. xxvi. 34.

Exercise 32

Learn the parts of ἔχω (69), καλέω (19), ἀποθνήσκω (53), βαίνω (48), πιστεύω (14), ἀγαπάω (15).
Learn Vocabulary 26.

1. τὸ ἀγαπᾶν τὸν θεὸν ἐξ ὅλης καρδίας καὶ τὸ ἀγαπᾶν τὸν πλησίον ὡς ἑαυτὸν περισσότερόν ἐστι πάντων τῶν ὁλοκαυτωμάτων[1] καὶ θυσιῶν. 2. προσεῖχον δὲ οἱ ὄχλοι τοῖς λεγομένοις ὑπὸ τοῦ Φιλίππου ἐν τῷ ἀκούειν αὐτοὺς καὶ βλέπειν τὰ σημεῖα ἃ ἐποίει. 3. πρὸ γὰρ τοῦ ἐλθεῖν τινὰς ἀπὸ Ἰακώβου μετὰ τῶν ἐθνῶν συνήσθιεν ὁ Πέτρος. 4. καὶ διὰ τὸ πληθυνθῆναι τὴν ἀνομίαν ψυγήσεται[2] ἡ ἀγάπη τῶν πολλῶν. 5. μετὰ δὲ τὸ σιγῆσαι αὐτοὺς ἀπεκρίθη Ἰάκωβος. 6. τίνα λέγουσιν οἱ ἄνθρωποι εἶναι τὸν υἱὸν τοῦ ἀνθρώπου; 7. οὐκ ὀφείλομεν νομίζειν χρυσῷ ἢ ἀργύρῳ ἢ λίθῳ τὸ θεῖον[3] εἶναι ὅμοιον. 8. καὶ λιθάσαντες τὸν Παῦλον ἔσυρον ἔξω τῆς πόλεως, νομίζοντες αὐτὸν τεθνηκέναι[4]. 9. ἐὰν δὲ εἴπωμεν Ἐξ ἀνθρώπων, ὁ λαὸς ἅπας καταλιθάσει ἡμᾶς, πιστεύει γὰρ Ἰωάνην προφήτην εἶναι. 10. ὁ μὲν οὖν Φῆστος ἀπεκρίθη τηρεῖσθαι τὸν Παῦλον ἐν Καισαρείᾳ, ἑαυτὸν δὲ μέλλειν ἐν τάχει[5] ἐκπορεύεσθαι. 11. καὶ ἐθαμβήθησαν ἅπαντες, ὥστε συζητεῖν αὐτοὺς λέγοντας Τί ἐστι τοῦτο; 12. ἀμὴν λέγω σοι ὅτι ἐν ταύτῃ τῇ νυκτὶ πρὶν ἀλέκτορα φωνῆσαι τρὶς ἀπαρνήσῃ με. 13. καὶ γνωστὸν ἐγένετο πᾶσι τοῖς κατοικοῦσιν Ἰερουσαλήμ, ὥστε κληθῆναι τὸ χωρίον[6] ἐκεῖνο Ἀχελδαμάχ. 14. κύριε, κατάβηθι πρὶν ἀποθανεῖν τὸ παιδίον μου 15. ἤμελλεν ἑαυτὸν ἀναιρεῖν[7] νομίζων ἐκπεφευγέναι τοὺς δεσμίους.

1. For to fear the Lord and to walk in his ways is good for the sons of men. 2. But while the elders were coming we remained in the fields. 3. The young men did not enter the temple because the priest

[1] ὁλοκαύτωμα, -ατος, τό "a whole burnt offering"
[2] ψυγήσεται, fut. mid. from ψύχω "shall grow cold."
[3] τὸ θεῖον "the divine Being."
[4] τεθνηκέναι perf. inf. act. from θνήσκω "I die."
[5] ἐν τάχει "quickly." [6] χωρίον "place." [7] ἀναιρεῖν "to slay."

was dead. 4. And after Paul had spoken Festus answered him. 5. Before the king saw the city he sent three messengers to its rulers. 6. But we all feared, so that we hid among the trees. 7. All the people believe that Moses wrote these things. 8. Depart from the house before the publican comes. 9. But after the multitude gave heed to the apostles they did many signs among them. 10. We think that he benefited this people by teaching them to obey the king. 11. And he healed the blind man so that all men wondered. 12. The young man died before the prophet came. 13. We believe that Peter is an apostle. 14. They stoned Paul because he preached the Gospel to them. 15. To love the Lord is better than gold or silver. 16. While he was coming down from the mountain he commanded his disciples to tell the vision to no man before they came to Jerusalem. 17. And now I have told you all these things before they come to pass. 18. All the Jews cried out that Paul ought not to live any longer[1]. 19. But I perceived that he was a wise and good man. 20. The people gave heed to John for they believed that he was a prophet.

LESSON XXXIII

THE VERBS IN μι, δίδωμι

Besides the verbs in ω there are a few verbs of very frequent occurrence which are called verbs in μι from the ending of the 1st sing. of the Pres. Ind. Act.

These verbs have endings differing from those of the verbs in ω in the Present and 2nd Aorist tenses. In the other tenses their endings are practically the same as those of the verbs in ω.

It is especially important in the case of the verbs in μι to remember the distinction laid down in Lesson XVII between the verbal stem from which most of the tenses of the verb are formed and the present stem from which the present tense is formed.

The verbal stems of the three principal verbs in μι are as follows

Present	Meaning	Stem
δίδωμι	I give	δο
τίθημι	I place	θε
ἵστημι	I cause to stand	στα

[1] μηκέτι.

δίδωμι

It will be noticed that the present stem is a reduplicated and lengthened form of the verbal stem in all three cases. ἵστημι stands for σίστημι, the rough breathing taking the place of the σ.

The Present and 2nd Aorist forms should be carefully learnt. The other tenses can readily be formed from the verbal stem.

Present and Imperfect Active of δίδωμι "I give"

Ind.	Imperf.	Imperat.	Subjunctive
δίδωμι	ἐδίδουν		διδῶ
δίδως	ἐδίδους	δίδου	διδῷς
δίδωσι	ἐδίδου	διδότω	διδῷ
δίδομεν	ἐδίδομεν		διδῶμεν
δίδοτε	ἐδίδοτε	δίδοτε	διδῶτε
διδόασι	ἐδίδοσαν or ἐδίδουν	διδότωσαν	διδῶσι

Optative	Infinitive	Part.
(διδοίην	διδόναι	διδούς, διδοῦσα, διδόν
διδοίης		Gen. διδόντος etc.
διδοίη		
διδοῖμεν		
διδοῖτε		
διδοῖεν)		

2nd Aorist Active

Indic.	Imperat.	Subjunctive	Optative	Infinitive	Part.
—		δῶ	(δοίην	δοῦναι	δούς
—	δός	δῷς	δοίης		δοῦσα
—	δότω	δῷ, δώῃ	δοίη, δοῖ, δῴη		δόν
ἔδομεν		δῶμεν	δοῖμεν		
ἔδοτε	δότε	δῶτε	δοῖτε		
ἔδοσαν	δότωσαν	δῶσι	δοῖεν)		

Notes. The singular of the 2nd Aor. Ind. is not used, its place is taken by the 1st Aor. ἔδωκα, ἔδωκας, ἔδωκε.

ω is found in all the endings of the Subjunctive.

The forms of the verbs in -μι which are enclosed in brackets need not be learnt by those who only intend to study the New Testament.

δίδωμι

Present and Imperfect Middle and Passive

Ind.	Imperf.	Imperat.	Subj.
δίδομαι	ἐδιδόμην		διδῶμαι
δίδοσαι	ἐδίδοσο	δίδοσο	διδῷ
δίδοται	ἐδίδοτο	διδόσθω	διδῶται
διδόμεθα	ἐδιδόμεθα		διδώμεθα
δίδοσθε	ἐδίδοσθε	δίδοσθε	διδῶσθε
δίδονται	ἐδίδοντο	διδόσθωσαν	διδῶνται

Opt.	Infin.	Part.
(διδοίμην	δίδοσθαι	διδόμενος
διδοῖο		διδομένη
διδοῖτο		διδόμενον
διδοίμεθα		
διδοῖσθε		
διδοῖντο)		

Notice the similarity of these endings to those of the Perfect Passive.

2nd Aorist Middle[1]

Indic.	[Imperat.	Subj.	Opt.	Infin.	Part.
ἐδόμην		δῶμαι	(δοίμην	δόσθαι	δόμενος, η, ον
ἔδου	δοῦ	δῷ	δοῖο		
ἔδοτο	δόσθω	δῶται	δοῖτο		
ἐδόμεθα		δώμεθα	δοίμεθα		
ἔδοσθε	δόσθε	δῶσθε	δοῖσθε		
ἔδοντο	δόσθωσαν]	δῶνται	δοῖντο)		

Notice the prevalence of the vowels ω and ο throughout.

The other tenses of δίδωμι are as follows: they are formed regularly from the stem δο with the following exceptions:

(1) The consonant inserted before the endings of the 1st Aor. Act. is κ and not σ.

(2) The short vowel of the stem is not lengthened before the endings of the 1st Aor. Pass., the Future Pass. or the Perf. Pass.

Future Act.	δώσω
1st Aor. Act.	ἔδωκα
Perf. Act.	δέδωκα
Fut. Mid.	δώσομαι
Fut. Pass.	δοθήσομαι
1st Aor. Pass.	ἐδόθην
Perf. Mid. or Pass.	δέδομαι

[1] The 2nd Aor. Mid. need not be learned at first.

Exercise 33

Learn the parts of δίδωμι (61), πίπτω (26).
Learn Vocabulary 27.

1. ὁ δὲ Ἰησοῦς ἐδίδου τὸν ἄρτον τοῖς μαθηταῖς ἵνα διδῶσιν αὐτὸν τοῖς ὄχλοις. 2. ὁ γὰρ θεὸς δίδωσι τὸ πνεῦμα τὸ ἅγιον τοῖς αἰτοῦσιν αὐτόν. 3. εἰπὲ ἡμῖν ἐν ποίᾳ ἐξουσίᾳ ταῦτα ποιεῖς, ἢ τίς ἐστιν ὁ δούς σοι τὴν ἐξουσίαν ταύτην. 4. ἀπολύετε καὶ ἀπολυθήσεσθε, δίδοτε καὶ δοθήσεται ὑμῖν. 5. καὶ διὰ τί οὐκ ἔδωκάς μου τὸ ἀργύριον ἐπὶ τράπεζαν[1]; 6. ὑμῖν δέδοται γνῶναι τὰ μυστήρια τῆς βασιλείας. 7. ἀπόδος μοι εἴ τι ὀφείλεις. 8. ὁ δὲ οὐκ ἤθελεν, ἀλλὰ ἀπελθὼν ἔβαλεν αὐτὸν εἰς φυλακὴν ἕως ἀποδῷ τὸ ὀφειλόμενον. 9. ἔξεστιν ἡμᾶς Καίσαρι φόρον[2] δοῦναι; δῶμεν ἢ μὴ δῶμεν; 10. ἐδόθη μοι πᾶσα ἐξουσία ἐν οὐρανῷ καὶ ἐπὶ γῆς. 11. ὁ πατὴρ ἀγαπᾷ τὸν υἱόν, καὶ πάντα δέδωκεν ἐν τῇ χειρὶ αὐτοῦ. 12. μακάριόν ἐστι μᾶλλον δοῦναι ἢ λαμβάνειν. 13. τίς ἡ σοφία ἡ δοθεῖσα τούτῳ; 14. εἰπέ μοι εἰ τοσούτου* τὸ χωρίον ἀπέδοσθε; 15. ταῦτα πάντα σοι δώσω ἐὰν πεσὼν προσκυνήσῃς μοι. 16. καὶ ὅταν ἄγωσιν ὑμᾶς παραδιδόντες, μὴ προμεριμνᾶτε τί λαλήσητε, ἀλλ' ὃ ἐὰν δοθῇ ὑμῖν ἐν ἐκείνῃ τῇ ὥρᾳ τοῦτο λαλεῖτε. 17. καὶ νῦν εἴρηκα ὑμῖν πρὶν γενέσθαι, ἵνα ὅταν γένηται πιστεύσητε.

1. I give you power over unclean spirits to cast them out. 2. This dog was given to me by my father. 3. We wish to give the gold to the high-priests. 4. Do not give good things to the wicked. 5. The field was being sold to the soldiers by the publicans. 6. They went about giving garments to the lepers. 7. I will in no wise give that which is thine to the Lord. 8. Thou gavest me water when I was thirsty[3]. 9. Let us keep the commands which have been given to us. 10. He who gives bread to the hungry[4] shall in no wise lose[5] his reward. 11. We were giving the money to the servants that they might give it to the widows. 12. The king has given us this city that we may live in it, let us not betray it to his enemies. 13. Sell all that thou hast and give to the poor. 14. If ye ask bread will your father give you a stone? 15. Whatever we ask will be given to us. 16. Give and it shall be given to you. 17. This money has been given to thee that thou mayest buy the field. 18. Give us, O Lord, thy grace that we may worship thee in spirit and in truth. 19. What is the wisdom that is given to this man?

---

[1] ἐπὶ τράπεζαν = "to the bank."   [2] φόρος -ου, ὁ, "tribute."
[3] διψάω.   [4] "I am hungry," πεινάω.   [5] ἀπολέσῃ.
* τοσούτου Genitive of value, "for so much."

LESSON XXXIV

THE VERBS IN μι, τίθημι "I place"

Present and Imperfect Active

Ind.	Imperf.	Imperat.	Subjunctive
τίθημι	ἐτίθην		τιθῶ
τίθης	ἐτίθεις	τίθει	τιθῇς
τίθησι	ἐτίθει	τιθέτω	τιθῇ
τίθεμεν	ἐτίθεμεν		τιθῶμεν
τίθετε	ἐτίθετε	τίθετε	τιθῆτε
τιθέασι	ἐτίθεσαν or ἐτίθουν	τιθέτωσαν	τιθῶσι

Optative	Inf.	Participle
(τιθείην	τιθέναι	τιθείς
τιθείης		τιθεῖσα
τιθείη		τιθέν
τιθείμεν		
τιθεῖτε		
τιθεῖεν)		

2nd Aorist Active

Indic.	Imperat.	Subj.	Opt.	Infin.	Part.
—		θῶ	(θείην	θεῖναι	θείς
—	θές	θῇς	θείης		θεῖσα
—	θέτω	θῇ	θείη		θέν
ἔθεμεν		θῶμεν	θεῖμεν		
ἔθετε	θέτε	θῆτε	θεῖτε		
ἔθεσαν	θέτωσαν	θῶσι	θεῖεν)		

Present and Imperfect Middle and Passive

Ind.	Imperf.	Imperat.	Subj.
τίθεμαι	(ἐτιθέμην		(τιθῶμαι
τίθεσαι	ἐτίθεσο	(τίθεσο	τιθῇ
τίθεται	ἐτίθετο	τιθέσθω	τιθῆται
τιθέμεθα	ἐτιθέμεθα		τιθώμεθα
τίθεσθε	ἐτίθεσθε	τίθεσθε	τιθῆσθε
τίθενται	ἐτίθεντο)	τιθέσθωσαν)	τιθῶνται)

Opt.	Infin.	Part.
(τιθείμην	τίθεσθαι	τιθέμενος
τιθεῖο		τιθεμένη
τιθεῖτο		τιθέμενον
τιθείμεθα		
τιθεῖσθε		
τιθεῖντο)		

τίθημι

2nd Aorist Middle

Indic.	Imperat.	Subj.	Opt.	Infin.	Part.
ἐθέμην		(θῶμαι	(θείμην	(θέσθαι)	(θέμενος, η, ον)
ἔθου	(θοῦ	θῇ	θεῖο		
ἔθετο	θέσθω	θῆται	θεῖτο		
ἐθέμεθα		θώμεθα	θείμεθα		
ἔθεσθε	θέσθε	θῆσθε	θεῖσθε		
ἔθεντο	θέσθωσαν)	θῶνται)	θεῖντο)		

Observe the general similarity between the endings of τίθημι and those of δίδωμι with the exception that ε and not o is the characteristic vowel.

The other tenses of τίθημι are as follows: they have the same peculiarities as the corresponding tenses of δίδωμι. Stem θε.

Notice that the vowel in the Perfect is ει and not η.

Future Act.	θήσω
1st Aor. Act.	ἔθηκα
Perf. Act.	τέθεικα
Fut. Mid.	θήσομαι
Fut. Pass.	τεθήσομαι
1st Aor. Pass.	ἐτέθην
Perf. Mid. or Pass.	τέθειμαι

Note that in the Fut. and 1 Aor. Pass. the θ of the stem is changed to τ to prevent two θ's coming together.

Exercise 34

Learn the parts of τίθημι (63), αἴρω (36), φέρω (73).
Learn Vocabulary 28.

1. οὐ καίουσιν λύχνον καὶ τιθέασιν αὐτὸν ὑπὸ τὸν μόδιον[1] ἀλλ' ἐπὶ τὴν λυχνίαν[2]. 2. καὶ λαβὼν τὸ σῶμα ὁ Ἰωσὴφ ἔθηκεν αὐτὸ ἐν τῷ καινῷ αὐτοῦ μνημείῳ. 3. μήτι ἔρχεται ὁ λύχνος ἵνα ὑπὸ τὸν μόδιον τεθῇ; 4. καὶ ὅπου ἂν εἰσεπορεύετο ἐν ταῖς ἀγοραῖς ἐτίθεσαν τοὺς ἀσθενοῦντας. 5. καὶ ἐναγκαλισάμενος[3] τὰ παιδία κατευλόγει τιθεὶς τὰς χεῖρας ἐπ' αὐτά. 6. ὁ ποιμὴν ὁ καλὸς τὴν ψυχὴν αὐτοῦ τίθησιν ὑπὲρ τῶν προβάτων. 7. ἦραν τὸν κύριον ἐκ τοῦ μνημείου, καὶ οὐκ οἴδαμεν[4] ποῦ ἔθηκαν αὐτόν. 8. οὐχ ὑμῶν ἐστὶ γνῶναι χρόνους ἢ καιροὺς οὓς ὁ πατὴρ ἔθετο ἐν τῇ ἰδίᾳ ἐξουσίᾳ. 9. καὶ ἔκλασεν τοὺς ἄρτους καὶ ἐδίδου τοῖς μαθηταῖς ἵνα παρατιθῶσιν αὐτοῖς.

[1] μόδιος -ου, ὁ, "a measure."
[2] λυχνία -ας, ἡ, "a lamp-stand."
[3] ἐναγκαλίζω "I take in my arms."
[4] οἴδαμεν "we know."

THE VERBS IN μι

10. καὶ εἰς ἣν ἂν πόλιν εἰσέρχησθε καὶ δέχωνται ὑμᾶς, ἐσθίετε τὰ παρατιθέμενα ὑμῖν. 11. καὶ ἰδοὺ ἄνδρες φέροντες ἐπὶ κλίνης ἄνθρωπον ὃς ἦν παραλελυμένος, καὶ ἐζήτουν αὐτὸν εἰσενεγκεῖν καὶ θεῖναι αὐτὸν ἐνώπιον αὐτοῦ. 12. καὶ αὐτὸς ἀπεσπάσθη ἀπ' αὐτῶν ὡσεὶ λίθου βολήν[1], καὶ θεὶς τὰ γόνατα προσηύχετο. 13. κύριε διὰ τί οὐ δύναμαί σοι ἀκολουθεῖν ἄρτι[2]; τὴν ψυχήν μου ὑπέρ σου θήσω. 14. ἔφερον τὰς τιμὰς τῶν χωρίων καὶ ἐτίθουν παρὰ τοὺς πόδας τῶν ἀποστόλων. 15. κάθου[3] ἐκ δεξιῶν μου ἕως ἂν θῶ τοὺς ἐχθρούς σου ὑποπόδιον[4] τῶν ποδῶν σου.

1. We set beside them wine and water in cups. 2. We wished to place the sick in the market-places. 3. And falling upon his knees he prayed to the God of heaven. 4. How shall we place the paralytic before his feet? 5. They used to place the books in the synagogue. 6. We will place the lamp under the measure. 7. Thou didst place me in a good land. 8. Behold all these laid down their lives for the brethren. 9. Do not place this writing upon the cross. 10. This is the throne that was placed in the temple. 11. Place the body of the prophet in the tomb of his fathers. 12. The sword is placed in the hand of the king. 13. The apostles placed their hands upon us and blessed us. 14. I will come down that I may place my hands upon her, and she shall live. 15. The lamps shall be placed in the house of the elder. 16. The nets were placed by the side of the ship. 17. The sick man was brought in on a bed and placed before him. 18. I am he that placed my hands upon your head when you were a boy. 19. Ye shall in no wise eat that which is set before you. 20. The bread was broken and set before them.

LESSON XXXV

THE VERBS IN μι, ἵστημι

The following points should be specially noticed in connexion with this verb.

(1) This is one of the few verbs which has both a 1st and a 2nd Aorist in use. These tenses always differ in meaning in the case of this verb.

---

[1] ὡσεὶ λίθου βολὴν "about a stone's cast."
[2] ἄρτι "now, at this moment." [3] κάθου "sit down."
[4] ὑποπόδιον -ον, τό, "a footstool."

ἵστημι   113

The Present, Imperfect, Future and 1st Aorist tenses of the active voice of ἵστημι are transitive and mean "I cause to stand" or "I place" etc.

The **Perfect** and **Pluperfect are intransitive** and are used in the sense of the Present and Imperfect with the meaning of "I stand" etc. The **2nd Aorist** is also **intransitive** and means "I stood."

The **Passive** is used in the sense of "I am caused to stand," "I am placed," hence simply "I stand."

Practically the only passive tense used in the N.T. is the 1st Aorist.

(2) In the tenses in which there is reduplication (the Present, and the Perfect) the first σ is omitted and a rough breathing put in its place: Present ἵστημι for σίστημι, Perfect ἕστηκα for σέστηκα.

The breathings should be watched with special care in the case of this verb. There is a rough breathing on all the moods of the Present and Perfect tenses, and a smooth breathing on the augmented tenses of the 1st and 2nd Aorist.

The Present Middle and Passive is only given for completeness, and need not be learnt at first.

Notice that in the 1st Aor. Act. the usual σ, and not κ, is found.

Present and Imperfect Active

Ind.	Imperfect	Imperat.	Subjunct.
ἵστημι	(ἵστην		(ἱστῶ
ἵστης	ἵστης	(ἵστη	ἱστῇς
ἵστησι	ἵστη	ἱστάτω	ἱστῇ
ἵσταμεν	ἵσταμεν		ἱστῶμεν
ἵστατε	ἵστατε	ἵστατε	ἱστῆτε
ἱστᾶσι	ἵστασαν)	ἱστάτωσαν)	ἱστῶσι)

Opt.	Infinitive	Participle
(ἱσταίην	(ἱστάναι)	(ἱστάς
ἱσταίης		ἱστᾶσα
ἱσταίη		ἱστάν)
ἱσταῖμεν		
ἱσταῖτε		
ἱσταῖεν)		

ἵστημι

Second Aorist Active

Indicative	Imperat.	Subjunctive	Optative	Infinitive	Part.
ἔστην		στῶ	(σταίην	στῆναι	στάς
ἔστης	στῆθι	στῇς	σταίης		στᾶσα
ἔστη	στήτω	στῇ	σταίη		στάν
ἔστημεν		στῶμεν	σταίμεν		
ἔστητε	στῆτε	στῆτε	σταῖτε		
ἔστησαν[1]	στήτωσαν	στῶσι	σταῖεν)		

Present and Imperfect Middle and Passive

Ind.	Imperf.	Imperat.	Subj.
(ἵσταμαι	(ἱστάμην		(ἱστῶμαι
ἵστασαι	ἵστασο	(ἵστασο	ἱστῇ
ἵσταται	ἵστατο	ἱστάσθω	ἱστῆται
ἱστάμεθα	ἱστάμεθα		ἱστώμεθα
ἵστασθε	ἵστασθε	ἵστασθε	ἱστῆσθε
ἵστανται)	ἵσταντο)	ἱστάσθωσαν)	ἱστῶνται)

Opt.	Infin.	Part.
(ἱσταίμην	(ἵστασθαι)	(ἱστάμενος
ἱσταῖο		ἱσταμένη
ἱσταῖτο		ἱστάμενον)
ἱσταίμεθα		
ἱσταῖσθε		
ἱσταῖντο)		

The other tenses of ἵστημι are as follows.

Future Active. στήσω I shall cause to stand.
1st Aorist Act. ἔστησα I caused to stand.
Perfect Act. ἕστηκα I stand. 2nd Perf. Part. ἑστώς, ἑστῶσα, ἑστός
Pluperfect Act. ἑστήκειν often written εἱστήκειν I was standing.
Future Middle. στήσομαι I shall stand.
Future Passive. σταθήσομαι I shall stand.
1st Aor. Pass. ἐστάθην I stood.

[1] Note that the 3rd pl. of the 1st and 2nd Aorists of ἵστημι are the same in form. Their meaning must be inferred from the context. Examples are given in the last three sentences of exercise B. The verb in sentence 12 is 2nd Aor. and that in sentence 13 1st Aor.

EXERCISES

Exercise 35

Learn the parts of ἵστημι (62), πάσχω (72), ἀγγέλλω (33), φαίνω (38), βαίνω (48).

Learn Vocabulary 29.

A

1. τότε παραλαμβάνει αὐτὸν ὁ διάβολος εἰς τὴν ἁγίαν πόλιν καὶ ἔστησεν αὐτὸν ἐπὶ τὸ πτερύγιον[1] τοῦ ἱεροῦ. 2. ταῦτα δὲ αὐτῶν λαλούντων αὐτὸς ἔστη ἐν μέσῳ αὐτῶν. 3. ἔβλεψαν σὺν αὐτοῖς ἑστῶτα τὸν ἄνθρωπον τὸν τεθεραπευμένον. 4. εἰ δὲ ὁ Σατανᾶς τὸν Σατανᾶν ἐκβάλλει, ἐφ' ἑαυτὸν ἐμερίσθη· πῶς οὖν σταθήσεται ἡ βασιλεία αὐτοῦ; 5. τὰ νῦν παραγγέλλει ὁ θεὸς τοῖς ἀνθρώποις πάντας πανταχοῦ μετανοεῖν, καθ' ὅτι ἔστησεν ἡμέραν ἐν ᾗ μέλλει κρίνειν τὴν οἰκουμένην ἐν δικαιοσύνῃ. 6. ὁ Φαρισαῖος σταθεὶς ταῦτα πρὸς ἑαυτὸν προσηύχετο. 7. ὁ δὲ τελώνης μακρόθεν[2] ἑστὼς οὐκ ἤθελεν οὐδὲ τοὺς ὀφθαλμοὺς ἐπᾶραι εἰς τὸν οὐρανόν. 8. ὁ δὲ Ἰησοῦς ἐστάθη ἔμπροσθεν τοῦ ἡγεμόνος. 9. θεὶς δὲ τὰ γόνατα ἔκραξεν φωνῇ μεγάλῃ Κύριε μὴ στήσῃς αὐτοῖς ταύτην τὴν ἁμαρτίαν. 10. μετὰ ταῦτα ἀνέστη Ἰούδας ὁ Γαλιλαῖος ἐν ταῖς ἡμέραις τῆς ἀπογραφῆς[3] καὶ ἀπέστησε λαὸν ὀπίσω αὐτοῦ. 11. εἰ Μωυσέως καὶ τῶν προφητῶν οὐκ ἀκούουσιν, οὐδ' ἐάν τις ἐκ νεκρῶν ἀναστῇ πεισθήσονται. 12. εἶπεν δὲ τῷ ἀνδρὶ τῷ ξηρὰν ἔχοντι τὴν χεῖρα Ἔγειρε καὶ στῆθι εἰς τὸ μέσον· καὶ ἀναστὰς ἔστη.

B

1. ἄνθρωπε, τίς με κατέστησεν κριτὴν ἢ μεριστὴν[4] ἐφ' ὑμᾶς; 2. οὐδεὶς δύναται ἐλθεῖν πρός με ἐὰν μὴ ὁ πατὴρ ὁ πέμψας με ἑλκύσῃ αὐτόν, καὶ ἀναστήσω αὐτὸν ἐν τῇ ἐσχάτῃ ἡμέρᾳ. 3. ἡ μήτηρ καὶ οἱ ἀδελφοὶ αὐτοῦ εἱστήκεισαν ἔξω ζητοῦντες αὐτῷ λαλῆσαι. 4. οἱ ὑποκριταὶ φιλοῦσιν ἐν ταῖς συναγωγαῖς ἑστῶτες προσεύχεσθαι, ὅπως φανῶσιν τοῖς ἀνθρώποις. 5. δοὺς δὲ αὐτῇ χεῖρα ἀνέστησεν αὐτήν. 6. τὸ δὲ πνεῦμα ῥητῶς[5] λέγει ὅτι ἐν ὑστέροις καιροῖς ἀποστήσονταί τινες τῆς πίστεως. 7. πῶς ὁμοιώσωμεν τὴν βασιλείαν τοῦ θεοῦ, ἢ ἐν τίνι αὐτὴν παραβολῇ θῶμεν; 8. ὁ δὲ Ἰησοῦς ἐπιλαβόμενος παιδίον ἔστησεν αὐτὸ παρ' ἑαυτῷ. 9. πορεύεσθε καὶ σταθέντες λαλεῖτε ἐν τῷ ἱερῷ τῷ λαῷ πάντα τὰ ῥήματα τῆς ζωῆς ταύτης. 10. καὶ καταβαινόντων αὐτῶν ἐκ τοῦ ὄρους ἐνετείλατο[6] αὐτοῖς ὁ Ἰησοῦς λέγων

---

[1] πτερύγιον -ου, τό, "pinnacle."
[2] μακρόθεν "afar off."
[3] ἀπογραφή -ῆς, ἡ, "enrolment."
[4] μεριστής -οῦ, ὁ, "a divider."
[5] ῥητῶς "expressly."
[6] ἐνετείλατο, 3rd sing. 1st Aor. Mid. from ἐντέλλομαι.

Μηδενὶ εἴπητε τὸ ὅραμα ἕως οὗ ὁ υἱὸς τοῦ ἀνθρώπου ἐκ νεκρῶν ἀναστῇ. 11. οἷς καὶ παρέστησεν ἑαυτὸν ζῶντα μετὰ τὸ παθεῖν αὐτὸν ἐν πολλοῖς τεκμηρίοις. 12. καὶ προσελθὼν ἥψατο τῆς σοροῦ[1], οἱ δὲ βαστάζοντες ἔστησαν. 13. καὶ ἔστησαν μάρτυρας ψευδεῖς λέγοντας Ὁ ἄνθρωπος οὗτος οὐ παύεται λαλῶν ῥήματα κατὰ τοῦ τόπου τοῦ ἁγίου. 14. ἀγάγοντες δὲ αὐτοὺς ἔστησαν ἐν τῷ συνεδρίῳ.

1. I will cause thee to stand before Caesar for my name's sake[2]. 2. The righteous shall stand in the kingdom of their Father. 3. Paul therefore stood before Festus[3]. 4. The priests caused the publican to stand in the midst of the marketplace. 5. But Peter stood up and preached the word to the multitude. 6. He is not here, for he has risen[4] from the dead. 7. Who appointed thee to be the ruler of this people? 8. Then we arose and departed from the city. 9. You made the king to stand in the Holy Place. 10. In the last days many departed from the faith. 11. We stood without[5], wishing to see the prophet. 12. Stand on thy feet and take up thy bed. 13. We hope to stand before the Lord in that day. 14. Then the spirit of the Lord lifted me up and caused me to stand on the waters. 15. After these things many robbers arose and led away much people after them. 16. If any man believes in me I will raise him up at the last day. 17. We commanded the soldiers to stand apart from the multitude. 18. How shall we stand in the day of his wrath[6]? 19. And standing up he cried with a loud voice, "Stand apart from these men, and make them to stand beside the king." 20. Those that heard these things stood still.

LESSON XXXVI

OTHER VERBS IN μι, οἶδα

The verb ἵημι occurs in the New Testament only in compounds, the most common of which are

ἀφίημι "I send away, I let go, I forgive, I allow."
συνίημι "I understand."

The verbal stem of ἵημι is ἑ. The rough breathing passes to the

[1] σορός -οῦ, ἡ, "a bier."
[2] "for the sake of" ἕνεκα followed by a Genitive.
[3] Φῆστος.
[4] "has risen" 2 Aor. ἀνίστημι.
[5] "without" ἔξω.
[6] "wrath" ὀργή -ῆς, ἡ.

οἶδα

reduplicating syllable ι in the Present and Imperfect, and the stem vowel is lengthened before the ending μι as in τίθημι.

All parts of the verb have therefore a rough breathing.

The forms of ἀφίημι given below are those which occur most frequently in the New Testament. Some of them such as the 2nd sing. and the 1st and 3rd pl. of the Pres. Ind. are formed as if from ἀφίω or ἀφέω: a tendency on the part of the verbs in μι to assimilate their endings to those of the verbs in ω is very marked in the New Testament.

Note that in the Imperfect the preposition and not the stem receives the augment.

Pres. Ind. Act.
(ἀφίημι)
ἀφεῖς, ἀφίης
ἀφίησι
ἀφίεμεν, ἀφίομεν
ἀφίετε
ἀφίουσι, ἀφίασι

3rd. sing. Imperf. Ind. Act. ἤφιε
Pres. Inf. Act. ἀφιέναι
3rd pl. Pres. Ind. Pass. ἀφίενται
3rd pl. Perf. Ind. Pass. ἀφέωνται
2nd Aor. Imperat. Act. 2nd sing. ἄφες
                    2nd pl. ἄφετε
2nd Aor. Sub. Act. ἀφῶ etc.
2nd Aor. Part. ἀφείς ἀφεῖσα ἀφέν

Future Active. ἀφήσω
Future Passive. ἀφεθήσομαι
1st Aor. Act. ἀφῆκα
1st Aor. Pass. ἀφέθην

The forms of οἶδα "I know" which are found in the New Testament are as follows (not those in brackets):

οἶδα is a Perfect whose Present εἴδω is not in use.

Perf. Ind.	Pluperf.	Imperat.	Subj.	Inf.	Part.
οἶδα	ᾔδειν		εἰδῶ	εἰδέναι	εἰδώς
οἶδας	ᾔδεις	(ἴσθι)	εἰδῇς		εἰδυῖα
οἶδε	ᾔδει	(ἴστω)	εἰδῇ		εἰδός
οἴδαμεν	ᾔδειμεν		εἰδῶμεν		
ἴδατε, ἴστε	ᾔδειτε	ἴστε	εἰδῆτε		
οἴδασι, ἴσασι	ᾔδεισαν	(ἴστωσαν)	εἰδῶσι		

δύναμαι "I am able" and ἐπίσταμαι "I know" are conjugated like the Present Passive of ἴστημι.

OTHER VERBS IN μι

Present	Imperfect	Infinitive	Participle
δύναμαι	ἠδυνάμην	δύνασθαι	δυνάμενος, η, ον
δύνασαι, δύνῃ	ἠδύνασο		
δύναται	ἠδύνατο		
δυνάμεθα	ἠδυνάμεθα		
δύνασθε	ἠδύνασθε		
δύνανται	ἠδύναντο		

Notice that the Imperfect has a double augment. The Aorist ἠδυνήθην also generally has a double augment.

There is also another class of verbs in μι which inserts νυ (in stems ending in a vowel ννυ) between the verbal stem and the endings of the Present and Imperfect tenses.

Stem	Pres. Ind. Act.
δεικ	δείκνυμι
ὀλ	ὄλλυμι (ὄλνυμι)
ζω	ζώννυμι

These verbs tend generally in the N.T. to assimilate themselves to verbs in ω. Such μι forms as do occur are similar to those of τίθημι, allowing for the stem vowel υ instead of ε.

Exercise 36

Learn the parts of ἀφίημι (58), δύναμαι (10), δείκνυμι (59), γράφω (7). Learn Vocabulary 30.

1. καὶ νῦν λέγω ὑμῖν ἀπόστητε ἀπὸ τῶν ἀνθρώπων τούτων καὶ ἄφετε αὐτούς. 2. ὁ δὲ Ἰησοῦς εἶπεν αὐτῷ Ἄφες ἄρτι, οὕτω γὰρ πρέπον ἐστὶν ἡμῖν πληρῶσαι πᾶσαν δικαιοσύνην. τότε ἀφίησιν αὐτόν. 3. τότε συνῆκαν οἱ μαθηταὶ ὅτι περὶ Ἰωάνου τοῦ βαπτιστοῦ εἶπεν αὐτοῖς. 4. τίς δύναται ἀφιέναι ἁμαρτίας εἰ μὴ εἷς, ὁ θεός; 5. οἱ δὲ εὐθέως ἀφέντες τὰ δίκτυα ἠκολούθησαν αὐτῷ. 6. καὶ ἄφες ἡμῖν τὰ ὀφειλήματα ἡμῶν, ὡς καὶ ἡμεῖς ἀφήκαμεν τοῖς ὀφειλέταις ἡμῶν. 7. ἐὰν γὰρ ἀφῆτε τοῖς ἀνθρώποις τὰ παραπτώματα αὐτῶν, ἀφήσει καὶ ὑμῖν ὁ πατὴρ ὑμῶν ὁ οὐράνιος. 8. οἶδά σε τίς εἶ, ὁ ἅγιος τοῦ θεοῦ. 9. τότε δείκνυσιν αὐτῷ ὁ διάβολος πάσας τὰς βασιλείας τοῦ κόσμου. 10. πλανᾶσθε μὴ εἰδότες τὰς γραφὰς μηδὲ τὴν δύναμιν τοῦ θεοῦ. 11. ἐκείνοις δὲ τοῖς ἔξω ἐν παραβολαῖς τὰ πάντα γίγνεται, ἵνα ἀκούοντες ἀκούωσιν καὶ μὴ συνίωσιν. 12. θάρσει τέκνον, ἀφίενταί σοι αἱ ἁμαρτίαι. 13. τί ὅτι ἐζητεῖτέ με; οὐκ ᾔδειτε ὅτι ἐν τοῖς τοῦ πατρός μου δεῖ εἶναί με; 14. ᾔδει δὲ καὶ Ἰούδας ὁ παραδιδοὺς αὐτὸν τὸν τόπον.

THE OPTATIVE MOOD

15. πάτερ, εὐχαριστῶ σοι ὅτι ἤκουσάς μου, ἐγὼ δὲ ᾔδειν ὅτι πάντοτέ μου ἀκούεις. 16. ταῦτα ἔγραψα ὑμῖν ἵνα εἰδῆτε ὅτι ζωὴν ἔχετε αἰώνιον. 17. θέλω δὲ ὑμᾶς εἰδέναι ὅτι παντὸς ἀνδρὸς ἡ κεφαλὴ ὁ Χριστός ἐστι. 18. καὶ οὐκ ἤφιεν τὰ δαιμόνια λαλεῖν ὅτι ᾔδεισαν αὐτόν.

1. Master, we know that thou art true. 2. God will forgive all our sins if we believe on[1] his name. 3. Then the priests understood that he had spoken this parable against them. 4. But since they did not know this, they arose and went to Jerusalem. 5. Did ye understand all these things? 6. I forgave thee all that debt. 7. I write this to you that ye may know that ye are saved. 8. Let these men alone that they may worship the God of their fathers. 9. How shall I forgive thee for this? 10. He suffered not the man who had been healed to follow him. 11. Know well that the Lord will not allow thee to err. 12. I am not able to understand this unless[2] thou teach me. 13. Who is able to know all his faults? 14. They knew that their soldiers were of good courage. 15. Know that all your faults shall be forgiven.

LESSON XXXVII

THE OPTATIVE MOOD. PERIPHRASTIC TENSES

The Optative Mood

The Optative Mood is used rarely in the New Testament; its use is confined to the Present and Aorist tenses.

Its forms are given in the table of verbs on pages 144—150. The Optative of εἰμί is as follows: εἴην, εἴης, εἴη, εἶμεν or εἴημεν, εἶτε or εἴητε, εἶεν or εἴησαν.

It generally expresses a wish:

Example:

O boy, mayest thou become more fortunate than thy father.

ὦ παῖ, γένοιο πατρὸς εὐτυχέστερος.

It is also used in dependent questions in the writings of St Luke sometimes with the particle ἄν.

Examples:

And they began to discuss among themselves which it should be of them that should do this.

καὶ αὐτοὶ ἤρξαντο συζητεῖν πρὸς ἑαυτοὺς τὸ τίς ἄρα εἴη ἐξ αὐτῶν ὁ τοῦτο μέλλων πράσσειν. Lk. xxii. 23.

[1] "on" εἰς. [2] "unless" εἰ μή.

And while Peter was doubting within himself what the vision should be which he had seen, behold the men that had been sent by Cornelius... stood before the door.

ὡς δὲ ἐν ἑαυτῷ διηπόρει ὁ Πέτρος τί ἂν εἴη τὸ ὅραμα ὃ εἶδεν, ἰδοὺ οἱ ἄνδρες οἱ ἀπεσταλμένοι ὑπὸ τοῦ Κορνηλίου...ἐπέστησαν ἐπὶ τὸν πυλῶνα.

Acts x. 17.

See the author's *Syntax of N.T. Greek*, paragraphs 131, 160, 161.

Periphrastic Tenses

In New Testament Greek tenses are sometimes formed, as in English, of a part of the verb "to be" and a participle.

They are called "Periphrastic Tenses" because they are expressed in a roundabout way (περιφράζειν).

The commonest Periphrastic Tenses are:

The Periphrastic Imperfect formed of the Imperfect of εἶναι and the Present participle:

And Jesus was going before them.

καὶ ἦν προάγων αὐτοὺς ὁ Ἰησοῦς. Mk x. 32.

The Periphrastic Perfect formed of the Present of εἶναι and the Perfect participle:

The people will stone us, for they are persuaded that John is a prophet.

ὁ λαὸς καταλιθάσει ἡμᾶς, πεπεισμένος γάρ ἐστιν Ἰωάνην προφήτην εἶναι. Lk. xx. 6.

The Periphrastic Pluperfect formed of the Imperfect of εἶναι and the Perfect participle:

And John was clothed with camel's hair.

καὶ ἦν ὁ Ἰωάνης ἐνδεδυμένος τρίχας καμήλου. Mk i. 6.

The Periphrastic Future formed of the Future of εἶναι and the Present participle. This form of the tense has the force of a Future continuous, with the sense of continuity emphasised.

From henceforth thou shalt catch men.

ἀπὸ τοῦ νῦν ἀνθρώπους ἔσῃ ζωγρῶν. Lk. v. 10.

Exercise 37

Learn Vocabulary 31.

1. ἰδοὺ ἡ δούλη Κυρίου· γένοιτό μοι κατὰ τὸ ῥῆμά σου. 2. καὶ πάντες διελογίζοντο ἐν ταῖς καρδίαις αὐτῶν περὶ τοῦ Ἰωάνου, μή ποτε αὐτὸς εἴη ὁ Χριστός. 3. τὸ ἀργύριόν σου σὺν σοὶ εἴη εἰς ἀπώλειαν. 4. ἀκούσας δὲ ὄχλου διαπορευομένου[1] ἐπυνθάνετο τί ἂν εἴη τοῦτο. 5. ὁ δὲ θεὸς τῆς ὑπομονῆς δῴη[2] ὑμῖν τὸ αὐτὸ φρονεῖν ἐν ἀλλήλοις. 6. καὶ πᾶν τὸ πλῆθος ἦν τοῦ λαοῦ προσευχόμενον ἔξω τῇ ὥρᾳ τοῦ θυμιάματος[3]. 7. καὶ ἦν ὅλη ἡ πόλις ἐπισυνηγμένη πρὸς τὴν θύραν. 8. Ἰερουσαλὴμ ἔσται πατουμένη ὑπὸ τῶν ἐθνῶν. 9. ἐπηρώτων δὲ αὐτὸν οἱ μαθηταὶ αὐτοῦ τίς αὕτη εἴη ἡ παραβολή. 10. οὐ γάρ ἐστιν ἐν γωνίᾳ[4] πεπραγμένον τοῦτο. 11. καὶ ἦσαν οἱ μαθηταὶ Ἰωάνου νηστεύοντες. 12. εἶπεν δὲ ὁ Παῦλος Ἑστὼς ἐπὶ τοῦ βήματος[5] Καίσαρός εἰμι οὗ με δεῖ κρίνεσθαι. 13. ἦν γὰρ διδάσκων αὐτοὺς ὡς ἐξουσίαν ἔχων καὶ οὐχ ὡς οἱ γραμματεῖς αὐτῶν. 14. καὶ προσκαλεσάμενος ἕνα τῶν παίδων ἐπυνθάνετο τί ἂν εἴη ταῦτα.

1. Then the blind man asked what this might be. 2. The disciples of Jesus were eating and drinking. 3. This thing has been done before many witnesses. 4. May it happen to us according to thy will. 5. Thou shalt be walking in the way of righteousness. 6. The disciples disputed[6] who should be the greatest. 7. May all the workers of iniquity[7] perish[8]. 8. Then all the multitude was gathered together to the sea. 9. We desire to know what this saying may be. 10. May I become more like to thee, O Lord.

[1] διαπορευομένου "passing by."
[2] δῴη from δίδωμι.
[3] θυμίαμα, -ατος, τό, "incense."
[4] γωνία -ας, ἡ, "a corner."
[5] βῆμα -ατος, τό, "a judgement seat."
[6] συζητέω.
[7] ἀνομία.
[8] ἀπόλλοιντο.

LESSON XXXVIII

PREPOSITIONS

Prepositions are words joined with, and nearly always placed before, nouns or pronouns so that the preposition with the noun or pronoun forms a phrase equivalent to an adjective or adverb.

Examples: Phrase equivalent to an adjective—

The king of Britain.

"Of" is a preposition, and with the noun "Britain" it forms a phrase equivalent to an adjective. Compare the expression "His Britannic Majesty."

Phrases equivalent to an adverb—

> He walked for six hours.
> They sat by the sea.

The phrases "for six hours" and "by the sea" are equivalent to adverbs, for they qualify the verbs "walked" and "sat."

In English all prepositions are followed by a noun or pronoun in the accusative case, or "govern" an accusative case, as it is expressed sometimes.

Prepositions were originally **adverbs**, and are so still when they are compounded with verbs. Most of the local and other relations which are now expressed in Greek by a preposition followed by the Accusative, Genitive, or Dative case of a noun or pronoun were originally expressed by the use of a suitable case of the noun or pronoun alone.

In the language from which Greek is derived there were cases which, when standing by themselves, sufficed to denote local, temporal and other relations.

The **accusative** case denoted extension, or motion towards.

The **ablative** case denoted separation, or motion from.

The **locative** case denoted place where, or rest at.

The **instrumental** case denoted the means by which an action was accomplished, and it also had an idea of association.

In that form of the Greek language with which we are acquainted we find the form which we call the Genitive case used to express the meaning of the Ablative case as well as its own proper meaning.

The form which we call the Dative case expresses the meanings of the Locative and Instrumental cases as well as its own.

We are therefore justified in saying, as a practical rule, that the Genitive in Greek denotes **motion from,** and that the Dative denotes **rest at,** and can also be used to express the **instrument** of an action, although these are not the proper original meanings of these cases.

As we have already stated the Accusative denotes **motion towards.**

These cases called in the help of adverbs to make their meaning more precise, and, when these adverbs had become fixed in this use by

PREPOSITIONS

custom, they were treated as a separate part of speech, and called Prepositions.

Prepositions do not properly speaking "govern" the cases of the nouns which they precede. The case is really the governing element in the expression: the preposition only serves to make clear the exact sense in which it is used.

But as language developed the prepositions mastered the cases.

As the horse in the fable called in the man to help him against the stag, and allowed him to get on his back, and then found that he himself had lost his liberty, so the cases called in the help of the prepositions, and then found themselves weakened and finally destroyed.

In English, French, Italian, and to some extent in modern Greek the cases have disappeared, wholly, or in part, and the prepositions do the work which they once did. For example we say "of a man" where the Greeks said ἀνθρώπου and "to a man" where the Greeks said ἀνθρώπῳ.

In the New Testament we can see this process going on. Prepositions are used with the case of a noun where the case alone sufficed in Classical Greek.

For example the simple Dative was used in Classical Greek to express the instrument; but in New Testament Greek ἐν with the Dative is so used sometimes.

Example:

Κύριε, εἰ πατάξομεν ἐν μαχαίρᾳ;
Lord, shall we strike with the sword? Lk. xxii. 49.

In estimating the meaning of a prepositional phrase (i.e. a preposition followed by a noun) the proper course to adopt is first to consider the force of the **case of the noun** and then to add to this the **root meaning of the preposition**. The combination of the two ideas will generally explain the meaning of the phrase.

If the proper force of the case is kept in view it will explain how the same preposition can have such wholly different meanings with different cases. The meaning of the case is really far more important than the meaning of the preposition.

We may see the joint influence of the case of the noun and the root meaning of the preposition best by considering some preposition that is used with all three cases.

For example παρά means "beside."

When it is used with the Accusative it denotes **motion to beside** or **motion alongside of**.

When it is used with the Genitive it denotes **motion from beside**.

When it is used with the Dative it denotes **rest beside** and is translated "near," or "with."

Examples:

Accusative. περιπατῶν δὲ παρὰ τὴν θάλασσαν τῆς Γαλιλαίας εἶδεν δύο ἀδελφούς.

And walking along the side of the sea of Galilee he saw two brethren.

καὶ ἔριψαν αὐτοὺς παρὰ τοὺς πόδας αὐτοῦ.
And they cast them at his feet.

Genitive. ἐγένετο ἄνθρωπος ἀπεσταλμένος παρὰ θεοῦ.
There came into being a man sent from God.

δόξαν παρὰ ἀνθρώπων οὐ λαμβάνω.
I receive not glory from men.

Dative. ἐπιλαβόμενος παιδίον ἔστησεν αὐτὸ παρ' ἑαυτῷ.
Taking a child he placed him near him.

καὶ παρ' αὐτῷ ἔμειναν τὴν ἡμέραν ἐκείνην.
And they remained with him that day.

Prepositions connected with one case only

The uses of the prepositions given in the following tables are those which occur most frequently in New Testament Greek.

The use of Classical Greek is somewhat different.

The meaning printed in black type after each preposition may be regarded as indicating the root meaning of the preposition; it also generally indicates the meaning of the preposition when compounded with a verb etc. The student is advised to master these meanings thoroughly by learning them by heart, and to pick up the derived meanings in the course of his reading, remembering what has been stated above as to the importance of the meaning of the case in deciding the meaning of a prepositional phrase.

PREPOSITIONS

Prepositions connected with the **Accusative** only.

 ἀνά **up**. (Frequent in composition with verbs, but rare before a noun.)
 εἰς **into**.

Prepositions connected with the **Genitive** only.

 ἀντί **over against**, instead of, in return for.
 ἀπό **away from** (from the exterior).
 ἐκ **out of** (from the interior).
 πρό **in front of, before** of time or place.

Prepositions connected with the **Dative** only.

 ἐν **in** of time or place. In N.T. also of the instrument and even of the agent; I Cor. iv. 21, vi. 2, Acts xvii. 31.
 σύν **together with**.

Notes on the above prepositions

ἀνά occurs in the English word analysis (ἀνάλυσις) a thorough loosing or loosing up.

The likeness between the prepositions ἀντί, ἀπό, ἐκ, πρό, ἐν and the Latin prepositions ante, ab, ex, pro, in is obvious.

They occur in such English words as "antipope" a bishop set up over against, or as a rival to, the Pope, "antipathy" a feeling against a person or thing, "abstraction" a taking away, "expulsion" a driving out, "propulsion" a driving forward, "intrusion" a thrusting in.

σύν is found in many English words such as "sympathy," "symphony" (συμπάθεια, συμφωνία).

Prepositions connected with the Genitive and Accusative

 διά **through**. With the Acc. on account of, owing to.
       With the Gen. through, throughout, by means of,
 κατά **down**. With Acc. down along, during, with regard to, according to.
       With Gen. down from, down upon, against.
 μετά **among**. With Acc. after.
       With Gen. with, among.
 περί **around**. With Acc. about, around, of place or time.
       With Gen. about, concerning, on account of.
 ὑπέρ **over**. With Acc. above, beyond.
       With Gen. on behalf of, for the sake of, concerning.
 ὑπό **under**. With Acc. under.
       With Gen. under the influence of, hence "*by*" of the Agent after Passive verbs.

Notes on the above prepositions

διά is found in such words as "dialect" a language spoken through a district, "diagram" etc.

κατά is found in "catastrophe" which means a turning upside down.

μετά is found in the word "metaphysics" that science which is above or beyond the science of physics.

It is also found in the words "metaphor," "metamorphosis," but there it has the sense of change, of transference from one state to another, which it commonly has when compounded with a verb etc. in Greek. "Metaphor" means the transference of a word properly referring to one set of objects to another set of objects. "Metamorphosis" means a change of form.

περί is found in such words as "perimeter" the length of a thing all round, "peripatetic" a man who walks about.

ὑπέρ is the same word as the Latin "super." It occurs in such English words as "hypercritical," over critical.

Prepositions connected with the Accusative, Genitive, and Dative

ἐπί **upon.** With Acc. upon (placed on), up to, as far as.
With Gen. on, in the presence of, in the time of.
With Dat. on, at, on account of, in addition to.

παρά **beside.** With Acc. to the side of, beside, beyond, contrary.
With Gen. from beside, from (of persons).
With Dat. near (generally of persons).

πρός **towards.** With Acc. towards, up to, in reference to, with regard to, at home with (like Latin *apud* and French *chez*). See Jn. i. 2.
With Gen. from. (Very rare in N.T.)
With Dat. at, close to.

Notes on the above prepositions

ἐπί is found in the words "epitaph" an inscription on a tomb, "epigram" a writing on a given subject.

παρά is found in the word "parable" the placing of one thing beside another for comparison.

πρός is found in the word "proselyte" which means a person who passes from one type of opinion to another.

Prepositions compounded with verbs etc.

In English certain words which are generally classed as prepositions are joined with verbs and nouns to form compound words.

Examples: undertake, overtake, outbid, overcoat, outrigger.

But very frequently these "prepositions" are written after the word with which they go, and separately from it. In this case it is plain that these so-called "prepositions" are really adverbs.

Examples: They went away.
We took over the business.
This coat is quite worn out.

In Greek the "prepositions" are generally joined to the words which they qualify, and form compound words.

I send away, ἀποστέλλω.
I drive together, or gather together, συνάγω.
A synagogue (a gathering together), συναγωγή.
An assembly (a body of men called out), ἐκκλησία.
Chosen out, ἐκλεκτός.

In some cases two "prepositions" may be joined to one word:
ἀντιπαρέρχομαι   I pass by opposite to.

Consider the force of the "prepositions" in the following compound words:

ἀνέρχομαι	I go up.
ἀπέρχομαι	I go away.
διέρχομαι	I go through.
εἰσέρχομαι	I go into.
ἐξέρχομαι	I go out of.
ἐπέρχομαι	I come upon.
παρέρχομαι	I go by the side of.
προσέρχομαι	I go towards (especially of going towards people).
συνέρχομαι	I go with.
ἐμβαίνω	I go in.
καταβαίνω	I go down.
προβαίνω	I go before.
ἀντιλέγω	I speak against, I contradict.
ὑπερέχω	I have over, I excel.
ὑπομένω	I remain under, I endure.

Notice also:

ἀποκαλύπτω	I cover away from, I uncover, I reveal.
ἐπιστρέφω	I turn towards, I turn again, I return, I repent.
ἐπικαλέομαι	I call upon, I surname.
προσκαλέομαι	I call to myself, I summon.
προσκυνέω	I kiss my hand to, I worship.
προσεύχομαι	I pray to.

In all these examples of compound words the "prepositions" have the same meanings which they have when they are used before the case of a noun or pronoun.

Certain of them however have a somewhat extended or different meaning when they are used to form compound words.

For example ἀνά in composition means not only "up" but also "over again," "anew" (the Latin "re") and also "back," and "to and fro."

ἀναβλέπω	means not only "I look up" but also "I look anew," or "I receive my sight."
ἀναπίπτω	means "I fall back," or "I recline."

μετά in composition generally has the sense of change or alteration.

μεταβαίνω	I pass from one place to another, I remove, I depart.
μετανοέω	I change my mind, I repent.
μετάνοια	repentance.

παρά from its meaning of "beside" or "along" gets a further sense of passing on one side and so of averting, neglecting, transgressing.

παρέρχομαι	I pass by the side of, I pass from the side of, I pass away.
παραβαίνω	I go by the side of, I violate, I transgress.
παραιτέομαι	I avert by entreaty, I beg off, I refuse, I excuse myself.
παρακούω	I hear amiss, I disobey.

ὑπό from its meaning "under" gets the sense of subjection or inferiority.

ὑκακούω	I listen to, I obey, I submit to.
ὑπακοή	obedience.
ὑποτάσσομαι	I order myself under, I submit to.

Certain "prepositions" such as ἀπό, διά, κατά, σύν sometimes practically lose their local meaning in composition and denote that the action of the verb with which they are connected is to be regarded as fully accomplished.

Some such compound words are:

ἀποκτείνω	I kill.	κατεσθίω	I eat up.
ἀπόλλυμι	I destroy.	καταλείπω	I abandon.
ἀπολαμβάνω	I receive to the full.	κατοικέω	I inhabit.
διαμένω	I remain.	συντηρέω	I keep safe.
κατεργάζομαι	I perform.		

The following compound verbs which differ greatly in meaning from the simple verbs from which they are formed should be carefully learnt.

ἀναγινώσκω	I read.
ἀποκρίνομαι	I answer (I give a decision from myself).
ἐπαγγέλλομαι	I promise (I announce concerning myself).
παραγγέλλω	I command (I pass a message along a line).
παρακαλέω	I call to my side, I summon, I admonish, I exhort, I entreat, I comfort, I encourage.
ὑπάγω	I withdraw myself, I depart. (I drive or draw under.)
ὑπάρχει	He is (he begins below, he commences).

Notice also the derived nouns ἐπαγγελία a promise, παραγγελία a command, ὁ Παράκλητος the Advocate, or the Comforter.

Exercise 38

1. ἔπρεπεν γὰρ αὐτῷ, δι' ὃν τὰ πάντα καὶ δι' οὗ τὰ πάντα, τὸν ἀρχηγὸν τῆς σωτηρίας αὐτῶν διὰ παθημάτων τελειῶσαι.

2. εἰ δὲ Χριστὸς ἐν ὑμῖν, τὸ μὲν σῶμα νεκρὸν δι' ἁμαρτίαν, τὸ δὲ πνεῦμα ζωὴ διὰ δικαιοσύνην.

3. εἰσέλθετε διὰ τῆς στενῆς πύλης.

4. τινὲς μὲν καὶ διὰ φθόνον καὶ ἔριν, τινὲς δὲ καὶ δι' εὐδοκίαν τὸν Χριστὸν κηρύσσουσιν.

5. ἐπειδὴ γὰρ δι' ἀνθρώπου ὁ θάνατος, καὶ δι' ἀνθρώπου ἀνάστασις νεκρῶν.

6. καὶ χρηματισθέντες κατ' ὄναρ μὴ ἀνακάμψαι πρὸς Ἡρώδην, δι' ἄλλης ὁδοῦ ἀνεχώρησαν εἰς τὴν χώραν αὐτῶν.

7. καὶ ἰδού, ὥρμησε πᾶσα ἡ ἀγέλη τῶν χοίρων κατὰ τοῦ κρημνοῦ εἰς τὴν θάλασσαν.

PREPOSITIONS

8. καθ' ἡμέραν πρὸς ὑμᾶς ἐκαθεζόμην διδάσκων ἐν τῷ ἱερῷ.
9. ἡ γὰρ σὰρξ ἐπιθυμεῖ κατὰ τοῦ πνεύματος, τὸ δὲ πνεῦμα κατὰ τῆς σαρκός.
10. εἰ ὁ θεὸς ὑπὲρ ἡμῶν, τίς καθ' ἡμῶν;
11. κατὰ τὴν πίστιν ὑμῶν γενηθῇ ὑμῖν.
12. ὃς γὰρ οὐκ ἔστι καθ' ἡμῶν, ὑπὲρ ἡμῶν ἐστιν.
13. μὴ κρίνετε κατ' ὄψιν, ἀλλὰ τὴν δικαίαν κρίσιν κρίνετε.
14. καὶ κατὰ πάσας τὰς συναγωγὰς πολλάκις τιμωρῶν αὐτούς, ἠνάγκαζον βλασφημεῖν.
15. τὸ δὲ πέλαγος τὸ κατὰ τὴν Κιλικίαν καὶ Παμφυλίαν διαπλεύσαντες, κατήλθομεν εἰς Μύρα.
16. καὶ ἀπολαβόμενος αὐτὸν ἀπὸ τοῦ ὄχλου κατ' ἰδίαν, ἔβαλε τοὺς δακτύλους αὐτοῦ εἰς τὰ ὦτα αὐτοῦ.
17. καὶ καλέσουσιν τὸ ὄνομα αὐτοῦ Ἐμμανουὴλ ὅ ἐστι μεθερμηνευόμενον Μεθ' ἡμῶν ὁ θεός.
18. ἔπειτα μετὰ ἔτη τρία ἀνῆλθον εἰς Ἱεροσόλυμα.
19. ἄγωμεν καὶ ἡμεῖς ἵνα ἀποθάνωμεν μετ' αὐτοῦ.
20. καὶ περὶ ἐνδύματος τί μεριμνᾶτε;
21. καὶ ἐκάθητο περὶ αὐτὸν ὄχλος.
22. περὶ δὲ τῆς ἡμέρας ἐκείνης οὐδεὶς οἶδεν.
23. καὶ ἐξελθὼν περὶ τρίτην ὥραν εἶδεν ἄλλους ἑστῶτας ἀργούς.
24. οὐ περὶ τούτων δὲ ἐρωτῶ μόνον.

Exercise 38 a

1. ὁ ποιμὴν ὁ καλὸς τὴν ψυχὴν αὐτοῦ τίθησιν ὑπὲρ τῶν προβάτων.
2. οὐκ ἔστι μαθητὴς ὑπὲρ τὸν διδάσκαλον.
3. τοῦτό ἐστι τὸ σῶμά μου τὸ ὑπὲρ ὑμῶν διδόμενον.
4. ὁ φιλῶν πατέρα ἢ μητέρα ὑπὲρ ἐμὲ οὐκ ἔστι μου ἄξιος.
5. διὸ καὶ ὁ θεὸς αὐτὸν ὑπερύψωσεν, καὶ ἐχαρίσατο αὐτῷ ὄνομα τὸ ὑπὲρ πᾶν ὄνομα.
6. καὶ γὰρ ἐγὼ ἄνθρωπός εἰμι ὑπὸ ἐξουσίαν, ἔχων ὑπ' ἐμαυτὸν στρατιώτας.
7. ἐγενόμην τοῖς ὑπὸ νόμον ὡς ὑπὸ νόμον, μὴ ὢν αὐτὸς ὑπὸ νόμον, ἵνα τοὺς ὑπὸ νόμον κερδήσω.

EXERCISES

8. ἵνα πληρωθῇ τὸ ῥηθὲν ὑπὸ Κυρίου διὰ τοῦ προφήτου.
9. ὁ ἐπὶ τοῦ δώματος μὴ καταβάτω ἆραι τὰ ἐκ τῆς οἰκίας αὐτοῦ.
10. καὶ ὁ πεσὼν ἐπὶ τὸν λίθον τοῦτον συνθλασθήσεται.
11. ἐπὶ τοῦ βήματος Καίσαρος ἑστώς εἰμι.
12. οὐδὲ καίουσιν λύχνον καὶ τιθέασιν αὐτὸν ὑπὸ τὸν μόδιον, ἀλλ' ἐπὶ τὴν λυχνίαν.
13. καὶ πολλοὶ λεπροὶ ἦσαν ἐν τῷ Ἰσραὴλ ἐπὶ Ἐλισαίου τοῦ προφήτου.
14. ἐξεπλήσσοντο οἱ ὄχλοι ἐπὶ τῇ διδαχῇ αὐτοῦ.
15. παραγγέλλω σοι ἐνώπιον Χριστοῦ Ἰησοῦ τοῦ μαρτυρήσαντος ἐπὶ Ποντίου Πειλάτου τὴν καλὴν ὁμολογίαν.
16. καὶ πολλοὶ ἐπὶ τῇ γενέσει αὐτοῦ χαρήσονται.
17. ἐγένετο ἄνθρωπος ἀπεσταλμένος παρὰ θεοῦ.
18. ἤνεγκεν τὸ χρῆμα καὶ ἔθηκεν παρὰ τοὺς πόδας τῶν ἀποστόλων.
19. ὁ δὲ Ἰησοῦς, ἐπιλαβόμενος παιδίου, ἔστησεν αὐτὸ παρ' ἑαυτῷ.
20. ἕτεροι δὲ πειράζοντες, σημεῖον ἐξ οὐρανοῦ ἐζήτουν παρ' αὐτοῦ.
21. εἴ τις ὑμᾶς εὐαγγελίζεται παρ' ὃ παρελάβετε, ἀνάθεμα ἔστω.
22. παρὰ ἀνθρώποις τοῦτο ἀδύνατόν ἐστιν, παρὰ δὲ τῷ θεῷ πάντα δυνατά.
23. δοκεῖτε ὅτι οἱ Γαλιλαῖοι οὗτοι ἁμαρτωλοὶ παρὰ πάντας τοὺς Γαλιλαίους ἐγένοντο, ὅτι τοιαῦτα πεπόνθασιν;
24. καὶ διαφημίσθη ὁ λόγος οὗτος παρὰ Ἰουδαίοις μέχρι τῆς σήμερον.

Exercise 38 b

1. ἠλάττωσας αὐτὸν βραχύ τι παρ' ἀγγέλους.
2. καὶ νῦν δόξασόν με σύ, Πάτερ, παρὰ σεαυτῷ τῇ δόξῃ ᾗ[1] εἶχον πρὸ τοῦ τὸν κόσμον εἶναι παρὰ σοί.
3. παρὰ τὸν νόμον οὗτος ἀναπείθει τοὺς ἀνθρώπους σέβεσθαι τὸν θεόν.
4. θεμέλιον γὰρ ἄλλον οὐδεὶς δύναται θεῖναι παρὰ τὸν κείμενον.
5. καὶ ἔρχεται πρὸς τοὺς μαθητὰς καὶ εὑρίσκει αὐτοὺς καθεύδοντας.
6. εἶπεν δὲ πρὸς αὐτὸν ὁ ἄγγελος· Μὴ φοβοῦ, Ζαχαρία.
7. πᾶν ὃ δίδωσί μοι ὁ Πατὴρ πρὸς ἐμὲ ἥξει, καὶ τὸν ἐρχόμενον πρός με οὐ μὴ ἐκβάλω ἔξω.
8. δικαιωθέντες οὖν ἐκ πίστεως εἰρήνην ἔχομεν πρὸς τὸν θεὸν διὰ τοῦ Κυρίου ἡμῶν Ἰησοῦ Χριστοῦ.

[1] Short Syntax, § 63.

PREPOSITIONS

9. ὁ καιρός μου ἐγγύς ἐστιν, πρὸς σὲ ποιῶ τὸ πάσχα.
10. ὦ γενεὰ ἄπιστος, ἕως πότε πρὸς ὑμᾶς ἔσομαι; φέρετε αὐτὸν πρός με.
11. ταῦτα δὲ πάντα τυπικῶς συνέβαινεν ἐκείνοις, ἐγράφη δὲ πρὸς νουθεσίαν ἡμῶν.
12. καὶ ἐάν τις ἁμάρτῃ, παράκλητον ἔχομεν πρὸς τὸν Πατέρα.
13. τίς κοινωνία φωτὶ πρὸς σκότος;
14. ἐὰν αὐτὸν θέλω μένειν ἕως ἔρχομαι, τί πρὸς σέ;
15. οὗτος ἦν ἐν ἀρχῇ πρὸς τὸν θεόν.
16. ἀναστὰς πορεύσομαι πρὸς τὸν πατέρα μου.
17. δεῦτε πρός με πάντες οἱ κοπιῶντες.

Exercise 38 c

1. καὶ ἀναβλέψας ἔλεγεν· Βλέπω τοὺς ἀνθρώπους, ὅτι ὡς δένδρα ὁρῶ περιπατοῦντας.
2. καὶ ὁ Ἰησοῦς εἶπεν αὐτῷ· Ἀνάβλεψον, ἡ πίστις σου σέσωκέ σε.
3. πολύς τε ὄχλος τῶν ἱερέων ὑπήκουον τῇ πίστει.
4. ἐὰν δὲ παρακούσῃ αὐτῶν, εἶπον τῇ ἐκκλησίᾳ.
5. ἐν τῷ νόμῳ τί γέγραπται; πῶς ἀναγιγνώσκεις;
6. ὁ δὲ ἐπιτιμήσας αὐτοὺς παρήγγειλεν μηδενὶ λέγειν.
7. οἱ δὲ ἀκούσαντες ἐχάρησαν καὶ ἐπηγγείλαντο αὐτῷ ἀργύριον δοῦναι.
8. μακάριοι οἱ πενθοῦντες, ὅτι αὐτοὶ παρακληθήσονται.
9. καὶ ἔρχεται πρὸς αὐτὸν λεπρός, παρακαλῶν αὐτόν.
10. παρακαλῶ οὖν ὑμᾶς ἐγὼ ὁ δέσμιος ἐν Κυρίῳ, ἀξίως περιπατῆσαι τῆς κλήσεως.
11. αὐτὸς ἄρχων τῆς συναγωγῆς ὑπῆρχε.
12. ἡμῶν γὰρ ἡ πολίτευμα ἐν οὐρανοῖς ὑπάρχει.
13. ὁ γὰρ μικρότερος ἐν πᾶσιν ὑμῖν ὑπάρχων, οὗτός ἐστιν μέγας.
14. ὕπαγε σεαυτὸν δεῖξον τῷ ἱερεῖ.
15. καὶ ὁ περιπατῶν ἐν τῇ σκοτίᾳ οὐκ οἶδεν ποῦ ὑπάγει.
16. ὁ μὲν υἱὸς τοῦ ἀνθρώπου ὑπάγει καθὼς γέγραπται περὶ αὐτοῦ.
17. διατί καὶ ὑμεῖς παραβαίνετε τὴν ἐντολὴν τοῦ θεοῦ διὰ τὴν παράδοσιν ὑμῶν;
18. καὶ ἤρξαντο πάντες παραιτεῖσθαι.
19. εἰ μὲν οὖν ἀδικῶ καὶ ἄξιον θανάτου πέπραχά τι, οὐ παραιτοῦμαι τὸ ἀποθανεῖν.
20. μετανοεῖτε· ἤγγικε γὰρ ἡ βασιλεία τῶν οὐρανῶν.
21. ἡμεῖς οἴδαμεν ὅτι μεταβεβήκαμεν ἐκ τοῦ θανάτου εἰς τὴν ζωήν.

LESSON XXXIX

CONDITIONAL SENTENCES

Conditional Sentences are sentences which contain a subordinate clause which states a supposition and a principal clause which states the result of the fulfilment of this supposition.

The subordinate clause is called the **protasis**, and the principal clause is called the **apodosis**.

Example: If you do this you will become rich.

Here "If you do this" is the Protasis, and "you will become rich" is the Apodosis.

The Protasis is introduced by εἰ "if."

The particle ἄν is regularly joined to εἰ in the Protasis when the verb in the Protasis is in the Subjunctive mood: εἰ combined with ἄν forms ἐάν, ἤν, ἄν.

The negative of the Protasis is μή and that of the Apodosis is οὐ. In the New Testament, however, οὐ is sometimes found in a Protasis, especially when the verb is in the Indicative mood.

The construction of Conditional sentences varies according as the time of the supposition is Past, Present, or Future.

Future suppositions and one class of Present and Past suppositions have already been treated of, and will cause no difficulty.

Examples: Supposition in Present or Past time implying nothing as to the fulfilment of the condition. The Indicative mood is used in the Protasis just as in English; any part of the finite verb may stand in the Apodosis.

If thou art the son of God, command this stone...
εἰ υἱὸς εἶ τοῦ θεοῦ, εἰπὲ τῷ λίθῳ τούτῳ...   Lk. iv. 3.

For if Abraham was justified by works, he hath whereof to glory.
εἰ γὰρ Ἀβραὰμ ἐξ ἔργων ἐδικαιώθη, ἔχει καύχημα.   Rom. iv. 2.

Supposition in Future time. Either εἰ with the Future Indicative in the Protasis and the Future Indicative or some other form expressing

CONDITIONAL SENTENCES

future time in the Apodosis, or ἐάν with the Subjunctive in the Protasis and the Future or some form expressing future time in the Apodosis. The latter form is the more common. Note that in English we seldom use the Future in the Protasis of such sentences as these, but the Present, which has acquired a certain future sense.

> If we deny him, he will deny us.
> εἰ ἀρνησόμεθα, κἀκεῖνος ἀρνήσεται ἡμᾶς.   2 Tim. ii. 12.

If all shall be offended in thee, I never will be offended.
εἰ πάντες σκανδαλισθήσονται ἐν σοί, ἐγὼ οὐδέποτε σκανδαλισθήσομαι.
Mt. xxvi. 33.

> If thou wilt thou canst make me clean.
> ἐὰν θέλῃς δύνασαί με καθαρίσαι.   Mk i. 40.

All this will I give thee, if thou wilt fall down and worship me.
ταῦτά σοι πάντα δώσω, ἐὰν πεσὼν προσκυνήσῃς μοι.   Mt. iv. 9.

> If I must die with thee, I will never deny thee.
> ἐὰν δέῃ με συναποθανεῖν σοι, οὐ μή σε ἀπαρνήσομαι.
> Mk xiv. 31.

It will be noticed that in all the sentences given above nothing is implied as to the fulfilment or non-fulfilment of the condition stated in the Protasis.

But in some conditional sentences it is distinctly implied that the condition **is not**, or **was not fulfilled**.

Examples. Present time:
> If you were wise, you would not do this.

Past time:
> If you had been wise, you would not have done this.

In Greek such sentences as these have a construction which is so different from that which is found in English that it demands special attention.

The form which such sentences take in English is no guide whatever to the way in which they should be translated into Greek.

The rules given below must be carefully mastered and remembered.

EXERCISES

When the Protasis states a present or past supposition implying that the condition is not or was not fulfilled, the **secondary tenses** of the **indicative** are used both in the protasis and the apodosis.

The verb in the apodosis nearly always has the adverb ἄν.

The Imperfect denotes continued action.

The Aorist simple fact.

The time of the action is implied in the **context** rather than expressed by the tense of the verb[1].

Examples. Present time:

This man, if he were a prophet, would know who and what the woman is...

οὗτος εἰ ἦν προφήτης, ἐγίνωσκεν ἂν τίς καὶ ποταπὴ ἡ γυνή...

Lk. vii. 39.

If thou knewest the gift of God, and who it is that speaketh with thee, thou wouldst have asked him...

εἰ ᾔδεις τὴν δωρεὰν τοῦ θεοῦ, καὶ τίς ἐστιν ὁ λέγων σοι,...σὺ ἂν ᾔτησας αὐτόν... Jn iv. 10.

If ye believed Moses ye would believe me.

εἰ γὰρ ἐπιστεύετε Μωϋσεῖ, ἐπιστεύετε ἂν ἐμοί. Jn v. 46.

Past time:

For if they had known, they would not have crucified the Lord of Glory.

εἰ γὰρ ἔγνωσαν, οὐκ ἂν τὸν κύριον τῆς δόξης ἐσταύρωσαν.

1 Cor. ii. 8.

Exercise 39

1. ἡ βασιλεία ἡ ἐμὴ οὐκ ἔστιν ἐκ τοῦ κόσμου τούτου, εἰ ἐκ τοῦ κόσμου τούτου ἦν ἡ βασιλεία ἡ ἐμή, οἱ ὑπηρέται οἱ ἐμοὶ ἠγωνίζοντο ἂν ἵνα μὴ παραδοθῶ τοῖς Ἰουδαίοις. 2. εἰ ἤμεθα ἐν ταῖς ἡμέραις τῶν πατέρων ἡμῶν, οὐκ ἂν ἤμεθα κοινωνοὶ ἐν τῷ αἵματι τῶν προφητῶν. 3. εἰ ᾔδει ὁ οἰκοδεσπότης ποίᾳ

---

[1] (But as a rough rule it may be said that the Imperfect expresses an unfulfilled condition in present time, and the Aorist expresses an unfulfilled condition in past time.)

136 CONDITIONAL SENTENCES

φυλακῇ ὁ κλέπτης ἔρχεται, ἐγρηγόρησεν ἄν. 4. εἰ ἠγαπᾶτέ με ἐχάρητε ἂν ὅτι πορεύομαι πρὸς τὸν πατέρα. 5. ἐὰν ᾖ ἐξ ἀνθρώπων ἡ βουλὴ αὕτη, καταλυθήσεται, εἰ δὲ ἐκ θεοῦ ἐστίν, οὐ δυνήσεσθε καταλῦσαι αὐτήν. 6. εἰ γὰρ ἐγνώκειτε τί ἐστιν Ἔλεος θέλω καὶ οὐ θυσίαν, οὐκ ἂν κατεδικάσατε τοὺς ἀναιτίους. 7. οὐαί σοι Χοραζείν, οὐαί σοι Βηθσαιδάν, ὅτι εἰ ἐν Τύρῳ καὶ Σιδῶνι ἐγένοντο αἱ δυνάμεις αἱ γενόμεναι ἐν ὑμῖν, πάλαι ἂν ἐν σάκκῳ καὶ σποδῷ μετενόησαν. 8. ἐὰν δὲ τὸ ἅλας μωρανθῇ, ἐν τίνι ἁλισθήσεται; 9. Κύριε, εἰ ἦς ὧδε, οὐκ αν ἀπέθανεν ὁ ἀδελφός μου. 10. ἐὰν μὴ περισσεύσῃ ὑμῶν ἡ δικαιοσύνη πλεῖον τῶν γραμματέων καὶ Φαρισαίων, οὐ μὴ εἰσέλθητε εἰς τὴν βασιλείαν τῶν οὐρανῶν. 11. εἰ ἐμὲ ᾔδειτε, καὶ τὸν πατέρα μου ἂν ᾔδειτε. 12. ἐὰν γὰρ ἀφῆτε τοῖς ἀνθρώποις τὰ παραπτώματα αὐτῶν, ἀφήσει καὶ ὑμῖν ὁ πατὴρ ὑμῶν ὁ οὐράνιος. 13. εἰ τυφλοὶ ἦτε οὐκ ἂν εἴχετε ἁμαρτίαν. 14. εἰ θέλεις εἰσελθεῖν εἰς τὴν ζωήν, τήρει τὰς ἐντολάς. 15. εἰ ὁ θεὸς πατὴρ ὑμῶν ἦν, ἠγαπᾶτε ἂν ἐμέ, ἐγὼ γὰρ ἐκ τοῦ θεοῦ ἐξῆλθον καὶ ἥκω. 16. εἰ κακῶς ἐλάλησα, μαρτύρησον περὶ τοῦ κακοῦ. 17. εἰ ἔτι ἀνθρώποις ἤρεσκον, Χριστοῦ δοῦλος οὐκ ἂν ἤμην. 18. εἰ νεκροὶ οὐκ ἐγείρονται, οὐδὲ Χριστὸς ἐγήγερται. 19. εἰ υἱὸς εἶ τοῦ θεοῦ, κατάβηθι ἀπὸ τοῦ σταυροῦ.

READING EXERCISES

These pieces for reading are taken from the *Shepherd of Hermas*, an early piece of allegorical writing, attributed by some to the first and by some to the early second century, and from the so-called *Second Epistle of Clement*, which is now generally supposed to be a sermon by one of the early Bishops of Rome.

The references marked S. are to paragraphs in the writer's *N.T. Syntax*.

READING EXERCISES

I

Νηστεύων καὶ καθήμενος εἰς ὄρος τι καὶ εὐχαριστῶν τῷ Κυρίῳ περὶ πάντων ὧν[1] ἐποίησε μετ' ἐμοῦ, βλέπω τὸν ποιμένα παρακαθήμενόν[2] μοι καὶ λέγοντα· Τί ὀρθρινὸς ὧδε ἐλήλυθας; Ὅτι, φημί, κύριε, στατίωνα[3] ἔχω. Τί, φησίν, ἐστὶ στατίων; Νηστεύω, φημί, κύριε. Νηστεία δέ, φησί, τί ἐστιν αὕτη, ἣν[4] νηστεύετε; Ὡς εἰώθειν[5], φημί, κύριε, οὕτω νηστεύω. Οὐκ οἴδατε, φησί, νηστεύειν τῷ Κυρίῳ, οὐδέ ἐστι νηστεία αὕτη ἡ ἀνωφελής, ἣν νηστεύετε αὐτῷ. Διατί, φημί, κύριε, τοῦτο λέγεις; Λέγω σοι, φησίν, ὅτι οὐκ ἔστιν αὕτη νηστεία, ἣν δοκεῖτε νηστεύειν. ἀλλὰ ἐγώ σε διδάξω τί ἐστι νηστεία δεκτὴ καὶ πλήρης τῷ Κυρίῳ. ἄκουε, φησίν, ὁ θεὸς οὐ βούλεται τοιαύτην νηστείαν ματαίαν· οὕτω γὰρ νηστεύων τῷ θεῷ οὐδὲν ἐργάσῃ τῇ δικαιοσύνῃ. νήστευσον δὲ τῷ θεῷ νηστείαν τοιαύτην· μηδὲν πονηρεύσῃ[6] ἐν τῇ ζωῇ σου. ἀλλὰ δούλευσον τῷ Κυρίῳ ἐν καθαρᾷ καρδίᾳ· τήρησον τὰς ἐντολὰς αὐτοῦ πορευόμενος ἐν τοῖς προστάγμασιν[7] αὐτοῦ καὶ μηδεμία ἐπιθυμία πονηρὰ ἀναβήτω ἐν τῇ καρδίᾳ σου, πίστευσον δὲ τῷ θεῷ, ὅτι ἐὰν ταῦτα ἐργάσῃ καὶ φοβηθῇς αὐτὸν καὶ ἐγκρατεύσῃ ἀπὸ παντὸς πονηροῦ πράγματος, ζήσῃ τῷ θεῷ· καὶ ταῦτα ἐὰν ἐργάσῃ, μεγάλην νηστείαν ποιήσεις καὶ δεκτὴν τῷ θεῷ.

II

Πορευομένου μου εἰς Κώμας περιπατῶν ἀνεμνήσθην[8] τῆς ὁράσεως, καὶ πάλιν με αἴρει Πνεῦμα καὶ ἀποφέρει εἰς τὸν αὐτὸν τόπον. ἐλθὼν οὖν εἰς τὸν τόπον τίθω τὰ γόνατα καὶ ἠρξάμην προσεύχεσθαι τῷ Κυρίῳ καὶ δοξάζειν αὐτοῦ τὸ ὄνομα, ὅτι με ἄξιον ἡγήσατο καὶ ἐγνώρισέν μοι τὰς ἁμαρτίας μου τὰς πρότερον. μετὰ δὲ τὸ ἐγερθῆναί με ἀπὸ τῆς προσευχῆς βλέπω ἀπέναντί μου τὴν πρεσβυτέραν, ἣν καὶ πρότερον ἑωράκειν[9], περιπατοῦσαν καὶ ἀναγιγνώσκουσαν βιβλίον, καὶ λέγει μοι· Δύνῃ ταῦτα τοῖς ἐκλεκτοῖς τοῦ

---

[1] Attraction of relative, S. 63 [2] παρακάθημαι, I sit by.
[3] στατίων, the Latin word "statio," a technical Christian term for a fast.
[4] Cognate accusative, S. 17.
[5] εἰώθειν, 1st person pluperfect from ἔθω.
[6] πονηρεύω, I do wrong. [7] πρόσταγμα, a command.
[8] ἀναμιμνήσκω, I remind: in pass., I remember, followed by a genitive.
[9] ἑωράκειν, pluperfect from ὁράω.

θεοῦ ἀναγγεῖλαι; λέγω αὐτῇ· Κυρία, τοσαῦτα μνημονεῦσαι οὐ δύναμαι. δὸς δέ μοι τὸ βιβλίον, ἵνα μεταγράψωμαι[1] αὐτό. Λάβε, φησίν, καὶ ἀποδώσεις μοι. ἔλαβον ἐγώ, καὶ εἴς τινα τόπον τοῦ ἀγροῦ ἀναχωρήσας μετεγραψάμην πάντα. τελέσαντος οὖν τὰ γράμματα τοῦ βιβλίου ἡρπάγη[2] μου ἐκ τῆς χειρὸς τὸ βιβλίον· ὑπὸ τίνος δὲ οὐκ εἶδον.

III

ἔδειξέ μοι δένδρα πολλὰ μὴ ἔχοντα φύλλα, ἀλλ' ὡσεὶ ξηρὰ[3] ἐδόκει μοι εἶναι· ὅμοια γὰρ ἦν[3] πάντα. καὶ λέγει μοι· Βλέπεις τὰ δένδρα ταῦτα; Βλέπω, φημί, κύριε, ὅμοια ὄντα καὶ ξηρά. ἀποκριθείς μοι λέγει· Ταῦτα τὰ δένδρα ἃ βλέπεις, οἱ κατοικοῦντές εἰσιν ἐν τῷ αἰῶνι τούτῳ. Διατί οὖν, φημί, κύριε, ὡσεὶ ξηρά εἰσι καὶ ὅμοια; Ὅτι, φησίν, οὔτε οἱ δίκαιοι φαίνονται οὔτε οἱ ἁμαρτωλοὶ ἐν τῷ αἰῶνι τούτῳ, ἀλλ' ὅμοιοί εἰσιν· ὁ γὰρ αἰὼν οὗτος τοῖς δικαίοις χειμών ἐστι, καὶ οὐ φαίνονται μετὰ τῶν ἁμαρτωλῶν κατοικοῦντες. ὥσπερ γὰρ ἐν τῷ χειμῶνι τὰ δένδρα ἀποβεβληκότα τὰ φύλλα ὅμοιά εἰσι καὶ οὐ φαίνονται τὰ ξηρὰ ποῖά εἰσιν, ἢ τὰ ζῶντα· οὕτως ἐν τῷ αἰῶνι τούτῳ οὐ φαίνονται οὔτε οἱ δίκαιοι οὔτε οἱ ἁμαρτωλοί, ἀλλὰ πάντες ὅμοιοί εἰσιν.

IV

ὑπῆγον εἰς ἀγρόν, καὶ ἰδού, βλέπω κονιορτὸν ὡς εἰς τὸν οὐρανὸν καὶ ἠρξάμην λέγειν ἐν ἐμαυτῷ· Μήποτε κτήνη ἔρχονται καὶ κονιορτὸν ἐγείρουσιν; οὕτω δὲ ἦν ἀπ' ἐμοῦ ὡς ἀπὸ σταδίου.

γινομένου μείζονος καὶ μείζονος κονιορτοῦ ἐπενόησα[4] εἶναί τι θεῖον· μικρὸν ἐξέλαμψεν ὁ ἥλιος καὶ ἰδού, βλέπω θηρίον μέγιστον καὶ ἐκ τοῦ στόματος αὐτοῦ ἀκρίδες πύριναι ἐξεπορεύοντο· ἦν δὲ τὸ θηρίον τῷ μήκει ὡσεὶ ποδῶν ἑκατόν, τὴν δὲ κεφαλὴν εἶχεν ὡσεὶ κεράμου. καὶ ἠρξάμην κλαίειν καὶ ἐρωτᾶν τὸν Κύριον, ἵνα με λυτρώσηται ἀπ' αὐτοῦ. ἐνδυσάμενος οὖν τὴν πίστιν τοῦ Κυρίου, θαρσήσας εἰς τὸ θηρίον ἐμαυτὸν ἔδωκα. ἔρχομαι

---

[1] μεταγράφω, I transcribe.
[2] ἡρπάγη, 2 aor. pass. from ἁρπάζω.
[3] Neuter plural nouns may be followed by a singular verb.
[4] ἐπινοέω, I perceive.

ἐγγὺς αὐτοῦ, καὶ τὸ θηρίον ἐκτεῖναι ἑαυτὸ χαμαὶ καὶ οὐδὲν εἰ μὴ τὴν γλῶσσαν προέβαλλεν καὶ ὅλως οὐκ ἐκινήθη μέχρις ὅτε παρῆλθον αὐτό. εἶχεν δὲ τὸ θηρίον ἐπὶ τῆς κεφαλῆς χρώματα[1] τέσσαρα μέλαν, εἶτα πυροειδὲς[2] καὶ αἱματῶδες[3], εἶτα χρυσοῦν, εἶτα λευκόν. μετὰ δὲ τὸ παρελθεῖν με τὸ θηρίον[4] καὶ προελθεῖν ὡσεὶ πόδας τριάκοντα ὑπαντᾷ μοι παρθένος κεκοσμημένη ὡς ἐκ νυμφῶνος ἐκπορευομένη. ἔγνων ἐγὼ ἐκ τῶν προτέρων ὁραμάτων, ὅτι ἡ Ἐκκλησία ἐστίν, καὶ ἱλαρώτερος ἐγενόμην. ἀσπάζεταί με λέγουσα· Χαῖρε σύ, ἄνθρωπε. καὶ ἐγὼ αὐτὴν ἀντησπασάμην[5]· Κυρία, χαῖρε. ἀποκριθεῖσά μοι λέγει· Οὐδέν σοι ἀπήντησεν; λέγω αὐτῇ· Κυρία, τηλικοῦτο θηρίον, δυνάμενον λαοὺς διαφθεῖραι· ἀλλὰ τῇ δυνάμει τοῦ Κυρίου καὶ τῇ πολυσπλαγχνίᾳ[6] αὐτοῦ ἐξέφυγον αὐτό. Καλῶς ἐξέφυγες, φησίν, ὅτι τὴν μέριμνάν σου ἐπὶ τὸν θεὸν ἐπέριψας καὶ τὴν καρδίαν σου ἤνοιξας πρὸς τὸν Κύριον, πιστεύσας ὅτι δι' οὐδενὸς δύνῃ σωθῆναι εἰ μὴ διὰ τοῦ μεγάλου καὶ ἐνδόξου ὀνόματος. μεγάλην θλίψιν ἐκπέφευγας[7] διὰ τὴν πίστιν σου καὶ ὅτι τηλικοῦτο θηρίον ἰδὼν οὐκ ἐδιψύχησας[8]. ὕπαγε οὖν καὶ ἐξήγησαι τοῖς ἐκλεκτοῖς τοῦ Κυρίου τὰ μεγαλεῖα αὐτοῦ καὶ εἰπὲ αὐτοῖς ὅτι τὸ θηρίον τοῦτο τύπος ἐστὶν θλίψεως τῆς μελλούσης τῆς μεγάλης· ἐὰν οὖν προετοιμάσησθε καὶ μετανοήσητε ἐξ ὅλης καρδίας ὑμῶν πρὸς τὸν Κύριον, δυνήσεσθε ἐκφυγεῖν αὐτήν, ἐὰν ἡ καρδία ὑμῶν γένηται καθαρὰ καὶ ἄμωμος καὶ τὰς λοιπὰς τῆς ζωῆς ἡμέρας ὑμῶν δουλεύσητε τῷ Κυρίῳ ἀμέμπτως.

V

ἀδελφοί, οὕτως δεῖ ἡμᾶς φρονεῖν περὶ Ἰησοῦ Χριστοῦ, ὡς περὶ θεοῦ, ὡς περὶ κριτοῦ ζώντων καὶ νεκρῶν· καὶ οὐ δεῖ ἡμᾶς μικρὰ φρονεῖν περὶ τῆς σωτηρίας ἡμῶν. ἐν τῷ γὰρ φρονεῖν ἡμᾶς μικρὰ περὶ αὐτοῦ, μικρὰ καὶ ἐλπίζομεν λαβεῖν. καὶ ἡμεῖς ἁμαρτάνομεν οὐκ εἰδότες πόθεν ἐκλήθημεν, καὶ ὑπὸ τίνος, καὶ εἰς ὃν τόπον, καὶ ὅσα ὑπέμεινεν Ἰησοῦς Χριστὸς παθεῖν ἕνεκα

[1] χρῶμα, colour.
[2] πυροειδής, like fire.
[3] αἱματώδης, like blood.
[4] S. 173.
[5] ἀντασπάζομαι, I greet in return.
[6] πολυσπλαγχνία, lovingkindness.
[7] ἐκπέφευγας, 2nd perf. from ἐκφεύγω.
[8] διψυχέω, I doubt, I am of double mind.

ἡμῶν. τίνα οὖν ἡμεῖς αὐτῷ δώσομεν ἀντιμισθίαν, ἢ τίνα καρπὸν ἄξιον οὗ[1] ἡμῖν αὐτὸς ἔδωκεν; τὸ φῶς γὰρ ἡμῖν ἐχαρίσατο, ὡς πατὴρ υἱοὺς ἡμᾶς προσηγόρευσεν, ἀπολλυμένους ἡμᾶς ἔσωσεν. πηροὶ ὄντες τῇ διανοίᾳ, προσκυνοῦντες λίθους καὶ ξύλα καὶ χρυσὸν καὶ ἄργυρον καὶ χαλκόν, ἔργα ἀνθρώπων. καὶ ὁ βίος ἡμῶν ὅλος ἄλλο οὐδὲν ἦν εἰ μὴ θάνατος. ἠλέησεν γὰρ ἡμᾶς καὶ σπλαγχνισθεὶς ἔσωσεν, θεασάμενος ἐν ἡμῖν πολλὴν πλάνην καὶ ἀπώλειαν. ἐκάλεσεν γὰρ ἡμᾶς οὐκ ὄντας[2] καὶ ἠθέλησεν ἐκ μὴ ὄντος εἶναι[2] ἡμᾶς.

[1] S. 63.

[2] οὐκ ὄντας, μὴ ὄντος, εἶναι. All these parts of εἶναι are used here in the sense of "existing," and are not simple copulatives; for example, μὴ ὄντος should be translated "non-existence."

ACCENTUATION

There are three accents in Greek, the Acute accent ', the Grave accent `, and the Circumflex accent ˆ.

The Acute accent can stand on any of the last three syllables of a word, the Circumflex accent can only stand on one of the last two syllables of a word, the Grave accent can only stand on the last syllable of a word.

A word with an Acute accent on the last syllable is said to be **oxytone** or sharp toned, if the accent is on the last syllable but one the word is said to be **paroxytone**, if the accent is on the last syllable but two the word is said to be **proparoxytone.**

A word with a Circumflex accent on the last syllable is said to be **perispomenon**, if the accent is on the last syllable but one the word is said to be **properispomenon.**

A word with a Grave accent on the last syllable is said to be **barytone** or flat toned.

The last syllable but two cannot be accented unless the last syllable is short.

If the last syllable but one contains a long vowel or a diphthong and at the same time the last syllable is short, the last syllable but one is accented with a circumflex accent, if it has an accent at all, except in a few special words.

A word which has an acute accent on the last syllable changes this to a grave accent unless it is the last word in a clause or sentence.

For purposes of accentuation final οι and αι are reckoned as short vowels except in the Optative mood.

Examples: ἄνθρωποι, νῆσοι: but ποιήσοι (Opt. Mood).

Accentuation of Nouns and Adjectives

The place of the accent on the Nominative singular must be learnt. All other cases are accented on the same syllable as the Nom. sing. as far as the length of the last syllable permits.

Examples: ἄνθρωπος, ἀνθρώπου,
πρᾶγμα, πράγματος, πραγμάτων.

Exceptions. (1) The Gen. and Dat. of Oxytone nouns of the 1st and 2nd declensions are circumflexed.

Examples: ἀρχή, ἀρχῆς, ἀρχῇ, ἀρχῶν, ἀρχαῖς.
θεός, θεοῦ, θεῷ, θεῶν, θεοῖς.
δίκη, δικῶν.

(2) The Gen. pl. of all nouns of the 1st declension is circumflexed.

(3) Most monosyllables of the 3rd declension accent the last syllable of the Gen. and Dat. in both numbers.

Example: ἅλς, ἁλός, ἁλί, ἁλῶν, ἁλσί.

Accent of Verbs

Verbs throw back their accent as far as the length of the last syllable will permit.

Examples: δουλεύω, δουλεύουσι, δούλευε, ἐδούλευον.

The accent of a verb compounded with a preposition can never precede the augment.

Example: παρεῖχον, not πάρειχον.

For the accentuation of contracted verbs see pages 23, 24.

Exceptions. (1) Participles in inflection are accented as nouns.

Example: βουλεύων, neut. βουλεῦον, not βούλευον.

(2) The 1st Aor. Inf. Act., the 2nd Aor. Inf. Mid., Perf. Pass. Inf. and Part. and Infinitives ending in ναι accent the last syllable but one.

Examples: βουλεῦσαι, γενέσθαι, λελύσθαι, λελυμένος,
ἱστάναι, διδόναι, λελυκέναι.

(3) The 2nd Aor. Participle Active and Participles of the 3rd dec. except the Pres. Part. Act. and the 1st Aor. Part. Act. are accented like Oxytone adjectives.

(4) The 2nd Aor. Inf. Act. ending in ειν and the 2nd sing. 2nd Aor. Imperat. Mid. ending in ου have the circumflex accent on the last syllable.

Examples: εἰπεῖν, γενοῦ.

Enclitics

An Enclitic is a word which loses its own accent and is pronounced as if it were part of the preceding word.

The Enclitics which principally occur in the N.T. are:

(1) The oblique cases of the Personal pronouns of the 1st and 2nd person singular: με, μου, μοι, σε, σου, σοι.

(2) The Indefinite pronouns τις, τι, the Indefinite adverbs ποτε, που, πως, etc., and the conjunction τε.

(3) The Pres. Ind. of εἰμι I am, except the 2nd person singular.

The word before an Enclitic does not change a final Acute accent to a Grave accent.

If the last syllable of the preceding word is accented the accent of the Enclitic is dropped.

Examples: σοφός τις, καλόν ἐστι.

If the preceding word has an Acute accent on the last syllable but two, or a Circumflex accent on the last syllable but one, it receives an Acute accent from the Enclitic on the last syllable as a second accent.

Examples: ἄνθρωπός τις, οὗτός ἐστι.

If the preceding word has an Acute accent on the last syllable but one, it receives no second accent. A monosyllabic Enclitic here drops its accent, a disyllabic Enclitic retains it.

Examples: λόγος τις, λόγοι τινές.

Parts of εἰμί coming after οὐ retain their accent.

Example: οὐκ ἐστὶν οὗτος ἀγαθὸς ἄνθρωπος.

Proclitics

A Proclitic is a word which has no accent; it receives the accent of a following enclitic: εἴ τις.

The most important are the Articles ὁ, ἡ, οἱ, αἱ, the prepositions εἰς, ἐκ ἐξ, ἐν, and the words εἰ, ὡς, οὐ.

Words differing in accent or breathing

ἀλλά	but.
ἄλλα	other things.
αὐτή	nom. fem. sing. of αὐτός.
αὕτη	nom. fem. sing. of οὗτος.
αὐταί	nom. fem. pl. of αὐτός.
αὗται	nom. fem. pl. of οὗτος.
εἰ	if. εἶ thou art.
εἰς	to. εἷς one (masc.).
ἔξω	on the outside; without.
ἕξω	1st sing. fut. act. from ἔχω.
ἐν	in. ἕν one (neuter).
ἡ	nom. fem. sing. of the definite article.
ἥ	nom. fem. sing. of the relative pronoun.
ἤ	or.
ᾗ	dat. fem. sing. of the relative pronoun.
ᾖ	3rd sing. subj. from εἶναι.
ἦν	1st sing. imperf. from εἶναι.
ἤν	another form of ἐάν.
ἥν	acc. fem. sing. of the relative pronoun.
ὁ	nom. masc. sing. of the definite article.
ὅ	nom. and acc. neut. sing. of the relative pronoun.
ὄν	nom. and acc. neut. sing. pres. participle of εἰμί.
ὅν	acc. masc. sing. of the relative pronoun.
οὐ	not.
οὗ	gen. masc. and neut. sing. of the relative pronoun.
ταῦτα	nom. and acc. neut. pl. of οὗτος.
ταὐτά	contracted for τὰ αὐτά.
τίς, τί, etc.	who? what?
τις, τι, etc.	a certain man, a certain thing.
ὦ, ὤ	O, Oh.
ὦ	1st sing. subj. from εἶναι.
ᾧ	dat. masc. and neut. sing. of the relative pronoun.
ὤν	nom. sing. masc. pres. participle of εἰμί.
ὧν	gen. pl. of the relative pronoun.

TABLES OF VERBS

THE REGULAR VERB

As there is no single verb in Greek which is found in every tense, it has been found necessary in the following table to give tenses from several verbs in order to present it complete.

The tenses of the verb λύω are given as far as possible, and the tenses which do not occur in that verb are supplied from the verbs πάσχω, γίνεσθαι, σπείρειν.

The names of the tenses given in brackets are those by which they are commonly called in Greek grammars. They are however in many cases misleading (*Short Syntax*, sections 83, 84).

It is unfortunate that we are compelled by the uses of grammarians to use the name "tense" in connection with the forms of the Greek verb. It directs our attention too much to the time of the action of the verb, whereas it was the **state**[1], rather than the **time**[1], that was most prominently before the mind of a Greek. The time of the action of the verb is often left to be inferred from the context, and cannot be certainly told from the form of the verb. This is almost invariably the case with moods other than the Indicative, and is sometimes the case in the Indicative mood itself.

To the Greek mind the forms to which we give the names "Present" and "Imperfect" denoted **continuous or repeated** action.

The forms to which we give the name "Perfect," or "Pluperfect" denoted action **complete** at the time of speaking, the results of which were regarded as still existing.

The forms to which we give the name "Aorist" denoted a **simple, indefinite** action, and were always used where no stress was laid on the continuity, completion, or incompletion of the action denoted by the verb.

The Future tense in Greek, as in English, refers to future time in all its moods, and is thus an exception to the principle that the tenses of the moods other than the Indicative do not denote time in Greek.

[1] See pages xx, xxi.

THE REGULAR VERB

Tenses denoting continuous or repeated action

Active Voice

(1) In Present time.
(Present Indicative)
λύω
λύεις
λύει
λύομεν
λύετε
λύουσι

(2) In Past time.
(Imperfect Indicative)
ἔλυον
ἔλυες
ἔλυε
ἐλύομεν
ἐλύετε
ἔλυον

(3) At a time denoted by the context.

(Present Imperative)
λῦε
λυέτω
λύετε
λυέτωσαν or λυόντων

(Present Subjunctive)
λύω
λύῃς
λύῃ
λύωμεν
λύητε
λύωσι

(Present Optative)
λύοιμι
λύοις
λύοι
λύοιμεν
λύοιτε
λύοιεν

(Present Infinitive)
λύειν

(Present Participle)
λύων, λύουσα, λῦον
λύοντος κ.τ.λ. (see p. 72).

Middle and Passive Voice

(1) In Present time.
(Present Indicative)
λύομαι
λύῃ or λύει
λύεται
λυόμεθα
λύεσθε
λύονται

(2) In Past time.
(Imperfect Indicative)
ἐλυόμην
ἐλύου
ἐλύετο
ἐλυόμεθα
ἐλύεσθε
ἐλύοντο

(3) At a time determined by the context.

(Present Imperative)
λύου
λυέσθω
λύεσθε
λυέσθωσαν or λυέσθων

(Present Subjunctive)
λύωμαι
λύῃ
λύηται
λυώμεθα
λύησθε
λύωνται

(Present Optative)
λυοίμην
λύοιο
λύοιτο
λυοίμεθα
λύοισθε
λύοιντο

(Present Infinitive)
λύεσθαι

(Present Participle)
λυόμενος, η, ον

Tenses denoting action in Future time

Active Voice

(Future Indicative)	(Future Optative)	(Future Infinitive)	(Future Participle)
λύσω	λύσοιμι	λύσειν	λύσων, λύσουσα, λῦσον
λύσεις	λύσοις		λύσοντος κ.τ.λ. (see p. 72, as λύων).
λύσει	λύσοι		
λύσομεν	λύσοιμεν		
λύσετε	λύσοιτε		
λύσουσι	λύσοιεν		

Middle Voice

(Future Indicative)	(Future Optative)	(Future Infinitive)	(Future Participle)
λύσομαι	λυσοίμην	λύσεσθαι	λυσόμενος, η, ον
λύσῃ or λύσει	λύσοιο		
λύσεται	λύσοιτο		
λυσόμεθα	λυσοίμεθα		
λύσεσθε	λύσοισθε		
λύσονται	λύσοιντο		

Passive Voice

(Future Indicative)	(Future Optative)	(Future Infinitive)	(Future Participle)
λυθήσομαι	λυθησοίμην	λυθήσεσθαι	λυθησόμενος, η, ον
λυθήσῃ or λυθήσει	λυθήσοιο		
λυθήσεται	λυθήσοιτο		
λυθησόμεθα	λυθησοίμεθα		
λυθήσεσθε	λυθήσοισθε		
λυθήσονται	λυθήσοιντο		

Tenses denoting simple or indefinite action

Active Voice

(1) In past time.

(First Aorist Indicative)	(Second Aorist Indicative)
ἔλυσα	ἔπαθον
ἔλυσας	ἔπαθες
ἔλυσε	ἔπαθε
ἐλύσαμεν	ἐπάθομεν
ἐλύσατε	ἐπάθετε
ἔλυσαν	ἔπαθον

THE REGULAR VERB

(2) At a time determined by the context.

(First Aorist Imperative)	(First Aorist Subjunctive)	(First Aorist Optative)
λῦσον	λύσω	λύσαιμι
λυσάτω	λύσῃς	λύσαις or λύσειας
λύσατε	λύσῃ	λύσαι or λύσειε
λυσάτωσαν or λυσάντων	λύσωμεν	λύσαιμεν
	λύσητε	λύσαιτε
	λύσωσι	λύσαιεν or λύσειαν

(First Aorist Infinitive)
λῦσαι

(First Aorist Participle)
λύσας, λύσασα, λῦσαν
λύσαντος κ.τ.λ. (see p. 73).

(Second Aorist Imperative)	(Second Aorist Subjunctive)	(Second Aorist Optative)
πάθε	πάθω	πάθοιμι
παθέτω	πάθῃς	πάθοις
πάθετε	πάθῃ	πάθοι
παθέτωσαν or παθόντων	πάθωμεν	πάθοιμεν
	πάθητε	πάθοιτε
	πάθωσι	πάθοιεν

(Second Aorist Infinitive)
παθεῖν

(Second Aorist Participle)
παθών, παθοῦσα, παθόν
παθόντος κ.τ.λ. (see p. 72, as λύων).

Middle Voice

(1) In past time.

(First Aorist Indicative)	(Second Aorist Indicative)
ἐλυσάμην	ἐγενόμην
ἐλύσω	ἐγένου
ἐλύσατο	ἐγένετο
ἐλυσάμεθα	ἐγενόμεθα
ἐλύσασθε	ἐγένεσθε
ἐλύσαντο	ἐγένοντο

THE REGULAR VERB

(2) At a time determined by the context.

(First Aorist Imperative)	(First Aorist Subjunctive)	(First Aorist Optative)
λῦσαι	λύσωμαι	λυσαίμην
λυσάσθω	λύσῃ	λύσαιο
λύσασθε	λύσηται	λύσαιτο
λυσάσθωσαν or λυσάσθων	λυσώμεθα	λυσαίμεθα
	λύσησθε	λύσαισθε
	λύσωνται	λύσαιντο

(First Aorist Infinitive) (First Aorist Participle)
λύσασθαι   λυσάμενος, η, ον

(Second Aorist Imperative)	(Second Aorist Subjunctive)	(Second Aorist Optative)
γενοῦ	γένωμαι	γενοίμην
γενέσθω	γένῃ	γένοιο
γένεσθε	γένηται	γένοιτο
γενέσθωσαν or γενέσθων	γενώμεθα	γενοίμεθα
	γένησθε	γένοισθε
	γένωνται	γένοιντο

(Second Aorist Infinitive) (Second Aorist Participle)
γενέσθαι   γενόμενος, η, ον

Passive Voice

(1) In Past time.

(First Aorist Indicative)	(Second Aorist Indicative)
ἐλύθην	ἐσπάρην
ἐλύθης	ἐσπάρης
ἐλύθη	ἐσπάρη
ἐλύθημεν	ἐσπάρημεν
ἐλύθητε	ἐσπάρητε
ἐλύθησαν	ἐσπάρησαν

(2) At a time determined by the context.

(First Aorist Imperative)	(First Aorist Subjunctive)	(First Aorist Optative)
λύθητι	λυθῶ	λυθείην
λυθήτω	λυθῇς	λυθείης
λύθητε	λυθῇ	λυθείη
λυθήτωσαν or λυθέντων	λυθῶμεν	λυθείημεν or λυθεῖμεν
	λυθῆτε	λυθείητε or λυθεῖτε
	λυθῶσι	λυθείησαν or λυθεῖεν

THE REGULAR VERB 149

(First Aorist Infinitive)
λυθῆναι

(First Aorist Participle)
λυθείς, λυθεῖσα, λυθέν
λυθέντος κ.τ.λ. (see p. 73).

(Second Aorist Imperative)	(Second Aorist Subjunctive)	(Second Aorist Optative)
σπάρηθι	σπαρῶ	σπαρείην
σπαρήτω	σπαρῇς	σπαρείης
σπάρητε	σπαρῇ	σπαρείη
σπαρήτωσαν or σπαρέντων	σπαρῶμεν	σπαρείημεν or σπαρεῖμεν
	σπαρῆτε	σπαρείητε or σπαρεῖτε
	σπαρῶσι	σπαρείησαν or σπαρεῖεν

(Second Aorist Infinitive)
σπαρῆναι

(Second Aorist Participle)
σπαρείς, σπαρεῖσα, σπαρέν
σπαρέντος κ.τ.λ. (see p. 73, as λυθείς).

Tenses denoting perfect or completed action

Active Voice

(1) In Present time.

(First Perfect Indicative)	(Second Perfect Indicative)
λέλυκα	πέπονθα
λέλυκας	πέπονθας
λέλυκε	πέπονθε
λελύκαμεν	πεπόνθαμεν
λελύκατε	πεπόνθατε
λελύκασι	πεπόνθασι

(2) In Past time.

(Pluperfect Indicative)
ἐλελύκειν
ἐλελύκεις
ἐλελύκει
ἐλελύκειμεν
ἐλελύκειτε
ἐλελύκεσαν or ἐλελύκεισαν

THE REGULAR VERB

(3) At a time determined by the context.

(Perfect Imperative)
λέλυκε
λελυκέτω
λελύκετε
λελυκέτωσαν or λελυκόντων

(Perfect Subjunctive)
λελύκω
λελύκῃς
λελύκῃ
λελύκωμεν
λελύκητε
λελύκωσι

(Perfect Optative)
λελύκοιμι
λελύκοις
λελύκοι
λελύκοιμεν
λελύκοιτε
λελύκοιεν

(Perfect Infinitive)
λελυκέναι

(Perfect Participle)
λελυκώς, λελυκυῖα, λελυκός
λελυκότος κ.τ.λ. (see p. 91).

Middle and Passive Voice

(1) In Present time.
(Perfect Indicative)
λέλυμαι
λέλυσαι
λέλυται
λελύμεθα
λέλυσθε
λέλυνται

(2) In Past time.
(Pluperfect Indicative)
ἐλελύμην
ἐλέλυσο
ἐλέλυτο
ἐλελύμεθα
ἐλέλυσθε
ἐλέλυντο

(3) At a time determined by the context.

(Perfect Imperative)
λέλυσο
λελύσθω
λέλυσθε
λελύσθωσαν or λελύσθων

(Perfect Subjunctive)
λελυμένος ᾦ
 „   ᾖς
 „   ᾖ
λελυμένοι ὦμεν
 „   ἦτε
 „   ὦσι

(Perfect Optative)
λελυμένος εἴην
 „   εἴης
 „   εἴη
λελυμένοι εἴημεν or εἶμεν
 „   εἴητε or εἶτε
 „   εἴησαν or εἶεν

(Perfect Infinitive)
λελύσθαι

(Perfect Participle)
λελυμένος, η, ον

The forms of verbs given in the above tables are those used in Classical Greek. Some of them are not found in N.T. Greek. The tables scattered throughout the book give the N.T. forms.

CLASSES OF VERBS.

Class 1. Verbs in which the verbal stem and the present stem are the same.

	Present	Future	Aorist	Perf. Act.	Perf. Pass.	Aorist Pass.	Meaning
1.	ἄγω	ἄξω	ἤγαγον ἦξα	ἦχα	ἦγμαι	ἤχθην	drive or lead
2.	ἀκούω	ἀκούσομαι also in N.T. ἀκούσω	ἤκουσα	ἀκήκοα		ἠκούσθην	hear
3.	ἀνοίγω	ἀνοίξω	ἤνοιξα (ἀνέῳξα ἠνέῳξα)	ἀνέῳγα		ἠνοίχθην ἀνεῴχθην ἠνεῴχθην	open
4.	ἄρχομαι	ἄρξομαι	ἠρξάμην				begin
5.	βλέπω	βλέψω	ἔβλεψα				see
6.	βούλομαι					ἐβουλήθην ἠβουλήθην	wish
7.	γράφω	γράψω	ἔγραψα	γέγραφα	γέγραμμαι	ἐγράφθην	write
8.	δέχομαι	δέξομαι	ἐδεξάμην		δέδεγμαι ‡		receive
9.	διδάσκω	διδάξω	ἐδίδαξα			ἐδιδάχθην	teach
10.	δύναμαι	δυνήσομαι	ἠδυνάμην (Attic Imperfect) (ἐδυνάμην)			ἠδυνήθην	am able
11.	θέλω	θελήσω	ἠθέλησα				will
12.	πείθω	πείσω	ἔπεισα	πέποιθα	πέπεισμαι	ἐπείσθην	persuade
13.	πέμπω	πέμψω	ἔπεμψα		πέμπομαι	ἐπέμφθην	send
14.	πιστεύω	πιστεύσω	ἐπίστευσα	πεπίστευκα	πεπίστευμαι	ἐπιστεύθην	believe
15.	ἀγαπάω	ἀγαπήσω	ἠγάπησα	ἠγάπηκα			love

Most verbs in αω are conjugated like ἀγαπάω.

CLASSES OF VERBS

	Present	Future	Aorist	Perf. Act.	Perf. Pass.	Aorist Pass.	Meaning
16.	ζάω	ζήσω	ἔζησα	Present Ind. ζῶ, ζῇς, ζῇ, Inf. ζῆν			live
17.	ποιέω	ποιήσω	ἐποίησα	πεποίηκα	πεποίημαι	ἐποιήθην	make or do
			Most verbs in εω are conjugated like ποιέω.				
18.	δοκέω		ἔδοξα				seem
19.	καλέω	καλέσω	ἐκάλεσα	κέκληκα	κέκλημαι	ἐκλήθην	call
20.	πληρόω	πληρώσω	ἐπλήρωσα	πεπλήρωκα	πεπλήρωμαι	ἐπληρώθην	fill
			Verbs in οω are conjugated like πληρόω.				

Class 2. Verbs with mute stems which have a diphthong or long vowel ει, ευ in all tenses except the second aorist where the vowels are short ι, υ.

21.	φεύγω	φεύξομαι	ἔφυγον (2nd Aor.)				flee
22.	καταλείπω	καταλείψω	κατέλειψα				leave
			κατέλιπον (2nd Aor.)				

Class 3. Verbs which add τ to the verbal stem in order to form the present stem.

23.	ἀποκαλύπτω	ἀποκαλύψω	ἀπεκάλυψα			ἀπεκαλύφθην	reveal
24.	ἐκκόπτω	ἐκκόψω	ἐξέκοψα			ἐξεκόπην	cut out
25.	κρύπτω	κρύψω	ἔκρυψα	κέκρυφα	κέκρυμμαι	ἐκρύφθην	hide
						ἐκρύβην	
26.	πίπτω	πεσοῦμαι	ἔπεσον	πέπτωκα			fall
27.	τίκτω	τέξομαι	ἔτεκον			ἐτέχθην	bring forth

Class 4. Verbs in which the verbal stem ends in a guttural κ, γ, χ which is softened to σσ in the present stem.

28.	κηρύσσω	κηρύξω	ἐκήρυξα	κεκήρυχα	κεκήρυγμαι	ἐκηρύχθην	proclaim
29.	πράσσω	πράξω	ἔπραξα	πέπραχα	πέπραγμαι	ἐπράχθην	make or do

CLASSES OF VERBS

Class 5. Verbs ending in ζω in the present, these are formed from stems ending in δ with futures in σω, or from stems ending in γ or γγ with futures in ξω.

	Present	Future	Aorist	Perf. Act.	Perf. Pass.	Aorist Pass.	Meaning
30.	βαπτίζω	βαπτίσω	ἐβάπτισα		βεβάπτισμαι	ἐβαπτίσθην	baptise
31.	σώζω	σώσω	ἔσωσα	σέσωκα	σέσωσμαι	ἐσώθην	save
32.	κράζω	κεκράξομαι κρίξω	ἔκραξα	κέκραγα			cry

Most verbs in ζω in the N.T. are conjugated like βαπτίζω.

Class 6. Verbs in which the verbal stem ends in a liquid λ, μ, ν, ρ.

Division 1, stems ending in λ which becomes λλ in the present.

						2nd Aor. Pass.	
33.	ἀπαγγέλλω	ἀπαγγελῶ	ἀπήγγειλα			ἀπηγγέλην	announce
34.	βάλλω	βαλῶ	ἔβαλον	βέβληκα	βέβλημαι	ἐβλήθην	throw
35.	στέλλω	στελῶ	ἔστειλα	ἔσταλκα	ἔσταλμαι	ἐστάλην	send

Division 2, presents in αυω and αιρω formed from verbal stems in αυ- and αρ-.

36.	αἴρω	ἀρῶ	ἦρα	ἦρκα	ἦρμαι	ἤρθην	take away
37.	κερδαίνω	κερδανῶ κερδήσω	ἐκέρδανα ἐκέρδησα (these are the N.T. forms)				gain
38.	φαίνω	φανοῦμαι				ἐφάνην	show forth
39.	χαίρω	χαρήσομαι				ἐχάρην	rejoice

Division 3, presents in ευνω, ειρω, ῑνω, ῑρω, υνω, υρω, from stems in εν, ερ, ῑν, ῑρ, υν, υρ.

40.	ἀποκτείνω	ἀποκτερῶ	ἀπέκτεινα			ἀπεκτάνθην	kill
41.	γίνομαι	γενήσομαι	ἐγενόμην	γέγονα	γεγένημαι	ἐγενήθην	become

CLASSES OF VERBS

	Present	Future	Aorist	Perf. Act.	Perf. Pass.	Aorist Pass.	Meaning
42.	ἐγείρω	ἐγερῶ	ἤγειρα	ἐγήγερκα	ἐγήγερμαι	ἠγέρθην	arouse
43.	κρίνω	κρινῶ	ἔκρῑνα	κέκρικα	κέκριμαι	ἐκρίθην	judge
44.	σπείρω	σπερῶ	ἔσπειρα		ἔσπαρμαι	ἐσπάρην	sow
45.	φθείρω	φθερῶ	ἔφθειρα			ἐφθάρην	destroy

Class 7. Verbs which add ν or αν to the verbal stem to form the present stem.

46.	ἁμαρτάνω	ἁμαρτήσω	ἡμάρτησα	ἡμάρτηκα			sin
			ἥμαρτον				
47.	αὐξάνω	αὐξήσω	ηὔξησα			ηὐξήθην	increase
48.	βαίνω	βήσομαι	ἔβην	βέβηκα			go
49.	πίνω	πίομαι	ἔπιον	πέπωκα			drink

If the last vowel of the stem is short another ν which changes to μ or γ before a labial or guttural is added after the vowel.

50.	λαμβάνω	λήμψομαι	ἔλαβον	εἴληφα	εἴλημμαι	ἐλήφθην	take
	Verbal stem λαβ, double augment instead of reduplication in the perfect.						
51.	μανθάνω	μαθήσομαι	ἔμαθον	μεμάθηκα			learn
52.	τυγχάνω	τεύξομαι	ἔτυχον				happen

Class 8. Verbs which add σκ or ισκ to the verbal stem to form the present stem.

53.	ἀποθνήσκω	ἀποθανοῦμαι	ἀπέθανον				die
54.	ἀρέσκω	ἀρέσω	ἤρεσα				please
55.	γινώσκω	γνώσομαι	ἔγνων	ἔγνωκα	ἔγνωσμαι	ἐγνώσθην	know
56.	εὑρίσκω	εὑρήσω	εὗρον	εὕρηκα		εὑρέθην	find

CLASSES OF VERBS

Class 9. Verbs in μι.

	Present	Future	Aorist	Perf. Act.	Perf. Pass.	Aorist Pass.	Meaning
57.	ἀπολλύω	ἀπολέσω (ἀπολῶ)	ἀπώλεσα ἀπωλόμην 2nd Aor. Mid.	ἀπολωλώς = lost ἀπόλωλα			destroy, lose
58.	ἀφίημι	ἀφήσω	ἀφῆκα		ἀφέωνται (Doric 3rd pl.)	ἀφέθην	forgive
59.	δείκνυμι	δείξω	ἔδειξα				show
60.	δείκνύω						
61.	δίδωμι	δώσω	ἔδωκα	δέδωκα	δέδομαι	ἐδόθην	give
62.	ἵστημι	στήσω	ἔστησα ἔστην	ἕστηκα	ἕσταμαι	ἐστάθην	cause to stand
63.	τίθημι	θήσω	ἔθηκα	τέθεικα	τέθειμαι	ἐτέθην	place
64.	εἰμί	ἔσομαι	Imperfect ἦν				be
65.	φημί		Imperfect ἔφην				say

Class 10. Defective verbs whose parts are formed by putting together tenses formed from several distinct verbal stems of the same meaning.

	Present	Future	Aorist	Perf. Act.	Perf. Pass.	Aorist Pass.	Meaning
66.	ἀναιρέω	ἀνελῶ	ἀνεῖλον			ἀνῃρέθην	take up, kill
67.	ἔρχομαι	ἐλεύσομαι	ἦλθον, ἤλθα	ἐλήλυθα			come or go
68.	ἐσθίω	φάγομαι	ἔφαγον				eat
69.	ἔχω	ἕξω	ἔσχον	ἔσχηκα Imperfect εἶχον			have
70.	λέγω	λέξω ἐρῶ	ἔλεξα εἶπον, εἶπα	εἴρηκα	λέλεγμαι εἴρημαι	ἐλέχθην ἐρρέθην ἐρρήθην	say
71.	ὁράω	ὄψομαι	εἶδον	ἑώρακα ἑόρακα		ὤφθην	see
72.	πάσχω		ἔπαθον	πέπονθα			suffer
73.	φέρω	οἴσω	ἤνεγκον ἤνεγκα	ἐνήνοχα		ἠνέχθην	bear

VOCABULARIES

For the meaning of the asterisks see p. 22, note 1

Vocabulary 1

ἀκούω	(akouo)	I hear. (acoustics.)
*ἀποθνήσκω	(apothnēsko)	I die.
*ἀποστέλλω	(apostello)	I send. (apostle.)
βάλλω	(ballo)	I throw, I cast.
βλέπω	(blepo)	I look at, I see.
γράφω	(grapho)	I write. (graphic, telegraph.)
ἐγείρω	(ĕgeiro)	I rouse, I raise.
ἐσθίω	(ĕsthio)	I eat.
εὑρίσκω	(heurisko)	I find.
ἔχω	(ĕcho)	I have.
κρίνω	(krīno)	I judge. (critic.)
λαμβάνω	(lambano)	I take, I receive.
λέγω	(lĕgo)	I say. (Latin "lego" and words derived from it like "lecture.")
μένω	(mĕno)	I remain, I abide, I continue.
πιστεύω	(pisteuo)	I believe.
σώζω	(sōzo)	I save.

Vocabulary 2

αἰτέω	(aiteo)	I ask.
ζητέω	(zēteo)	I seek, I seek for.
θεωρέω	(thĕōreo)	I behold. (theory.)
καλέω	(kăleo)	I call.
λαλέω	(lăleo)	I speak.
μαρτυρέω	(martureo)	I bear witness. (martyr.)
*παρακαλέω	(parakaleo)	I exhort, I comfort. (Paraclete.)
ποιέω	(poieo)	I make, I do. (poet.)
τηρέω	(tĕreo)	I keep safe, I keep, I observe.
φιλέω	(fīleo)	I love. (philosophy.)

VOCABULARIES

Vocabulary 3

ἄγγελος, ου	(angelos)	angel, or messenger. (same word.)
ἀδελφός, ου	(adelphos)	brother.
ἄνθρωπος, ου	(anthrōpos)	man. (anthropology.)
ἀπόστολος, ου	(apostolos)	apostle.
ἄρτος, ου	(artos)	bread, plural "loaves."
δοῦλος, ου	(doulos)	slave, servant.
θάνατος, ου	(thanatos)	death.
θεός, ου	(theos)	God. (theist, theology.)
καί	(kai)	and.
κόσμος, ου	(kosmos)	world. (cosmic.)
κύριος, ου	(kurios)	lord.
λαός, ου	(laos)	people. (laity.)
λόγος, ου	(logos)	word, reason. (The termination "logy" in such words as "theology" comes from this word.)
νόμος, ου	(nomos)	law. (The termination "nomy" in such words as "astronomy" comes from this word.)
οἶκος, ου	(oikos)	house.
ἔρημος, ου fem.	(erēmos)	desert.
ὁδός, ου fem.	(hodos)	way.
παρθένος, ου fem.	(parthenos)	maiden, virgin.
φίλος, ου masc.	(philos)	friend.

N.B. The ου is the termination of the Genitive case. It should be learnt with the words thus—ἄγγελος, ἀγγέλου "an angel." It is useful to learn nouns in this way because the termination of the Genitive shows to which declension they belong. All the nouns given above are masculine with the exception of the last three. For a further explanation see the next exercise.

Vocabulary 4

ἀργύριον, ου	(argurion)	silver, money.
βιβλίον, ου	(biblion)	book. (Bible.)
δαιμόνιον, ου	(daimonion)	devil, demon.
δένδρον, ου	(dendron)	tree.
ἔργον, ου	(ergon)	work.
εὐαγγέλιον, ου	(euangelion)	Gospel (evangelist, evangelical, the ευ in the Greek is transliterated into "ev" in Latin).

ἱερόν, ου	(hieron)	temple.
ἱμάτιον, ου	(himation)	garment.
παιδίον, ου	(paidion)	young child.
πλοῖον, ου	(ploion)	boat.
πρόβατον, ου	(probaton)	sheep.
πρόσωπον, ου	(prosōpon)	face.
σάββατον, ου	(sabbaton)	Sabbath.
σημεῖον, ου	(semeion)	sign, miracle.
τέκνον, ου	(teknon)	child.

All the nouns in the above table are neuter in spite of the fact that two of them mean "child."

Vocabulary 5

ἀγάπη, ης	love.
ἀλήθεια, ας	truth.
ἁμαρτία, ας	sin.
ἀρχή, ης	beginning.
βασιλεία, ας	kingdom.
γενεά, ᾶς	generation.
γῆ, γῆς	earth, land. (geology.)
γραφή, ης	writing, in the plural "the Scriptures."
δικαιοσύνη, ης	righteousness.
εἰρήνη, ης	peace. (Irene.)
ἐκκλησία, ας	church, assembly. (ecclesiastical.)
ἐντολή, ης	commandment.
ἐξουσία, ας	power, authority.
ἐπαγγελία, ας	promise.
ζωή, ης	life. (zoological.)
ἡμέρα, ας	day. (ephemeral.)
καρδία, ας	heart.
κεφαλή, ης	head.
παραβολή, ης	parable. (same word.)
σοφία, ας	wisdom. (philosophy, i.e. the love of wisdom.)
συναγωγή, ης	synagogue. (same word.)
φωνή, ης	voice, sound. (telephone.)
χαρά, ας	joy.
ψυχή, ης	soul. (psychology.)
ὥρα, ας	hour. (same word.)

Vocabulary 6

ἀλλά	but.
ἀπό	from. (followed by a Genitive case.)
βαπτιστής, ου	baptist. (same word.)
γάρ	for. (conjunction, never used as the first word in a sentence.)
γλῶσσα, ης	tongue, language. (glossary.)
δέ	but, and. (never used as the first word in a sentence.)
δεσπότης, ου	master. (despot.)
δόξα, ης	glory. (doxology.)
εἰς	to, into. (followed by the Accusative case.)
ἐκ, ἐξ	out of. (followed by the Gen. case; the second form is used before a word beginning with a vowel.)
ἐν	in, on. (followed by a Dative case.)
θάλασσα, ης	sea, lake.
μαθητής, ου	disciple. (mathematics.)
νεανίας, ου	young man.
οὐ	not. (οὐκ before a word beginning with a vowel with a smooth breathing, οὐχ before a word beginning with a vowel with a rough breathing.)
οὖν	therefore, then. (not used to denote time, or as the first word of a sentence.)
πρό	before. (followed by a Genitive case.)
προφήτης, ου	prophet. (same word.)
σύν	together with. (followed by a Dative case.)

Vocabulary 7

ἀγαθός, η, ον	good.
ἀγαπητός, η, ον	beloved.
ἅγιος, α, ον	holy. οἱ ἅγιοι the saints (hagiography).
αἰώνιος, ον	eternal. (aeonian.)
δίκαιος, α, ον	just, righteous.
ἔσχατος, η, ον	last. (eschatology.)
ἕτερος, α, ον	different, or another. (hetero-doxy.)
ἴδιος, α, ον	one's own.
κακός, η, ον	bad. (cacophony.)
πιστός, η, ον	faithful.
πονηρός, α, ον	wicked. ὁ πονηρός the Evil One.
πρῶτος, η, ον	first. (protagonist.)

αἰώνιος has only two endings. The masculine ending is used with feminine nouns. Compound adjectives, like ἀπιστός "faithless," have also only two endings.

Vocabulary 8

ἄγω	I drive, lead, or bring.
*ἀναγινώσκω	I read.
*ἀποκτείνω	I kill.
*ἀπολύω	I release.
αὐτός, η, ο	he, she, it, also himself etc. (see next exercise.)
βαπτίζω	I baptise.
διδάσκω	I teach.
δοξάζω	I glorify.
*ἐκβάλλω	I cast out.
ἐκεῖνος, η, ο	that. (see next exercise.)
[1] Ἰησοῦς, ου	Jesus.
Ἰουδαῖος, ου	a Jew.
Ἰωάνης	John.
κηρύσσω	I preach, or proclaim.
κράζω	I cry aloud.
λύω	I loose.
οὗτος, αὕτη, τοῦτο	this. (see next exercise.)
πείθω	I persuade.
πέμπω	I send.
*περιπατέω	I walk about.
*συνάγω	I drive together, gather, bring together.
υἱός, ου	son.
*ὑπάγω	I depart.
φέρω	I bear, carry, bring.
χαίρω	I rejoice.

The verbs marked * are compounded with prepositions, for the way in which they are augmented see page 22.

Vocabulary 9

διά	"through" of place or time, "by means of" when followed by a Genitive, "on account of," "because of" when followed by an Accusative.
διδάσκαλος, ου	a teacher.

---

[1] Ἰησοῦς is declined as follows: Nom. Ἰησοῦς, Voc. Ἰησοῦ, Acc. Ἰησοῦν, Gen. Ἰησοῦ, Dat. Ἰησοῦ. It often has the article before it: this article must not be translated in English.

VOCABULARIES

ἐργάτης, ου	a workman, a labourer.
εὐθύς	immediately.
θρόνος, ου	a throne. (same word.)
Ἱεροσόλυμα, ων Ἱερουσαλήμ	Jerusalem. {Neuter Plural. (indeclinable feminine noun.)
καρπός, ου	fruit.
κριτής, ου	a judge. (critic.)
λῃστής, ου	a robber.
λίθος, ου	a stone. (lithography.)
μετά	"together with," "in company with" when followed by a Genitive, "after" when followed by an Accusative.
οἰκοδεσπότης, ου	a householder.
οὐρανός, ου	heaven.
ὀφθαλμός, ου	an eye. (ophthalmic.)
ὄχλος, ου	a crowd, or multitude.
πρεσβύτερος, ου	an elder. (presbyter.)
πρός	"towards," "to" when followed by an Accusative.
τελώνης, ου	a tax-gatherer, a publican.
τόπος, ου	a place. (topic.)
ὑπό	"by" when followed by a Genitive.
ὑποκριτής, ου	a hypocrite. (same word.)
χρόνος, ου	time. (chronology, chronic.)

Vocabulary 10

ἀγρός, ου	a field. (Latin "ager," hence agriculture.)
ἀδικία, ας	injustice, wickedness.
ἁμαρτωλός, ου	a sinner.
*ἀπέρχομαι	I go away, I depart.
*ἀποκρίνομαι	I answer. (generally followed by a noun in the Dative.)
ἅπτομαι	I touch. (generally followed by a noun in the Genitive.)
ἀρνέομαι	I deny.
δέχομαι	I receive.
*διέρχομαι	I go through, I go about.
ἐργάζομαι	I work.
[1] εὐαγγελίζομαι	I preach the gospel.

[1] This is a compound word and is augmented like a verb compounded with a preposition. 1 Aor. Mid. εὐηγγελισάμην.

ἔρχομαι — I go, I come.
Ἰσραήλ — Israel. (Indeclinable noun, Masc. gender.)
μή — not.
οἰκοδομέω — I build.
ὅς, ἥ, ὅ — who, which.
πορεύομαι — I go, I come, I make a journey.

Vocabulary 11

ἄρχομαι — I begin. (Deponent Middle, see p. 42.)
βούλομαι — I wish.
γάμος, ου — a marriage. (polygamy.)
δεῖ — it is necessary; it is right, meet, or fitting. (impersonal verb always contracted.)
δέομαι — I beseech, I beg. (deponent verb, not contracted, followed by a noun in the Genitive.)
διάβολος, ου — the devil. (diabolical.)
δύναμαι — I am able. (dynamite.) (Pres. Ind. δύναμαι, δύνασαι, δύναται, δυνάμεθα, δύνασθε, δύνανται, Imperf. ἐδυνάμην, ἐδύνασο, ἐδύνατο, ἐδυνάμεθα, ἐδύνασθε, ἐδύναντο; also ἠδυνάμην etc.)
ἐγώ — I.
ἐκεῖ — there.
ἐλεύθερος, α, ον — free.
*ἔξεστι — it is lawful. (impersonal verb.)
ἡμεῖς — we.
[1] θέλω — I am willing, I wish.
θεραπεύω — I heal. (therapeutic.)
Ἰορδάνης, ου — Jordan.
καλός, ή, όν — good, beautiful. (caligraphy.)
κελεύω — I command, I bid. C. acc.
μέν — a word used to contrast a person, or thing, or a class of persons or things, with some person, thing, or class mentioned after. (generally not translated.)
οἰκία, ας — a house.
ὁμολογέω — I confess. (followed by a Dative of the person to whom the confession is made.)
*παραγγέλλω — I command. C. dat.
Παῦλος — Paul.

---

[1] Imperfect ἤθελον.

πειράζω	I tempt, I try.
πτωχός, η, ον	poor.
Σαμάρεια, ας	Samaria.
σύ	thou.
τυφλός, η, ον	blind.
ὑμεῖς	you.
*ὑπακούω	I obey. (followed by a Dative of the person or thing obeyed.)
ὦ	O.
ὧδε	here.

Vocabulary 12

ἀδικέω	I injure.
*ἀνοίγω	I open.
ἄρχω	I rule. (followed by a noun in the Genitive. The Middle Voice means "I begin," see Voc. 11.)
[1]διακονέω	I serve. (followed by a Dative.)
διάκονος, ου	a servant, a minister. (deacon.)
διώκω	I pursue.
ἐλεέω	I have mercy on. (eleemosynary.)
*ἐνδύω	I put on.
εὐλογέω	I bless, I praise. (eulogy.)
ἐχθρός, α, ον	hated, as a noun "an enemy."
*κατοικέω	I dwell in, I inhabit. (followed by an Accusative.)
ὅτι	because. (also "that," see page 53.)
*προφητεύω	I prophesy.
σοφός, η, ον	wise. (sophist.)

Vocabulary 13

ἁγιάζω	I sanctify.
ἀγοράζω	I buy.
*ἀπάγω	I drive away.
*ἀποκαλύπτω	I reveal. (apocalypse.)
βαστάζω	I carry.
ἐγγίζω	I draw near, generally followed by a noun in the Dative.
*ἐκκόπτω	I cut down.

[1] Although not really compounded with a preposition this verb generally has the form διηκόνουν in the Imperfect.

ἐλπίζω	I hope.
ἑτοιμάζω	I make ready.
θαυμάζω	I wonder at. (followed by an Accusative.)
καθαρίζω	I cleanse.
κρύπτω	I hide. (crypt.)
λεπρός, οῦ	a leper.
ποταμός, οῦ	a river. (Mesopotamia.)
πράσσω	I do. (practice.)
σκανδαλίζω	I cause to stumble, or offend. (scandalise.)
τάσσω	I set in order. (syntax.)
ταχέως	quickly, soon.
φυλάσσω	I guard.

Vocabulary 14

ἁμαρτάνω	I sin.
ἀμνός, οῦ	a lamb.
βαίνω	I go.
γινώσκω, γιγνώσκω	I know.
εἶδον	I saw.
εἶπον	I said, I spoke, I told.
ἔπαθον	I suffered.
ἔσχον	I had, I held.
ἔφαγον	I ate.
ἦλθον	I came, I went.
ἤνεγκον	I carried.
*καταλείπω	I leave.
μανθάνω	I learn.
οἶνος, ου	wine.
πάσχω	I suffer.
πίνω	I drink.
πίπτω	I fall.
πολλά	many things.
τίκτω	I bring forth.
φεύγω	I flee.
ὦ	O!

Vocabulary 15

ἀδύνατος, η, ον	impossible.
Αἴγυπτος, ου (fem.)	Egypt.
αἴρω	I take up, I take away.
*ἀπαγγέλλω	I announce.
Βηθλεέμ	Bethlehem. (indeclinable.)
δυνατός, όν	possible.
ἐμφανίζω	I manifest, Pass. I appear.
ἕως	while, until.
Ἡρώδης, ου	Herod.
Ἰωσήφ	Joseph. (indeclinable.)
καιρός, ου	time, season.
*κατακρίνω	I condemn.
κλίνη, ης	a bed, a couch.
Κορνήλιος, ου	Cornelius.
κώμη, ης	a village.
Μαριάμ } Μαρία, ας }	Mary. (indeclinable.)
μάχαιρα, ας	a sword.
ὀπίσω	after, behind. (followed by a Genitive case.)
ὅτε	when.
ὀφείλω	I owe, I ought (when followed by an Infinitive).
πάντα	all things.
παρά	when followed by an Acc. case "to the side of," "beside" (of places), when followed by a Genitive case "from beside," "from" (of persons), when followed by a Dat. case "near," "at the house of" (of persons).
παραλυτικός, οῦ	a paralytic.
ποτήριον, ου	a cup.
σπείρω	I sow.
σταυρός, οῦ	a cross.
στρατιώτης, ου	a soldier.
Φαρισαῖος, ου	a Pharisee.
φθείρω	I destroy.
φυλή, ῆς	a tribe.
χήρα, ας	a widow.
ὥς	when, as.

Vocabulary 16

(From this vocabulary onwards the gender of nouns is denoted by the gender of the article given after them.)

αἰών αἰῶνος, ὁ	an age.
ἀλέκτωρ ἀλέκτορος, ὁ	a cock.
ἀμπελών ἀμπελῶνος, ὁ	a vineyard.
ἄρχων ἄρχοντος, ὁ	a ruler. (monarchy.)
ἀστήρ ἀστέρος, ὁ	a star.
εἰκών εἰκόνος, ἡ	an image.
ἐλπίς ἐλπίδος, ἡ	hope.
ἡγεμών ἡγεμόνος, ὁ	a leader, a governor
θύρα, ας, ἡ	a door.
λαμπάς λαμπάδος, ἡ	a lamp.
μήν μηνός, ὁ	a month.
νυμφίος, ου, ὁ	a bridegroom.
νύξ νυκτός, ἡ	night.
ὀδούς ὀδόντος, ὁ	a tooth.
παῖς παιδός, ὁ or ἡ	a child, a boy or girl. (pedagogue.)
Πέτρος, ου, ὁ	Peter.
ποιμήν ποιμένος, ὁ	a shepherd.
σάλπιγξ σάλπιγγος, ὁ	a trumpet.
σάρξ σαρκός, ἡ	flesh.
σωτήρ σωτῆρος, ὁ	a saviour.
τρεῖς	three.
φύλαξ φύλακος, ὁ	a guard.
φωνέω	I call, I make a noise, (of a cock) I crow.
χάρις χάριτος, ἡ	grace, favour.
χιτών χιτῶνος, ὁ	a garment, especially an under garment or shirt.

Vocabulary 17

αἷμα αἵματος, τό	blood. (haemorrhage.)
ἀνήρ ἀνδρός, ὁ	a man, a husband.
ἄφεσις ἀφέσεως, ἡ	remission, forgiveness.
βάπτισμα βαπτίσματος, τό	baptism.
βασιλεύς βασιλέως, ὁ	a king.
γένος γένους, τό	a race, a nation.
γόνυ γόνατος, τό	a knee.
γράμμα γράμματος, τό	a letter (of the alphabet).
γραμματεύς γραμματέως, ὁ	a scribe.

VOCABULARIES

γυνή γυναικός, ἡ	a woman, wife. (gynaecology.)
ἐπιστολή, ἡ	a letter. (epistle.)
ἔτος ἔτους, τό	a year.
θέλημα θελήματος, τό	will.
θρίξ τριχός, ἡ	a hair.
θυγάτηρ θυγατρός, ἡ	a daughter.
ἰχθύς ἰχθύος, ὁ	a fish.
κύων κύνος, ὁ	a dog. (Cynic.)
κωφός, η, ον	dull, deaf, dumb.
μετάνοια, ας, ἡ	repentance.
μήτηρ μητρός, ἡ	a mother. (Latin "mater.")
οὖς ὠτός, τό	an ear.
πατήρ πατρός, ὁ	a father. (Latin "pater.")
πνεῦμα πνεύματος, τό	spirit, wind. (pneumatic.)
πόλις πόλεως, ἡ	a city. (politics.)
πούς ποδός, ὁ	a foot. (chiropodist.)
πῦρ πυρός, τό	a fire. (pyrotechny.)
τέρας τέρατος, τό	a wonder, a miracle.
ὕδωρ ὕδατος, τό	water. (hydraulic, hydropathy.)
φῶς φωτός, τό	light. (phosphorus.)
χείρ χειρός, ἡ	a hand. (chiropodist.)

Vocabulary 18

ἀληθής, ἀληθές	true.
ἀνάστασις ἀναστάσεως, ἡ	resurrection.
ἀρχιερεύς ἀρχιερέως, ὁ	a high priest.
ἀσθενής, ες	weak, sick.
ἄφρων, ἄφρον	foolish.
γονεύς γονέως, ὁ	a father, an ancestor, in the pl. parents.
Δαυείδ, Δαβίδ, ὁ	David. (indeclinable.)
ἔθνος ἔθνους, τό	a race, in the pl. the Gentiles.
εἰ	if.
εἷς, μία, ἕν	one.
ἤ	than.
ἱερεύς ἱερέως, ὁ	a priest.
κρίμα κρίματος, τό	a judgement, a sentence, a condemnation.
κρίσις κρίσεως, ἡ	a judgement.
μᾶλλον	more.
μέγας, μεγάλη, μέγα	great.

μηδείς, μηδεμία, μηδέν	no one (with the Imperative, Infinitive etc.).
μηκέτι	no more.
νεκρός, α, ον	dead. (necropolis.)
ὄνομα ὀνόματος, τό	a name. (synonym.)
ὄρος ὄρους, τό	a hill, a mountain.
οὐδείς, οὐδεμία, οὐδέν	no one. (with the Indicative.)
πᾶς, πᾶσα, πᾶν	all, every.
πίστις πίστεως, ἡ	faith.
πλήρης, ες	full.
πολύς, πολλή, πολύ	many, much. (polygon.)
ῥῆμα ῥήματος, τό	a word, a saying.
σκότος σκότους, τό	darkness.
σπέρμα σπέρματος, τό	a seed.
στόμα στόματος, τό	a mouth.
σῶμα σώματος, τό	a body.
ὑγιής ὑγιές	whole, healthy. (hygienic.)

Vocabulary 19

ἀκάθαρτος, ον	unclean.
*ἀμφιβάλλω	I throw round, I throw on this side and that, especially used of a net.
Ἀνανίας, ὁ	Ananias.
Ἀνδρέας, ου, ὁ	Andrew.
Γαλιλαία, ας, ἡ	Galilee.
*διασπείρω	I scatter abroad, I disperse.
*εἰσέρχομαι Fut. εἰσελεύσομαι	I go into, I enter.
*ἐξέρχομαι	I go out.
Ἠλείας, ὁ	Elijah.
μακάριος, α, ον	blessed.
Μωϋσῆς, εως, ὁ	Moses.
*παραγίνομαι	I become near, I am present, I approach, I go to.
¨παράγω	I pass by. (lit. I lead past.)
πεντακισχίλιοι	five thousand.
πῶς	how.
Σατανᾶς gen. Σατανᾶ, ὁ	Satan.
Σίμων Σίμωνος, ὁ	Simon.

VOCABULARIES

σπαράσσω	I tear.
*συνλαλέω	I speak with.
τεσσεράκοντα	forty. (indeclinable.)
φοβέομαι	I fear, I am afraid.
φόβος, ου, ὁ	fear.
χρῆμα χρήματος, τό	money, nearly always used in the plural.

Vocabulary 20

*ἀναχωρέω	I depart.
Ἅννας gen. Ἅννα, ὁ	Annas.
ἀπόκρισις, εως, ἡ	an answer.
διδαχή, ῆς, ἡ	teaching. (didactic.)
δίκτυον, ου, τό	a net.
δύναμις, εως, ἡ	power. (dynamics.)
δύο	two.
ἐγγύς	near.
*ἐκπλήσσομαι	I am astonished.
*ἐπέρχομαι	I come upon.
ἐπί	see Lesson 26.
*ἐπιθυμέω	I desire.
ἐπιστάτης, ου, ὁ	master.
ἔτι	still.
Ζαχαρίας, ου, ὁ	Zacharias.
Ἰόππη, ης, ἡ	Joppa.
Καιάφας gen. Καιάφα, ὁ	Caiaphas.
κατά	see Lesson 26.
κοπιάω	I toil, I labour.
κρατέω	I take hold of, I hold.
κυριακή, ῆς, ἡ	the Lord's day.
Λύδδα, ας, ἡ	Lydda.
μνημεῖον, ου, τό	a tomb.
νεφέλη, ης, ἡ	a cloud.
ὅλος, η, ον	whole.
ὅσος, η, ον	as much as, how great, as many as, how much.
*παραλαμβάνω	I take with me, I receive.
πέτρα, ας, ἡ	a rock.
*προσέρχομαι	I go towards.
*προσκαρτερέω	I remain, I endure.
στενός, ή, όν	narrow.

συνέδριον, ου, τό	a council. (Sanhedrin.)
τίς τί	who? which? what? τί also means "why?"
τις τι	a certain person, a certain thing.
τότε	then (at that time).
ὡσεί	as if, as it were.

Vocabulary 21

ἀληθῶς	truly.
*ἀπολούω	I wash away.
γίνομαι, γίγνομαι, Fut. γενήσομαι	I become.
ἐγένετο	it came to pass.
*ἐκλέγομαι	I choose.
*ἐπιβάλλω	I cast upon, I lay upon, I put upon.
ἰδού	behold, lo.
*ἐπικαλέω	I put a name on, I surname. Middle Voice, I call upon, I invoke.
ἰσχυρός, α, ον	strong.
*καταλαμβάνω	I lay hold of. Middle Voice, I perceive.
λοιπός, η, ον	when used with an article in the plural "the rest," "the persons or things remaining."
μέλλω	I am about to, I delay, I tarry.
μικρός, α, ον	little.
ναός, ου, ὁ	the shrine of a temple, the Holy Place.
νέος, α, ον	young, new.
νῦν, νυνί	now, at this present time.
ὁδοιπορέω	I go my way.
ὁράω	I see.
οὐχί	an emphatic form of οὐ "not," especially used in questions which expect the answer "yes."
παλαιός, α, ον	old.
*προσεύχομαι	I pray.
ῥίπτω	I throw, I cast.
Σολομῶν Σολομῶνος, ὁ	Solomon.
*συνβουλεύομαι	I take counsel together with.
σχίσμα, ατος, τό	a rent, a division. (schism.)
σωτηρία, ἡ	salvation.
τί	why?
τρία	neuter of τρεῖς "three."
τροφή, ης, ἡ	nourishment, meat, food.
ὑπέρ	when followed by an Accusative "above," "beyond," when followed by a Genitive, "on behalf of," "for."

Vocabulary 22

ἀγαλλιάομαι	I rejoice greatly.
ἀγαπάω	I love.
βοάω	I cry, I shout.
γεννάομαι	I am born.
δικαιόω	I justify.
ἐάω	I allow, I permit. Future ἐάσω; 1st Aor. εἴασα, Infinitive ἐᾶσαι.
ἔξοδος, ου, ἡ	departure. (exodus.)
ἐρωτάω	I ask, especially of asking a question.
ζάω	I live.
ἰάομαι	I heal.
πληρόω	I fill, I fulfil.
ποῦ	where ?
*προσκυνέω	I worship. (followed by a Dative.)
πυνθάνομαι	I inquire.
σταυρόω	I crucify.
ταπεινόω	I humble.
ὑψόω	I exalt.
φανερόω	I make manifest.

Vocabulary 23

*εἰσάγω	I lead in, I bring in.
Ἕλλην Ἕλληνος, ὁ	a Greek.
ἐπαγγέλλομαι	I promise.
*ἐπιγιγνώσκω	I know.
ἑπτά	seven. (heptarchy.)
καθώς	even as.
κλέπτω	I steal. (kleptomaniac.)
κοιμάομαι	I sleep.
κοινόω	I make common, I defile.
Λάζαρος, ου, ὁ	Lazarus.
Μαγδαληνή	Magdalene.
πειρασμός, οῦ, ὁ	temptation.
φίλος, ου, ὁ	friend.

VOCABULARIES

From this point verbs compounded with a preposition are no longer marked.

Vocabulary 24

ἀθετέω	I set aside, I disregard.
ἀπολέσει	3rd sing. fut. ind. from ἀπολλύω, I destroy, I lose.
δέω	I bind, I fasten.
εὖ	well. εὖ ποιεῖν means "to benefit." C. dat.
ὅμοιος, α, ον	like. (homogeneous.) C. dat.
πάντοτε	always.
παράδοσις, εως, ἡ	tradition.
ποτέ	ever.
τοιοῦτος	such.

Vocabulary 25

ἀγαθοποιέω	I do good.
ἅλας ἅλατος, τό	salt.
ἁλίζω	I salt.
αὔριον	an Adverb meaning "on the morrow," ἡ αὔριον = tomorrow (understand ἡμέρα).
γεύομαι	I taste. (generally followed by a Genitive.)
ἐνθάδε	here.
ἤ	or. ἤ...ἤ, either...or.
Καῖσαρ Καίσαρος, ὁ	Caesar.
καταλύω	I loose (thoroughly), destroy.
μεριμνάω	I am anxious for.
μισθός, ου, ὁ	reward, pay.
νομίζω	I think.
ὅραμα, ατος, τό	a vision.
ὅστις	whosoever, but in the N.T. practically the same as ὅς, who.
περιβάλλω	I cast round, Mid. I clothe myself.
περισσεύω	I surpass, I have in abundance.
σιωπάω	I am silent.

Vocabulary 26

ἀνομία, ας, ἡ	lawlessness, wickedness.
ἀπαρνέομαι	I deny.
ἄργυρος, ου, ὁ	silver.
Ἀχελδαμάχ	Acheldama.
γνωστός, η, ον	known.
δέσμιος, ου, ὁ	a prisoner.

VOCABULARIES

ἐκπορεύομαι	I go out.
ἐκφεύγω	I escape.
ἔξω	outside. (followed by the Genitive case.)
θαμβέομαι	I wonder, I am astonished.
θυσία, ας, ἡ	a sacrifice.
Ἰάκωβος, ου, ὁ	James.
Καισαρεία, ας, ἡ	Caesarea.
καταλιθάζω	I stone (thoroughly).
λιθάζω	I stone.
περισσός, η, ον	surpassing, great.
πληθύνω	I multiply.
πλησίον	an Adverb meaning "near," hence ὁ πλησίον, one's neighbour.
πρίν	before.
προσέχω	I give heed to. C. dat.
σιγάω	I am silent.
συνεσθίω	I eat with.
συνζητέω	I join in seeking, I discuss, I argue.
σύρω	I drag.
τρίς	thrice.
Φῆστος, ου, ὁ	Festus.
Φίλιππος, ου, ὁ	Philip.
χρυσός, ου, ὁ	gold
χωρίον, ου, τό	a piece of land, a field.
ὥστε	so that.

Vocabulary 27

ἀποδίδωμι	I give back: in the Middle, I give away for my own sake, hence "I sell."
δίδωμι	I give.
μυστήριον, ου, τό	a mystery.
παραδίδωμι	I give up, I betray.
ποῖος, α, ον	of what kind?
προμεριμνάω	I am anxious beforehand.
τοσοῦτος	so much.
φυλακή, ῆς, ἡ	a watch, a guard, a prison.

Vocabulary 28

ἀγορά, ᾶς, ἡ	a market place.
ἀκολουθέω	I follow. (with Dative.)
ἀποσπάω	I draw away.
ἀσθενέω	I am weak or sick.
βολή, ῆς, ἡ	a throwing, a cast.

δεξιός, ά, όν	on the right hand.
εἰσπορεύομαι	I go to.
εἰσφέρω	I carry to.
ἔμπροσθεν	before.
ἐνώπιον	before (of place). (followed by a Genitive.)
καινός, ή, όν	new.
καίω	I burn, I kindle.
κατευλογέω	I bless.
κλάω	I break.
λύχνος, ου, ὁ	a lamp.
παραλελυμένος, η, ον	paralysed. (Perf. part. from παραλύω.)
παρατίθημι	I place beside, I set beside, I set before (of food, c. Dat.)
τίθημι	I place, I lay down.
τιμή, ῆς, ἡ	honour, price.

Vocabulary 29

ἀνίστημι	In the Transitive tenses "I cause to stand up," "I raise up," Intransitive "I stand up, rise, arise."
ἀφίστημι	In the Transitive tenses "I cause to stand away," "I remove, separate," Intransitive "I stand away from."
ἕλκω	I drag.
ἔμπροσθεν	before. (followed by a Genitive.)
ἐντέλλω	I command.
ἐπαίρω	I raise up.
ἐπιλαμβάνω	I lay hold of.
ἵστημι	In the Transitive tenses "I cause to stand," in the Intransitive tenses "I stand."
καθίστημι	In the Transitive tenses "I set up," "I establish," "I appoint."
μάρτυς μάρτυρος, ὁ	a witness. (martyr.)
μερίζω	I divide.
μέσος, η, ον	middle.
μετανοέω	I change my mind, repent.
ξηρός, ά, όν	dry, withered.
οἰκουμένη, ης, ἡ	the inhabited land, the world.
ὁμοιόω	I make like, I compare.

VOCABULARIES

πανταχοῦ — everywhere.
παρίστημι — In the Transitive tenses "I cause to stand beside," "I present." Intr. "stand beside."
παύομαι — I cease.
τεκμήριον, ου, τό — a certain proof.
ὕστερος, α, ον — last.
ψευδής, ες — false.

Vocabulary 30

ἀκολουθέω — I follow. (followed by a Dative.)
ἀφίημι — I let go, I let alone, I allow, I forgive.
δείκνυμι — I show.
εὐθέως — immediately.
εὐχαριστέω — I thank. (Eucharist.)
θαρσέω — I am of good courage.
οἶδα — I know.
οὐράνιος, α, ον — heavenly.
ὀφειλέτης, ου, ὁ — a debtor.
ὀφείλημα, ατος, τό — a debt.
πάντοτε — always.
παράπτωμα, ατος, τό — a fault, a transgression.
πλανάομαι — I err. (planet.)
πρέπον — fitting.
συνίημι — I understand.

Vocabulary 31

ἀλλήλους, as, a — one another. (Nominative not in use.)
ἀπώλεια, ας, ἡ — destruction.
διαλογίζομαι — I discuss.
διαπορεύομαι — I make my way through.
ἐπερωτάω — I ask.
ἐπισυνάγω — I gather together to.
νηστεύω — I fast.
πατέω — I trample on.
πλῆθος, ους, τό — a great number, a multitude.
προσκαλέομαι — I call to, I summon.
ὑπομονή, ῆς, ἡ — patience.
φρονέω — I think.

ENGLISH-GREEK VOCABULARY

The numbers refer to the Vocabularies

I abide, μένω 1
I am able, δύναμαι 11
I am about, μέλλω 21
above, ὑπέρ with Acc. 21
according to, κατά foll. by Acc. 20
Acheldama, Ἀχελδαμάχ 26
I am afraid, φοβέομαι 19
after, μετά with Acc. 9; ὀπίσω 15
against, κατά with Gen. 20
age, αἰών 16
all, πᾶς 18
all things, πάντα 15
I allow, ἐάω 22; ἀφίημι 30
always, πάντοτε 24
Ananias, Ἀνανίας 19
and, καί 3; δέ 6
Andrew, Ἀνδρέας 19
angel, ἄγγελος 3
another, ἕτερος 7
Annas, Ἄννας 20
I announce, ἀπαγγέλλω 15
I answer, ἀποκρίνομαι 10
answer, ἀπόκρισις 20
I am anxious, μεριμνάω 25
I am anxious beforehand, προμεριμνάω 27
Apostle, ἀπόστολος 9
I appoint, καθίστημι 29
I approach, παραγίνομαι 19
I argue, συνζητέω 26
I arise, ἀνίσταμαι 29
as, καθώς 23
as much as, ὅσος 20
I ask, αἰτέω 2
I ask a question, ἐρωτάω 22; ἐπερωτάω 31
assembly, ἐκκλησία 5
I am astonished, ἐκπλήσσομαι 20; θαμβέομαι 26

I ate, ἔφαγον 14

bad, κακός 7
I baptise, βαπτίζω 8
baptism, βάπτισμα 17
Baptist, Βαπτιστής 6
I bear, φέρω 8
I bear witness, μαρτυρέω 2
beautiful, καλός 11
I become, γίνομαι 21
bed, κλίνη 15
before (preposition), πρό 6; ἐνώπιον 28; ἔμπροσθεν 29; πρίν 26
I beg, δέομαι 11
I begin, ἄρχομαι 11
beginning, ἀρχή 5
on behalf of, ὑπέρ with Gen. 21
I behold, θεωρέω 2
behold! ἰδού 21
I believe, πιστεύω 1
beloved, ἀγαπητός 7
I benefit, εὖ ποιέω 24
I beseech, δέομαι 11
beside, παρά 15
Bethlehem, Βηθλεέμ 15
I betray, παραδίδωμι 27
I bid, κελεύω 11
I bless, εὐλογέω 12; κατευλογέω 28
blessed, μακάριος 19
blind, τυφλός 11
blood, αἷμα 17
boat, πλοῖον 4
body, σῶμα 18
book, βιβλίον 4
I am born, γεννάομαι 22
boy, παῖς 15
bread, ἄρτος 3

ENGLISH-GREEK VOCABULARY

I break, κλάω 28
bridegroom, νυμφίος 16
I bring, ἄγω 8
I bring forth, τίκτω 14
I bring in, εἰσάγω 23
brother, ἀδελφός 3
I build, οἰκοδομέω 10
I burn, καίω 28
but, ἀλλά, δέ 6
I buy, ἀγοράζω 13
by, ὑπό 9
by means of, διά with Gen. 9

Caesar, Καῖσαρ 25
Caesarea, Καισαρεία 26
Caiaphas, Καιάφας 20
I call, καλέω 2 ; φωνέω 16
I call upon, ἐπικαλέομαι 21 ; προσκαλέω 31
I came, ἦλθον 14
I carry, φέρω 8 ; βαστάζω 13
I carry to, εἰσφέρω 28
I carried, ἤνεγκον 14
I cast, βάλλω 1 ; ῥίπτω 21
cast, βολή 28
I cast out, ἐκβάλλω 8
I cease, παύομαι 29
a certain man, τις 20
child, τέκνον 4 ; παῖς 16
child, young, παιδίον 4
I choose, ἐκλέγομαι 21
church, ἐκκλησία 5
city, πόλις 17
I cleanse, καθαρίζω 13
I clothe myself, περιβάλλομαι 25
cloud, νεφέλη 20
cock, ἀλέκτωρ 16
I comfort, παρακαλέω 2
I come, ἔρχομαι, πορεύομαι 10
I come upon, ἐπέρχομαι 20
to come to pass, γίνεσθαι 21
I command, κελεύω 11 ; παραγγέλλω 11 ; ἐντέλλω 29
commandment, ἐντολή 5
I compare, ὁμοιόω 29
I condemn, κατακρίνω 15

condemnation, κρίμα 18
I confess, ὁμολογέω 11
I continue, μένω 1
Cornelius, Κορνήλιος 15
couch, κλίνη 15
council, συνέδριον 20
I am of good courage, θαρσέω 30
cross, σταυρός 15
I crow, φωνέω 16
crowd, ὄχλος 9
I crucify, σταυρόω 23
I cry, βοάω 22
I cry aloud, κράζω 8
cup, ποτήριον 15
I cut down, ἐκκόπτω 13

darkness, σκότος 18
daughter, θυγάτηρ 17
David, Δανειδ, Δαβίδ 18
day, ἡμέρα 5
dead, νεκρός 18
deaf, κωφός 17
death, θάνατος 3
a debt, ὀφείλημα 30
debtor, ὀφειλέτης 30
I defile, κοινόω 23
I delay, μέλλω 21
demon, δαιμόνιον 4
deny, ἀρνέομαι 10
I depart, ὑπάγω 8 ; ἀπέρχομαι 10 ; ἀναχωρέω 20
departure, ἔξοδος 22
desert, ἔρημος 3
I desire, ἐπιθυμέω 20
I destroy, φθείρω 15 ; ἀπολλύω 24 ; καταλύω 25
destruction, ἀπώλεια 31
devil, δαιμόνιον 4 ; διάβολος 11
I die, ἀποθνήσκω 1
different, ἕτερος 7
disciple, μαθητής 6
I discuss, συνζητέω 26 ; διαλογίζομαι 31
disperse, διασπείρω 18
I disregard, ἀθετέω 24
I divide, μερίζω 29

ENGLISH-GREEK VOCABULARY

division, σχίσμα 21
I do, ποιέω 2; πράσσω 13
dog, κύων 17
door, θύρα 16
down, κατά, foll. by Gen. 20
I drag, σύρω 26; ἑλκύω 29
I draw away, ἀποσπάω 26
I draw near, ἐγγίζω 13
I drink, πίνω 14
I drive, ἄγω 8
I drive away, ἀπάγω 13
I drive together, συνάγω 8
dry, ξηρός 29
dumb, κωφός 17
dwell in, κατοικέω 12; μένω 1

ear, οὖς 17
earth, γῆ 5
I eat, ἐσθίω 1
I eat with, συνεσθίω 26
Egypt, Αἴγυπτος 15
elder, πρεσβύτερος 9
Elijah, Ἠλείας 19
I endure, προσκαρτερέω 20
enemy, ἐχθρός 12
I enter, εἰσέρχομαι 19
I err, πλανάομαι 30
I escape, ἐκφεύγω 26
I establish, καθίστημι 29
eternal, αἰώνιος 7
even as, καθώς 23
every, πᾶς 18
everywhere, πανταχοῦ 29
the Evil One, ὁ πονηρός 7
I exalt, ὑψόω 22
I exhort, παρακαλέω 2
eye, ὀφθαλμός 9

face, πρόσωπον 4
faith, πίστις 18
faithful, πιστός 7
I fall, πίπτω 14
false, ψευδής 29
I fast, νηστεύω 31
father, πατήρ 17
fault, παράπτωμα 30
favour, χάρις 16

field, ἀγρός 10; χωρίον 27
fill, πληρόω 22
I find, εὑρίσκω 1
fire, πῦρ 17
first, πρῶτος 7
fish, ἰχθύς 17
fitting, πρέπον 30
five thousand, πεντακισχίλιοι 19
I flee, φεύγω 14
flesh, σάρξ 16
I follow, ἀκολουθέω 30
food, τροφή 21
foolish, ἄφρων 18
foot, πούς 17
for (conj.), γάρ 6
for (prep.), πρό 6
I forgive, ἀφίημι 30
forgiveness, ἄφεσις 17
forty, τεσσαράκοντα 19
free, ἐλεύθερος 11
from, ἀπό 6
fruit, καρπός 9
fulfil, πληρόω 22
full, πλήρης

Galilee, Γαλιλαία 19
garment, ἱμάτιον 4; χιτών 16
I gather together, ἐπισυνάγω 31
generation, γενεά 5
Gentiles, τὰ ἔθνη 18
I give, δίδωμι 27
I give back, ἀποδίδωμι 27
I give up, παραδίδωμι 27
I glorify, δοξάζω 8
glory, δόξα 6
I go, ἔρχομαι, πορεύομαι 10; βαίνω 14
I go about, διέρχομαι 10
I go away, ἀπέρχομαι 10
I go into, εἰσέρχομαι 19; εἰσπορεύομαι 28
I go out, ἐξέρχομαι 19; ἐκπορεύομαι 26
I go through, διέρχομαι 10
I go towards, προσέρχομαι 20
God, θεός 3
gold, χρυσός 26

ENGLISH-GREEK VOCABULARY

good, ἀγαθός 7; καλός 11
Gospel, εὐαγγέλιον 4
Gospel, I preach the, εὐαγγελίζομαι 10
governor, ἡγεμών 16
grace, χάρις 16
great, μέγας 18
a Greek, Ἕλλην 23
I guard, φυλάσσω 13
guard, φύλαξ 16

I had, ἔσχον 14
hair, θρίξ 17
hand, χείρ 17
hated, ἐχθρός 12
I have, ἔχω 1
I have mercy on, ἐλεέω 12
he, she, it, αὐτός, αὐτή, αὐτό 8
head, κεφαλή 5
heal, θεραπεύω 11; ἰάομαι 22
healthy, ὑγιής 18
I hear, ἀκούω 1
heart, καρδία 5
heaven, οὐρανός 9
heavenly, οὐράνιος 30
I give heed to, προσέχω 26
I held, ἔσχον 14
here, ὧδε 11; ἐνθάδε 25
Herod, Ἡρώδης 15
I hide, κρύπτω 13
high-priest, ἀρχιερεύς 18
hill, ὄρος 18
himself etc., αὐτός 8
I hold, κρατέω 20
holy, ἅγιος 7
honour, τιμή 28
I hope, ἐλπίζω 13
hope, ἐλπίς 16
hour, ὥρα 5
house, οἶκος 3; οἰκία 11
householder, οἰκοδεσπότης 9
how, πῶς 19
I humble, ταπεινόω 22
husband, ἀνήρ 17
hypocrite, ὑποκριτής 9

I, ἐγώ 11

if, εἰ 18
image, εἰκών 16
immediately, εὐθύς 9; εὐθέως 30
impossible, ἀδύνατος 15
in, ἐν 6
inhabit, κατοικέω 12
I injure, ἀδικέω 12
injustice, ἀδικία 10
I inquire, πυνθάνομαι 22
into, εἰς 6
I invoke, ἐπικαλέομαι 21
Israel, Ἰσραήλ 10

James, Ἰάκωβος 26
Jerusalem, Ἱεροσόλυμα, Ἱερουσαλήμ 9
Jesus, Ἰησοῦς 8
Jew, Ἰουδαῖος 8
John, Ἰωάνης 8
Joppa, Ἰόππη 20
Jordan, Ἰορδάνης 11
Joseph, Ἰωσήφ 15
journey, I make a, πορεύομαι 10
joy, χαρά 5
I judge, κρίνω 1
judge, κριτής 9
judgement, κρίμα 18; κρίσις 18
just, δίκαιος 7
I justify, δικαιόω 22

I keep safe, τηρέω 2
I kill, ἀποκτείνω 8
I kindle, καίω 28
king, βασιλεύς 17
kingdom, βασιλεία 5
knee, γόνυ 17
I know, γινώσκω 14; ἐπιγινώσκω 23; οἶδα 30
known, γνωστός 26

I labour, κοπιάω 20
labourer, ἐργάτης 9
lake, θάλασσα 6
lamb, ἀμνός 14
lamp, λαμπάς 16; λύχνος 28
land, γῆ 5

language, γλῶσσα 6
last, ἔσχατος 7; ὕστερος 29
law, νόμος 3
it is lawful, ἔξεστι 11
lawlessness, ἀνομία 26
I lay down, τίθημι 28
I lay hold of, καταλαμβάνω 21; ἐπιλαμβάνω 29
I lay upon, ἐπιβάλλω 21
Lazarus, Λάζαρος 23
I lead, ἄγω 8
I lead in, εἰσάγω 23
leader, ἡγεμών 16
I learn, μανθάνω 14
learner, μαθητής 6
I leave, καταλείπω 14
leper, λεπρός 13
I let alone, ἀφίημι 30
I let go, ἀφίημι 30
letter, γράμμα 17; ἐπιστολή 17
light, φῶς 17
life, ζωή 5
like, ὅμοιος 24
I make like, ὁμοιόω 29
little, μικρός 21
I live, ζάω 22
loaves, ἄρτοι 3
I look at, βλέπω 1
I loose, λύω 9
lord, κύριος 3
I love, φιλέω 2; ἀγαπάω 22
love, ἀγαπή 5
Lydda, Λύδδα 20

Magdalene, Μαγδαληνή 23
maiden, παρθένος 3
I make, ποιέω 2
I make manifest, φανερόω 22
I make ready, ἑτοιμάζω 13
man, ἄνθρωπος 3; ἀνήρ 17
young man, νεανίας 6
I manifest, ἐμφανίζω, φανερόω 22
many, πολύς 18
many things, πολλά 14
market place, ἀγορά 28
marriage, γάμος 11

Mary, Μαριάμ, Μαρία 15
master, δεσπότης 6; ἐπιστάτης 20
meat, τροφή 21
mercy, I have, ἐλεέω 12
messenger, ἄγγελος 3
middle, μέσος 29
minister, διάκονος 12
miracle, σημεῖον 4; τέρας 17
money, ἀργύριον 4; τὰ χρήματα 19
month, μήν 16
more, μᾶλλον 18
Moses, Μωϋσῆς 19
mother, μήτηρ 17
mountain, ὄρος 18
mouth, στόμα 18
much, πολύς 18
I multiply, πληθύνω 23
multitude, ὄχλος 9
I must, see necessary
mystery, μυστήριον 27

name, ὄνομα 18
narrow, στενός 20
nation, γένος 17
near, ἐγγύς 20
necessary, it is, δεῖ 11
neighbour, ὁ πλησίον 26
net, δίκτυον 20
new, νέος 21; καινός 28
night, νύξ 16
no more, μηκέτι 18
no one, μηδείς, οὐδείς 18
not, οὐ 6; μή 10
nourishment, τροφή 21
now, νῦν 21

O, ὦ 14
I obey, ὑπακούω 11
I observe, τηρέω 2
I offend, σκανδαλίζω 13
old, παλαιός 21
on, ἐπί 20
on account of, διά with acc. 9
one, εἷς, μία, ἕν 18
one another, ἀλλήλους 31
one's own, ἴδιος 7
I open, ἀνοίγω 12

ENGLISH-GREEK VOCABULARY

other, ἕτερος 7
I ought, ὀφείλω 15
out of, ἐκ, ἐξ 6
outside, ἔξω 26
I owe, ὀφείλω 15

parable, παραβολή 5
paralytic, παραλυτικός 15; παραλελυμένος 28
parents, οἱ γονεῖς 18
I pass by, παράγω 19
patience, ὑπομονή 31
Paul, Παῦλος 11
pay, μισθός 25
peace, εἰρήνη 5
people, λαός 3
I perceive, καταλαμβάνομαι 21
I permit, ἐάω 22
I persuade, πείθω 8
Peter, Πέτρος 16
Pharisee, Φαρισαῖος 15
Philip, Φίλιππος 26
I place, τίθημι 28
I place beside, παρατίθημι 28
place, τόπος 9
poor, πτωχός 11
possible, δυνατός 15
power, ἐξουσία 5; δύναμις 20
I praise, εὐλογέω 12
I pray, προσεύχομαι 21
I preach, κηρύσσω 8
I preach the Gospel, εὐαγγελίζομαι 10
I present, παρίστημι 29
I am present, παραγίνομαι 19
priest, ἱερεύς 18
prison, φυλακή 27
prisoner, δέσμιος 26
I proclaim, κηρύσσω 8
promise, ἐπαγγελία 5
proof, τεκμήριον 29
I prophesy, προφητεύω 12
prophet, προφήτης 6
publican, τελώνης 9
I pursue, διωκω 12
I put on, ἐνδύω 12

I put upon, ἐπιβάλλω 21
quickly, ταχέως 13
race, γένος 17; ἔθνος 18
I raise, ἐγείρω 1; ἀνίστημι 29; ἐπαίρω 29
I read, ἀναγιγνώσκω 8
I make ready, ἑτοιμάζω 13
reason, λόγος 3
I receive, λαμβάνω 1; δέχομαι 10
I rejoice, χαίρω 8; ἀγαλλιάομαι 22
I release, ἀπολύω 8
I remain, μένω 1; προσκαρτερέω 20
remission, ἄφεσις 17
remove, ἀφίστημι 29
rent, σχίσμα 21
I repent, μετανοέω 29
repentance, μετάνοια 17
the rest, οἱ λοιποί 21
resurrection, ἀνάστασις 18
I reveal, ἀποκαλύπτω 13
reward, μισθός 25
on the right hand, δεξιός 28
righteous, δίκαιος 7
righteousness, δικαιοσύνη 5
I rise, ἀνίσταμαι 29
river, ποταμός 13
robber, λῃστής 9
rock, πέτρα 20
I rouse, ἐγείρω 1
I rule, ἄρχω 12
ruler, ἄρχων 16

Sabbath, σάββατον 4
sacrifice, θυσία 26
I keep safe, τηρέω 2
I said, εἶπον 14
saint, ἅγιος 7, see p. 20
I salt, ἁλίζω 25
salt, ἅλας 25
Samaria, Σαμάρεια 11
sanctify, ἁγιάζω 13
Satan, Σατανᾶς 19
save, σώζω 1
saviour, σωτήρ 16
I saw, εἶδον 14
I say, λέγω 1

saying, ῥῆμα 18
I scatter abroad, διασπείρω 19
scribe, γραμματεύς 17
scriptures, γραφαί 5
sea, θάλασσα 6
season, καιρός 15
I see, βλέπω 1; ὁράω 21
seed, σπέρμα 18
I seek, ζητέω 2
I sell, ἀποδίδομαι 27
I send, ἀποστέλλω 1; πέμπω 8
sentence, κρίμα 18
I separate, ἀφίστημι 29
servant, διάκονος 12; δοῦλος 3
I serve, διακονέω 12
I set aside, ἀθετέω 24
I set before, παρατίθημι 28
I set in order, τάσσω 13
I set up, καθίστημι 29
seven, ἑπτά 23
sheep, πρόβατον 4
shepherd, ποιμήν 16
ship, πλοῖον 4
I shout, βοάω 22
I show, φαίνω 15; δείκνυμι 30
shrine, ναός 21
sick, ἀσθενής 18
I am sick, ἀσθενέω 28
sign, σημεῖον 4
I am silent, σιωπάω 25
silver, ἀργύριον 4; ἄργυρος 26
Simon, Σίμων 19
I sin, ἁμαρτάνω 14
sin, ἁμαρτία 5
sinner, ἁμαρτωλός 10
slave, δοῦλος 3
I sleep, κοιμάω 23
soldier, στρατιώτης 15
Solomon, Σολομῶν 21
son, υἱός 8
soon, ταχέως 13
soul, ψυχή 5
sound, φωνή 5
I sow, σπείρω 15
I speak, λαλέω 2
I speak with, συνλαλέω 19
spirit, πνεῦμα 17

I spoke, εἶπον 14
I cause to stand, ἵστημι 29
I cause to stand away, ἀφίστημι 29
I stand away, ἀφίστημι 29
I cause to stand up, ἀνίστημι 29
I stand up, ἀνίσταμαι 29
star, ἀστήρ 16
I steal, κλέπτω 23
I stone, λιθάζω, καταλιθάζω 26
stone, λίθος 9
strong, ἰσχυρός 21
stumble, I cause to, σκανδαλίζω 13
I suffer, πάσχω 14
I suffered, ἔπαθον 14
I summon, προσκαλέω 31
I surname, ἐπικαλέω 21
I surpass, περισσεύω 25
surpassing, περισσός 26
sword, μάχαιρα 15
synagogue, συναγωγή 5

I take, λαμβάνω 1
I take counsel with, συνβουλεύομαι 21
I take hold of, κρατέω 20
I take up, or away, αἴρω 15
I take with, παραλαμβάνω 20
I tarry, μέλλω 21
I taste, γεύομαι 25
taxgatherer, τελώνης 9
I teach, διδάσκω 8
teacher, διδάσκαλος 9
teaching, διδαχή 20
I tear, σπαράσσω 19
temple, ἱερόν 4
tempt, πειράζω 11
temptation, πειρασμός 23
than, ἤ 18
I thank, εὐχαριστέω 30
that, ἐκεῖνος 8
then, τότε 28
there, ἐκεῖ 11
therefore, οὖν 6
I think, νομίζω 25; φρονέω 31
this, οὗτος 8
thou, σύ 11

three, τρεῖς 16; τρία 21
thrice, τρίς 26
throne, θρόνος 9
through, διά with Gen. 9
I throw, βάλλω 1; ῥίπτω 21
I throw round (of a net), ἀμφιβάλλω 19
time, χρόνος 9; καιρός 15
to (motion to), εἰς 6; πρός 9
to-morrow, ἡ αὔριον 25
I toil, κοπιάζω 20
I told, εἶπον 14
tomb, μνημεῖον 20
tongue, γλῶσσα 6
tooth, ὀδούς 16
I touch, ἅπτομαι 10
towards, πρός 9
tradition, παράδοσις 24
trample on, πατέω 31
transgression, παράπτωμα 30
tree, δένδρον 4
tribe, φυλή 15
true, ἀληθής 18
truly, ἀληθῶς 21
trumpet, σάλπιγξ 16
truth, ἀλήθεια 5
try, πειράζω 11
two, δύο 20

unclean, ἀκάθαρτος 19
I understand, συνίημι 30
until, ἕως 15

village, κώμη 15
vineyard, ἀμπελών 16
virgin, παρθένος 3
vision, ὅραμα 25
voice, φωνή 5

I walk about, περιπατέω 8
I wash away, ἀπολούω 21
watch, φυλακή 27
water, ὕδωρ 17
way, ὁδός 3
I go my way, ὁδοιπορέω 21
we, ἡμεῖς 11
weak, ἀσθενής 18
I am weak, ἀσθενέω 28

well, εὖ 24
I went, ἦλθον 14
what kind? ποῖος 27
when, ὅτε 15
where, ποῦ 22
while, ἕως 15
who, which, ὅς, ἥ, ὅ, 10; ὅστις 25
who? what? τίς, τί 20
whole (sound), ὑγιής 18
whole (complete), ὅλος 20
why?, τί
wicked, πονηρός 7
wickedness, ἀδικία 10; ἀνομία 26
widow, χήρα 15
wife, γυνή 17
wilderness, ἔρημος 3
will, θέλημα 17
I am willing, θέλω 11
wind, πνεῦμα 17
wine, οἶνος 14
wisdom, σοφία 5
wise, σοφός 12
I wish, βούλομαι, θέλω 11
with (together with), σύν 6; μετά with Gen. 9
withered, ξηρός 29
witness, μάρτυς 29
I bear witness, μαρτυρέω 2
woman, γυνή 17
I wonder at, θαυμάζω 13; θαμβέομαι 26
wonder, τέρας 17
word, λόγος 3; ῥῆμα 18
I work, ἐργάζομαι 10
work, ἔργον 4
workman, ἐργάτης 9
world, κόσμος 3; ἡ οἰκουμένη 29
I worship, προσκυνέω 22
I write, γράφω 1
writing, γραφή 5

year, ἔτος 17
you, ὑμεῖς 11
young, νέος 21
young child, παιδίον 4
young man, νεανίας 6

Zacharias, Ζαχαρίας 20

APPENDIX

THE FORMS OF THE SUBJUNCTIVE MOOD IN ENGLISH.

Special forms of the verb which denote that it is in the Subjunctive Mood are rare in English.

They are printed in heavy type in the tables of verbs given below.

The Present Subjunctive of ordinary verbs.

I love	We love.
Thou **love**	You love.
He **love**	They love.

As the second person singular is so seldom used, this table shows that there is practically only one form—that of the 3rd sing.—in which the forms of the Subjunctive mood differ from those of the Indicative mood.

The Subjunctive forms of the verb "to be".

Present Subjunctive.	Past Subjunctive.
I **be**	I **were**
Thou **be** or **beest**	Thou **wert**
He **be**	He **were**
We **be**	We were
You **be**	You were
They **be**	They were.

Examples of the use of the Subjunctive mood in English.

To express a wish:	God **save** the king.
To express purpose:	Go, that you **be** not late.
	Go, lest you **be** late.
To express concession:	**Be** it never so humble, there's no place like home.
	Do what he will, he cannot escape.
To express a condition:	If I **be** king, why am I not obeyed?
	Who stands, if freedom **fall**?
	Who dies, if England **live**?
	If I **were** you, I would not go.
To express a wish which cannot be fulfilled:	I wish I **were** not here.

In Noun clauses:

(1) As subject: It is not right that he **be** rewarded for such conduct.

(2) As object: I think it **were** a shame to do this.
I wish that he **be** sent home.
I wonder whether it **be** true.

Many of the uses given above are becoming obsolete, except the use to express a wish.

The ideas expressed in Latin by the Subjunctive and in Greek by the Subjunctive and the Optative or by the Past Indicative with ἄν are generally expressed in English by the compound forms of verbs which Dr Sonnenschein calls "Subjunctive Equivalents".

These compound forms are made with the auxiliary verbs *may, might, should, would*.

But it does not follow that a verb which is in the Subjunctive in Latin or Subjunctive or Optative (sometimes with ἄν) in Greek must be translated by a verb in the Subjunctive, or by a Subjunctive Equivalent, in English.

It must often be translated by a verb in the Indicative mood.

This is one reason why it is not wise to learn any definite meaning for the Subjunctive forms in Latin, or the Subjunctive and Optative forms in Greek.

The **function** which a verb in the Subjunctive mood in Latin or in the Subjunctive or Optative in Greek performs in a sentence **must** be understood before it is possible to decide what form of the verb must be used to translate it into English.

The general principle is that the Subjunctive mood is used in Latin and the Subjunctive or Optative mood in Greek to express an action or state which is **thought of**, or **imagined**, rather than described as actually happening; which is described as **improbable or remote** rather than as **certain**.

The difference may be briefly, if insufficiently, stated in the words: The Indicative mood expresses a **fact** and the Subjunctive mood a **thought**.

Again the Subjunctive or Optative moods are used in polite phrases in which a speaker suggests some action to another person as possible or desirable rather than compulsory.

Examples of the use of Subjunctive Equivalents in English:

> May the king live for ever.
> I am going to London that I may see my son.
> I was going to London that I might see my son.
> If I might go home to-day I should see my father.
> If my father were here, he would explain everything.

Contrast the following uses:

> I shall be home at twelve.   (Certainty.)
> I should be home at twelve.   (Uncertainty.)
> Give me the hammer.
> Would you give me the hammer?   (Polite use.)

CONTRACTED VERBS.

The contracted forms of verbs ending in -έω and of those given on p. 87 ending in -άω and -όω are the forms printed in the Greek texts of the N.T.

But the **uncontracted** form of the 1st person sing. of the Present indicative is the form of the verb given in dictionaries. **This form should be learnt** in this person only. The student will then know how to conjugate the verb.

THE ATTRIBUTIVE AND PREDICATIVE POSITION OF THE ADJECTIVE.

The order in which the Definite Article, the Adjective and the Noun are arranged in Greek is important, as different arrangements have different meanings.

If the Adjective defines the Noun and is used as an Attribute, the order is: Article, Adjective, Noun, or Article, Noun, another Article, Adjective.

Examples: ὁ ἀγαθὸς ἄνθρωπος
ὁ ἄνθρωπος ὁ ἀγαθός.

When the words are written in this order they mean

"The good man".

This is called "The Attributive Position".

But if the Adjective is part of the Predicate with some part of the verb "to be" omitted or understood, the order is:

APPENDIX

Definite Article, Noun, Adjective, or Adjective, Definite Article, Noun.

ὁ ἄνθρωπος ἀγαθός: ἀγαθὸς ὁ ἄνθρωπος.

When the words are written in this order they mean:

"The man is good".

This is called "The Predicative Position".

Examples for practice:

ἁγία ἡ παρθένος. ὁ πιστὸς δοῦλος. αἰώνιος ἡ σοφία τοῦ θεοῦ. ὁ ἄνθρωπος ὁ πονηρὸς ποιεῖ τὰ κακά. δίκαιος ὁ θεός. ὁ δεσπότης πρῶτος. ἔσχατος ὁ πρῶτος. καὶ ὁ πρῶτος ἔσχατος.

The just man. The man is just. The faithful virgin. The slave is wicked. The eternal wisdom of God. The master is last. The beloved disciple. The disciple is beloved. The holy prophets. The prophets are holy.

N.B. No part of the verb "to be" is to be used in these sentences, when translating from English to Greek.

USE OF αὐτός.

Experience has shown that the pronoun αὐτός causes so much trouble to students that it has been thought well to give the full declension of it here.

		Masc.	Fem.	Neut.
Sing.	N.V.	αὐτός	αὐτή	αὐτό
	Acc.	αὐτόν	αὐτήν	αὐτό
	G.	αὐτοῦ	αὐτῆς	αὐτοῦ
	D.	αὐτῷ	αὐτῇ	αὐτῷ
Plural.	N.V.	αὐτοί	αὐταί	αὐτά
	Acc.	αὐτούς	αὐτάς	αὐτά
	G.	αὐτῶν	αὐτῶν	αὐτῶν
	D.	αὐτοῖς	αὐταῖς	αὐτοῖς

αὐτός αὐτή αὐτό, especially in cases other than the Nominative, is the usual word used to translate He, She, It into Greek. It is used much more frequently in the Semitic Greek of the N.T. than in Hellenistic Greek.

In the Genitive case it is used as a Possessive pronoun of the 3rd person: αὐτοῦ his, αὐτῆς her, αὐτοῦ its, αὐτῶν their.

If a noun is followed by a Genitive form of αὐτός used in the sense of a Possessive pronoun, the noun generally has an article before it.

    His slave   ὁ δοῦλος αὐτοῦ.
    Their slaves οἱ δοῦλοι αὐτῶν.

It has been stated in the text that αὐτός, when connected with and agreeing with a noun, means "himself, herself, itself".

It should be added that αὐτός can also mean "himself" etc., especially in the Nominative case, when it stands by itself.

    He himself teaches the multitude.
    αὐτὸς διδάσκει τὸν ὄχλον.

Distinguish between αὐτή, which generally means "she herself", and the feminine αὕτη, which means "this woman", or simply "she"; also between αὐταί and αὗται.

For the distinction between αὑτοῦ and αὐτοῦ, αὑτῆς and αὐτῆς, see p. 45.

FORMATION OF THE FUTURE.

Verbal stems whose Present stems end in ζ generally contain a Dental letter. Hence their Futures are formed as shown below:

    Present θαυμάζω.
    Future   θαυμάσω.

Verbal stems whose Present stems end in σσ generally contain a Guttural letter. Hence their futures are formed as shown below:

    Present πράσσω τάσσω.
    Future   πράξω   τάξω.

Referring to page 52, the First Aorist endings of the 2nd sing. and 3rd pl. Indicative and the 2nd pl., 3rd sing. and 3rd pl. Imperative are found joined with the normally Second Aorist stem εἰπ- in some texts of the N.T. These forms are: εἶπας, εἶπαν, εἴπατε, εἰπάτω, εἰπάτωσαν, the last two very rare.

ENGLISH INDEX

Accentuation, 5, 23, 140, 143
Accusative case, 11
  with prepositions, 122
  as subject of the Infinitive, 104
Adjectives, xviii
  2nd declension, 19
  3rd declension, 65
Adverbs, 85
Agent, how expressed with passive verbs, 30
Alphabet, 1-2
Antecedent, 33
Apodosis, 133
Article, definite, 13, 16
Augment, 21
Auxiliary verbs, xx

Breathings, 5

Case in English, xviii
Clause, definition of, xxx
Clauses :
  Adjectival, xxxiii, 33-34
  Adverbial, xxxiv
    Conditional, 100, 133-136
    Consecutive, 104
    Final, 37, 96
    Substantival or Noun, xxxi, xxxvi; object, 53, 103; subject, 36
    Temporal, 56, 105; Indefinite Temporal, 97
Comparison of adjectives, 83-84
  of adverbs, 85
Complement, xxi
Compound verbs, 22, 127-129
Copulative verbs, xx

Dative case, 13
  with prepositions, 122-124

Declensions:
  first, 16, 18
  second, 10, 15
  third, 58-64
Deliberative subjunctive, 98
Dependent Commands, xxxii
  Questions, xxxii
  Statements, xxxii
Deponent verbs, xix
Double negatives, 100

Equivalents, xxix

Finite mood, 11

Genitive Absolute, 77
Genitive case, 13
  with prepositions, 122-124
Gerund, xxv

Hortatory subjunctive, 98

Imperative Mood, xxiii, 31, 32, 47, 48
Indicative Mood, xxiii
Infinitive Mood, xxv, xxxiii, 35-38, 102-105
Instrument, how expressed, 30, 123
Iota subscript, 5

Modal verbs, xxxiii
Moods, xxiii
  Imperative, xxiii
    Present, 31, 32
    Aorist, 47, 48
  Indicative, xxiii
  Infinitive, xxv, xxxii, 35-38, 102-105
    Present, 35, 36

Moods, Infinitive
  Aorist, 49
    with article, 102
  Optative, 119
  Subjunctive, xxiii, 95-101

Nouns, xvii

Object, direct, xviii, xxvii-xxviii
  indirect, xxviii, 13
Optative Mood, 119

Participles, xxiv, 72-77
  Adjectival, 74
  Adverbial, 74
  Tense of, 75
Periphrastic tenses, 120
Phrase, definition of, xxxi
Predicate, xxvi
Preparatory subject, xxxvi
Prepositions, 121-129
Prohibitions, 100
Pronouns:
  demonstrative, 25
  indefinite, 79
  interrogative, 78
  personal, 38
  possessive, 26, 39
  reflexive, 45
Protasis, 133

Sentences, definition of, xxvi, xxx
  Complex, xxx
  Compound, xxx, xxxi
  Simple, xxx
Subject, xxvi
Subjunctive Mood, xxiii, 95-101
  in English, 185

Tense, xxii-xxiii
  Aorist, 1st Act., 47; Middle, 82; Passive, 68
  Aorist, 2nd Act., 51; Middle, 83; Passive, 69
  Future Active, 40-41; Middle, 41; Passive, 69
  Imperfect, 21-23
  Perfect and Pluperfect, 91
  Periphrastic forms of, 120
  Present, 7; Continuous form, xix

Verbal nouns, xxv
Verbs, xvii-xxvi
  Contracted, 9, 23, 42, 87
  Liquid, 55
  in $\mu\iota$, 106-116
  "to be", xx, 20, 25, 42, 100
Voice:
  Active, xviii
  Middle, 40
  Passive, xix

GREEK INDEX

The numbers refer to the Vocabularies

Ἀγαθός 7
ἀγαλλιάω 22
ἀγαπάω 22
ἀγάπη 5
ἀγαπητός 7
ἄγγελος 3
ἁγιάζω 13
ἅγιος 7
ἀγορά 28
ἀγοράζω 13
ἀγρός 10
ἄγω 8
ἀδελφός 3
ἀδικέω 12
ἀδικία 10
ἀδύνατος 15
ἀθετέω 24
Αἴγυπτος 15
αἷμα 17
αἴρω 15
αἰτέω 2
αἰών 16
αἰώνιος 7
ἀκάθαρτος 19
ἀκολουθέω 30
ἀκούω 1
ἅλας 25
ἀλέκτωρ 16
ἀλήθεια 5
ἀληθής 18
ἀληθῶς 21
ἁλίζω 25
ἀλλά 6
ἀλλήλους 31
ἁμαρτάνω 14
ἁμαρτία 5

ἁμαρτωλός 10
ἀμνός 14
ἀμπελών 16
ἀμφιβάλλω 19
ἀναγιγνώσκω 8
Ἀνανίας 19
ἀνάστασις 18
ἀναχωρέω 20
Ἀνδρέας 19
ἀνήρ 17
ἄνθρωπος 3
ἀνίστημι 29
Ἄννας 20
ἀνοίγω 12
ἀνομία 26
ἀπαγγέλλω 15
ἀπάγω 13
ἀπαρνέομαι 26
ἀπέρχομαι 10
ἀπό 6
ἀποδίδωμι 27
ἀποθνῄσκω 1
ἀποκαλύπτω 13
ἀποκρίνομαι 10
ἀπόκρισις 20
ἀποκτείνω 8
ἀπολέσει 24
ἀπολούω 21
ἀπολύω 8
ἀποσπάω 28
ἀποστέλλω 1
ἀπόστολος 3
ἅπτομαι 10
ἀπώλεια 31
ἀργύριον 4
ἄργυρος 26

ἀρνέομαι 10
ἄρτος 3
ἀρχή 5
ἀρχιερεύς 18
ἄρχομαι 11
ἄρχω 12
ἄρχων 16
ἀσθενέω 28
ἀσθενής 18
ἀστήρ 16
αὔριον 25
αὐτός 8
ἄφεσις 17
ἀφίημι 30
ἀφίστημι 29
ἄφρων 18
Ἀχελδαμάχ 26

Βαίνω 14
βάλλω 1
βαπτίζω 8
βάπτισμα 17
βαπτιστής 6
βασιλεία 5
βασιλεύς 17
βαστάζω 13
Βηθλεέμ 15
βιβλίον 4
βλέπω 1
βοάω 22
βολή 28
βούλομαι 11

Γαλιλαία 19
γάμος 11
γάρ 6

GREEK INDEX

γεννάομαι 22
γένος 17
γεύομαι 25
γῆ 5
γιγνώσκω 14
γινώσκω 14
γίνομαι 21
γλῶσσα 6
γνωστός 26
γονεύς 18
γόνυ 17
γράμμα 17
γραμματεύς 17
γραφή 5
γράφω 1
γυνή 17

Δαβίδ 18
δαιμόνιον 4
Δανείδ 18
δέ 6
δεῖ 11
δείκνυμι 30
δένδρον 4
δεξιός 28
δέομαι 11
δέσμιος 26
δεσπότης 6
δέχομαι 10
δέω 24
διά 9
διάβολος 11
διακονέω 12
διάκονος 12
διαλογίζομαι 31
διασπείρω 19
διδάσκαλος 9
διδάσκω 8
διδαχή 20
δίδωμι 27
διέρχομαι 10
δίκαιος 7
δικαιοσύνη 5
δικαιόω 22
δίκτυον 20
διώκω 12

δόξα 6
δοξάζω 8
δοῦλος 3
δύναμαι 11
δύναμις 20
δυνατός 15
δύο 20

Ἐάω 22
ἐγγίζω 13
ἐγγύς 20
ἐγείρω 1
ἐγένετο 21
ἐγώ 11
ἔθνος 18
εἰ 18
εἶδον 14
εἰκών 16
εἶπον 14
εἰρήνη 5
εἰς 6
εἷς 18
εἰσάγω 23
εἰσέρχομαι 19
εἰσπορεύομαι 23
εἰσφέρω 28
ἐκ 6
ἐκβάλλω 8
ἐκεῖ 11
ἐκεῖνος 8
ἐκκλησία 5
ἐκκόπτω 13
ἐκλέγομαι 21
ἐκπλήσσομαι 20
ἐκπορεύομαι 26
ἐκφεύγω 26
ἐλεέω 12
ἐλεύθερος 11
ἑλκύω 29
Ἕλλην 23
ἐλπίζω 13
ἐλπίς 16
ἔμπροσθεν 29
ἐν 6
ἕν 18
ἐνδύω 12

ἐνθάδε 25
ἐντέλλω 29
ἐντολή 5
ἐνώπιον 28
ἐξέρχομαι 19
ἔξεστι 11
ἔξοδος 22
ἐξουσία 5
ἔξω 26
ἐπαγγελία 5
ἔπαθον 14
ἐπαίρω 29
ἐπέρχομαι 20
ἐπερωτάω 31
ἐπί 20
ἐπιβάλλω 21
ἐπιγινώσκω 23
ἐπιθυμέω 20
ἐπικαλέω 21
ἐπιλαμβάνομαι 29
ἐπιστάτης 20
ἐπισυνάγω 31
ἑπτά 23
ἐργάζομαι 10
ἐργάτης 9
ἔργον 4
ἔρημος 3
ἔρχομαι 10
ἐρωτάω 22
ἐσθίω 1
ἔσχατος 7
ἔσχον 14
ἕτερος 7
ἑτοιμάζω 13
ἔτος 17
εὖ 24
εὐαγγελίζομαι 10
εὐαγγέλιον 4
εὐθέως 30
εὐθύς 9
εὐλογέω 12
εὑρίσκω 1
εὐχαριστέω 30
ἔφαγον 14
ἐχθρός 12
ἔχω 1

GREEK INDEX

ἕως 15

Ζαχαρίας 20
ζάω 22
ζητέω 2
ζωή 5

Ἤ 18
ἡγεμών 16
Ἡλείας 19
ἦλθον 14
ἡμεῖς 11
ἡμέρα 5
ἤνεγκον 14
Ἡρώδης 15

θάλασσα 6
θαμβέομαι 26
θάνατος 3
θαρσέω 30
θαυμάζω 13
θέλημα 17
θέλω 11
θεός 3
θεραπεύω 11
θεωρέω 2
θρίξ 17
θρόνος 9
θυγάτηρ 17
θύρα 16
θυσία 26

Ἰάκωβος 26
ἰάομαι 22
ἴδιος 7
ἰδού 21
ἱερεύς 18
ἱερόν 4
Ἱερουσαλήμ 9
Ἰησοῦς 8
ἱμάτιον 4
Ἰόππη 20
Ἰορδάνης 11
Ἰουδαῖος 8
Ἰσραήλ 10
ἵστημι 29

ἰσχυρός 21
ἰχθύς ὁ 17
Ἰωάνης 8
Ἰωσήφ 15

Καθαρίζω 13
καθίστημι 29
καθώς 23
καί 3
Καιάφας 20
καινός 28
καιρός 15
Καῖσαρ 25
Καισαρεία 26
καίω 28
κακός 7
καλέω 2
καλός 11
καρδία 5
καρπός 9
κατά 20
κατακρίνω 15
καταλαμβάνω 21
καταλιθάζω 26
καταλείπω 14
καταλύω 25
κατευλογέω 28
κατοικέω 12
κελεύω 11
κεφαλή 5
κηρύσσω 8
κλάω 28
κλέπτω 23
κλίνη 15
κοινόω 23
κοπιάω 20
κοπιάζω 20
Κορνήλιος 15
κόσμος 3
κράζω 8
κρατέω 20
κρίμα 18
κρίνω 1
κρίσις 18
κριτής 9
κρύπτω 13

κύριος 3
κύων 17
κώμη 15
κωφός 17

Λάζαρος 23
λαλέω 2
λαμβάνω 1
λαμπάς 16
λαός 3
λέγω 1
λεπρός 13
λῃστής 9
λιθάζω 26
λίθος 9
λόγος 3
λοιπός 21
Λύδδα 20
λύχνος 28
λύω 9

Μαγδαληνή 23
μαθητής 6
μακάριος 19
μᾶλλον 18
μανθάνω 14
Μαρία 15
Μαριάμ 15
μαρτυρέω 2
μάρτυς 29
μάχαιρα 15
μέγας 18
μέλλω 21
μέν 11
μένω 1
μερίζω 29
μεριμνάω 25
μέσος 29
μετά 9
μετανοέω 29
μετάνοια 17
μή 10
μηδείς 18
μηκέτι 18
μήν 16
μήτηρ 17
μία 18

GREEK INDEX

μικρός 21
μισθός 25
μνημεῖον 20
μυστήριον 27
Μωϋσῆς 19

Ναός 21
νεανίας 6
νεκρός 18
νέος 21
νεφέλη 20
νηστεύω 31
νομίζω 25
νόμος 3
νυμφίος 16
νῦν, νυνί 21
νύξ 16

Ξηρός 29

Ὁδοιπορέω 21
ὁδός 3
ὁδούς 16
οἶδα 30
οἰκία 11
οἰκοδεσπότης 9
οἰκοδομέω 10
οἶκος 3
οἰκουμένη 29
οἶνος 14
ὅλος 20
ὅμοιος 24
ὁμοιόω 29
ὁμολογέω 11
ὄνομα 18
ὀπίσω 15
ὅραμα 25
ὁράω 21
ὄρος 18
ὅς 10
ὅσος 20
ὅστις 25
ὅτε 15
ὅτι 12
οὐ 6
οὐδείς 18

σύν 6
οὐράνιος 30
οὐρανός 9
οὖς 17
οὗτος 8
οὐχί 21
ὀφειλέτης 30
ὀφείλημα 30
ὀφείλω 15
ὀφθαλμός 9
ὄχλος 9

Παιδίον 4
παῖς 16
παλαιός 21
πάντα 15
πανταχοῦ 29
πάντοτε 24
παρά 15
παραβολή 5
παραγγέλλω 11
παραγίγνομαι 19
παράγω 19
παραδίδωμι 27
παράδοσις 24
παρακαλέω 2
παραλαμβάνω 20
παραλελυμένος 28
παραλυτικός 15
παράπτωμα 30
παρατίθημι 28
παρθένος 3
παρίστημι 29
πᾶς 18
πάσχω 14
πατέω 31
πατήρ 17
Παῦλος 11
παύομαι 29
πείθω 8
πειράζω 11
πειρασμός 23
πέμπω 8
πεντακισχίλιοι 19
περί see p. 125
περιβάλλω 25

περιπατέω 8
περισσεύω 25
περισσός 26
πέτρα 20
Πέτρος 16
πίνω 14
πίπτω 14
πιστεύω 1
πίστις 18
πιστός 7
πλανάομαι 30
πληθύνω 26
πληρόω 22
πλησίον 26
πλοῖον 4
πνεῦμα 17
ποιέω 2
ποιμήν 16
ποῖος 27
πόλις 17
πολλά 14
πολύς 18
πονηρός 7
πορεύομαι 10
ποταμός 13
ποτήριον 15
ποῦ 22
πούς 17
πράσσω 13
πρέπον 30
πρεσβύτερος 9
πρίν 26
πρό 6
πρόβατον 4
προμεριμνάω 27
πρός 9
προσέρχομαι 20
προσεύχομαι 21
προσέχω 26
προσκαλέομαι 31
προσκαρτερέω 20
προσκυνέω 22
πρόσωπον 4
προφητεύω 12
προφήτης 6
πρῶτος 7

GREEK INDEX

πτωχός 11
πυνθάνομαι 22
πῦρ 17
πῶς 19

'Ρῆμα 18
ῥίπτω 21

Σάββατον 4
σάλπιγξ 16
Σαμάρεια 11
σάρξ 16
Σατανᾶς 19
σημεῖον 4
Σίμων 19
σιωπάω 25
σκανδαλίζω 13
σκότος 18
Σολομών 21
σοφία 5
σοφός 12
σπαράσσω 19
σπείρω 15
σπέρμα 18
σταυρός 15
σταυρόω 22
στενός 20
στόμα 18
στρατιώτης 15
σύ 11
σύν 6
συνάγω 8
συναγωγή 5
συνβουλεύομαι 21
συνέδριον 20
συνεσθίω 26
συνζητέω 26
συνίημι 30
συνλαλέω 19
σύρω 26

σύρω 26
σχίσμα 21
σώζω 1
σῶμα 18
σωτήρ 16
σωτηρία 21

Ταπεινόω 22
τάσσω 13
ταχέως 13
τεκμήριον 20
τέκνον 4
τελώνης 9
τέρας 17
τεσσαράκοντα 19
τηρέω 2
τίθημι 28
τίκτω 14
τιμή 28
τίς 20
τις 20
τόπος 9
τότε 20
τρεῖς 16
τρία 21
τρίς 26
τροφή 21
τυφλός 11

Ὑγιής 18
ὕδωρ 17
υἱός 8
ὑμεῖς 11
ὑπάγω 8
ὑπακούω 11
ὑπέρ 21
ὑπό 9
ὑποκριτής 9
ὑπομονή 31
ὕστερος 29

ὕστερος 29
ὑψόω 22

Φανερόω 22
Φαρισαῖος 15
φέρω 8
φεύγω 14
Φῆστος 26
φθείρω 15
φιλέω 2
Φίλιππος 26
φοβέομαι 19
φόβος 19
φρονέω 31
φυλακή 27
φύλαξ 16
φυλάσσω 13
φυλή 15
φωνέω 16
φωνή 5
φῶς 17

Χαίρω 8
χαρά 5
χάρις 16
χείρ 17
χήρα 15
χιτών 16
χρῆμα 19
χρόνος 9
χρυσός 26
χωρίον 27

Ψευδής 29
ψυχή 5

Ὦ 14
ὧδε 11
ὥρα 5
ὥς 15
ὥστε 26

www.ingramcontent.com/pod-product-compliance
Lightning Source LLC
Chambersburg PA
CBHW051048160426
43193CB00010B/1106